'Written with warmth and care, and showing how young children with special needs can feel comfortable. I highly recommend any Early Years Teacher to read this book. It has prompted me as a mainstream Early Years Teacher to ensure that all children in my setting can have a "flying start".'

– *Lesley Bailey, Heatherside Preschool Supervisor and SENCO by the same author*

Literacy for Visual Learners
Teaching Children with Learning Differences to
Read, Write, Communicate and Create
Adele Devine
Illustrated by Quentin Devine
ISBN 978 1 84905 598 7
eISBN 978 1 78450 054 2

Colour Coding for Learners with Autism
A Resource Book for Creating Meaning through
Colour at Home and School
Adele Devine
Illustrated by Quentin Devine
ISBN 978 1 84905 441 6
eISBN 978 0 85700 812 1

of related interest

The Essential Manual for Asperger Syndrome
(ASD) in the Classroom
What Every Teacher Needs to Know
Kathy Hoopmann
Illustrated by Rebecca Houkamau
ISBN 978 1 84905 553 6
eISBN 978 0 85700 984 5

Sensory Stories for Children and Teens
with Special Educational Needs
A Practical Guide
Joanna Grace
ISBN 978 1 84905 484 3
eISBN 978 0 85700 874 9

Music for Special Kids
Musical Activities, Songs, Instruments and Resources
Pamela Ott
ISBN 978 1 84905 858 2
eISBN 978 0 85700 426 0

FLYING STARTS

for Unique Children

Top Tips for Supporting Children with SEN or Autism When They Start School

ADELE DEVINE

Jessica Kingsley *Publishers*
London and Philadelphia

First published in 2016
by Jessica Kingsley Publishers
73 Collier Street
London N1 9BE, UK
and
400 Market Street, Suite 400
Philadelphia, PA 19106, USA

www.jkp.com

Library of Congress Cataloging in Publication Data
Names: Devine, Adele, author.
Title: Flying starts for unique children : top tips for supporting children
    with SEN or autism when they start school / Adele Devine.
Description: London ; Philadelphia : Jessica Kingsley Publishers, [2016] |
    Includes bibliographical references and index.
Identifiers: LCCN 2016007161 | ISBN 9781785920011 (alk. paper)
Subjects: LCSH: Learning disabled children--Education (Early childhood) |
    Children with disabilities--Education (Early childhood) | Autistic
    children--Education (Early childhood) | Children with autism spectrum
    disorders--Education (Early childhood) | School environment. | Classroom
    environment. | Teachers of children with disabilities--Handbooks, manuals,
    etc.
Classification: LCC LC4704.73 .D48 2016 | DDC 371.9--dc23
LC record available at https://lccn.loc.gov/2016007161

British Library Cataloguing in Publication Data
A CIP catalogue record for this book is available from the British Library

ISBN 978 1 78592 001 1
eISBN 978 1 78450 241 6

Printed and bound in Great Britain

For parents,

who are so often unsung heroes...

Acknowledgements

As always my first thank you is to my amazing husband Quentin, who has supported every project and idea with his time and artistry. He is also an incredible 'Daddy' to our three children. Without him there would be no award-winning software and no books. He made me believe that I could change things…

Thanks to my wonderful parents who believe in us so wholeheartedly, support us at every twist and turn and show through their own example that 'work' can be 'love made visible'.

I thank Matthew Sartin (headteacher at Portesbery School) for listening to and encouraging new ideas. I thank Clare Walker (Early Years Coordinator) for her dedication, endless enthusiasm, support and friendship. I thank our students for filling school days with love, laughter and fun and for continually teaching us how to see things through different eyes. I thank the amazing staff I work with, who put every ounce of energy and love into making Portesbery such a happy, welcoming place.

I thank the parents and young people who have allowed me to share the case studies in this book and also those who have allowed me to include content from their books, blogs and articles. I'd like to acknowledge Gina Davies for her inspirational training and for kindly reading over the content on 'Attention Autism' that I have included in this book. We are all constantly learning and the more we share information the faster we can improve provisions for children with special education needs (SEN) and autism.

I thank all those at Jessica Kingsley Publishers who are always so thorough, so accurate, so polite, so patient and pay attention to every detail.

And finally I thank you for picking up this book and for making a difference. You, who will change so many lives…

Contents

An Introduction: Once Upon a Time...   11

1. First Impressions: The Difference First Impressions Can
    Make to a Child's School Experience   17

2. Keeping Mum: Supporting, Listening to and
    Learning from Parents   26

3. Good Communication Can Save You Time:
    Communication Boards, Books, Tick Lists,
    Emails, Phone Calls and More   38

4. Unlocking that Special Child: Observing,
    Investigating and Getting Creative   45

5. Colour-Coded Symbols   53

6. Show Them the Way: Using Visuals – Practical Ideas
    and Examples   61

7. What's Next? Seeing from All Angles – Understanding
    the Reasons Behind Behaviours   68

8. Be a Supermodel! Teaching Children Through Using Staff
    and Other Children as Positive Role Models   76

9. Toilet Training   84

10. Flower Power: Seeing Through a Child's Eyes
    and Finding Roots   95

11. If You're Good... A Positive Approach to Behaviour
    and Using Rewards   102

12. I Can't Wait! Teaching Waiting Skills   108

13. Choice Time: Helping Children Who Find It
    Difficult to Make Choices   116

14. Good Sitting: Supporting the Child
    Who Cannot Sit Still   122

15. Against the Clock: How Using Timers Can Enable a
    Special Child to Stay on Track   131

16. The Relationship with Technology: How to Use that Love
    of Technology   139

17. Volume Control: Ways to Help the Sound Sensitive Child
    Survive and Thrive at School   144

18. Space Invaders: Increasing Awareness
    of Personal Space   154

19. The Sixth Sense (Proprioception): Is that Bouncy Child
    Still Learning Where Their Body is in Space?   161

20. The Child who Chews: Strategies for the Child who
    Chews Toys or Clothes   172

21. When Clothes Hurt: Helping Children with Sensitivity
    to Clothes and Shoes   179

22. Personal Care Scares: Supporting the Child with Anxieties
    about Hair Washing, Hair Cuts and Brushing Teeth   185

23. Food Phobia! Children Who Refuse to Eat or Have
    Extremely Limited Diets   195

24. Recipes for Success: Cooking with Children with SEN   201

25. Eating Out: Taking Children with SEN to Restaurants   208

26. Retail Therapy: Taking Children with
    SEN to Real Shops   214

27. Pet Therapy: How Animals Can Encourage Interaction,
    Communication and Calm   221

28. Dealing with Different Days: Strategies and Supports for
    Halloween, Dress-Up days, Sports Days, Fireworks Night
    and Other Events   229

29. Planning for Christmas: Why Christmas Causes Anxieties
    and Ways to Help   238

30. The Christmas Play: Helping that Special Child Shine   244

31. Present Danger! Teaching Children to Handle
    Gift-Giving Times   251

32. A Change of Setting; Transition Tips for Your Special
    Children, Inspired by the Experiences of a Rescue Cat...   258

33. Reasons to be Hopeful: Changing Our Attitudes and
    Language Can Change Outcomes   267

34. Extending Learning: Extra Information on Attention
    Autism, Intensive Interaction, Makaton™, Social
    Stories™, PECS® and TEACCH   273

35. Happily Ever After   292

    References   299

    Useful Websites   303

    Index   304

An Introduction

Once Upon a Time...

To be of use to the world is the only way to be happy.

Hans Christian Andersen

When we were little

We delighted in making Louise laugh and loved her sense of humour. We became expert at reading her facial expressions, developing instinct and empathy so that she could communicate meaning without words.

Whatever we were doing we found a way to ensure that Louise could do it too. My Aunt and Uncle instilled in us all that there must always be a 'can', that there is always a way...

There were times when our belief in Lou's 'cans' got us into trouble. One winter's day we were watching the film version of Johanna Spyri's *Heidi*. There's a magical scene where Heidi and Peter (the goatherd) support her friend Clara (who is usually reliant on a wheelchair) to take steps and walk. I was sitting by the fire with my cousins Carrie and Louise (in her wheelchair). *Heidi* had got us thinking... What if we supported Louise to walk as Peter and Heidi had? Could we get her to take steps? Wouldn't that be wonderful! Despite Lou's profound physical disabilities, we became convinced that we could teach her. Louise was enthusiastic and responded with a big 'Ummm' (her sound for 'Yes'). I suspect that there was also a mischievous twinkle in her eye. We started to undo the straps supporting her. She had a heavy wheelchair, which was moulded to support her positioning because she could not sit up herself. We bent down so that our shoulders were under her arms. Louise, who is six years older, was significantly bigger than us (Carrie age six and me age seven) and could not hang on to us or aid our efforts in any way, but we were strong and oh so determined. 'One, two, three…', we counted, then lifted together. Louise was far too heavy for us and her feet did not go flat and bear weight as we'd hoped. They stayed as they were. There was a terrible 'What have we done?' moment before we all tumbled to the floor in a heavy heap. We were mortified. What *had* we done? Louise was breathing strangely, her body was making unusual convulsions on top of us and she was making pained, loud roaring noises that we had never heard before. As we took stock of the awful situation we saw that Lou's eyes were filled with tears. That's when we realised that the roars were actually Lou's uncontrollable, whole hearted laughter. Over 30 years have passed, but when we talk about that day Louise still finds it so funny. Our childhood was filled with moments like this…

Special education

Apart from a few distinctive sounds to communicate 'yes' and 'no' Louise has no recognisable speech. She was profoundly physically disabled from the neck down due to a lack of oxygen at birth and diagnosed with severe cerebral palsy. I grew up close to Louise and learnt to read and translate a lot of her thoughts by instinct. Some people never see beyond Lou's disabilities. But those who take the time find that she has a quick wit, a brilliant brain, a devilish sense of humour and a fearless, tireless determination to live her life. She also has a unique ability to inspire and transform the lives of others. I loved how my Aunt and Uncle fought for Lou's education and inclusion. When Louise learnt to use a communication board to speak to us we thought it was amazing.

She would wait patiently as a little light moved along a big board with different symbols until it reached the one she wanted and then she would press down with her chin. She was brilliant at this and often made us laugh with her funny, timely comments. Louise learned to use an electric wheelchair with chin controls. She loved having this new found independence and we enjoyed finding creative ways to include electric wheelchair antics in our play.

Louise has been a huge influence on me. She is funny, brilliant and determined to achieve every possible can.

Fast forward 15 years...

After university I took a job in a book shop. I loved the books and put my heart into making the children's department magical, but knew this was not going to be a forever job. I'd not yet discovered what I really wanted to do or who I was meant to be.

One day my Aunt came in and asked how I would feel about going on a boat with Louise as her companion/carer. My response was an instant 'Yes!'

'The ship that changes lives' – Puerto Rico

When I saw 'Nellie' (The Lord Nelson) it was love at first sight. I loved that tall sailing ship from those big billowing sails to the tiny port hole in our messy cabin. We were a part of the cabin crew and took turns with the duties on board. We scrubbed the decks, went right up the masts to fold the sails and even did night watch. The Jubilee Sailing Trust is a charity that has specifically designed inclusive ships to enable people with physical disabilities to experience sailing. Louise was able to experience everything. She even went up the mast to the crow's nest, hoisted up with ropes by the most determined and dedicated crew.

We all took turns doing night 'watch duty' in shifts. One night I was standing by the ship's wheel, watching Lou using chin controls to steer the ship. I loved seeing all these doors being opened for her. I loved seeing the crew put their heart into making things happen. I was looking up at the brightest stars through white sails. I felt so alive. I wanted more…

Camp Eagle Springs – Pennsylvania, USA

I returned to my bookshop and handed in my notice. I was on a mission to find a tough test. I signed up to go on a summer camp in America, which provided holidays for adults with learning difficulties and respite for their carers. They said that it would be the toughest, most amazing summer of my life and that was exactly the sort of challenge I wanted.

That summer of '99 at Camp Eagle Springs was a life changing experience. I felt an instinctive connection with autistic adults in our care. I would spend hours listening, laughing, observing and learning from them. They made me feel relaxed, inspired and at home.

Camp was exhausting, challenging and amazing. I loved it! I was so happy falling into bed exhausted every night – the unpredictability, the chance to create and make a difference to other lives…

Camp was also where I met my soul mate, my future husband and father to our three children – Quentin Devine.

Closing a window

After camp I started looking for a job doing care work. I believed that that this would be the most fulfilling work and I could make a real difference. Quentin and I took jobs in a care home in Manchester. He was activities coordinator. I was a carer. The reality of these jobs fell short of our expectations. I wanted to change lives and was frustrated with not having the time or resources or other staff sharing my ideals.

Not knowing what to do, I took on the most awful, soul destroying job – taking complaints in a call centre. I counted down the minutes during each shift and would come home every night after work and cry…

Opening a door...

'What do you really *want* to do?' asked Quentin.

I thought about it and suddenly I knew... 'I want to work with autistic children.' After seeing the difference a week could make with the adults on camp I'd become convinced that if I could have met them as children I could have really changed outcomes. Suddenly I knew exactly what I wanted to do, but how?

Quentin searched the internet, made some calls and somehow found me the contact number I needed. After a few phone calls I arranged to go and meet a family, who were hoping to train an extra tutor to work with their four-year-old son who had autism. I had an instant connection with them and their brilliant little boy. Two years working as a home tutor with children in Brighton and seeing them progress so much made me realise the job I was meant to do. More than anything I wanted to be a special needs teacher.

Teaching

Being a special needs teacher is *the* most amazing job in the world. Beyond that never-ending mountain of paper work, the tick boxes and the politics there are these brilliant children, who fill every day with magic and fun.

I love seeing what every child can do. I love the observing, the inventing, getting creative and non-stop learning. I love supporting the parents and sharing all the fantastically exciting things their children get up to at school. Every day is special. We are a part of something magical and see wow after wow after wow.

I love teaching in Early Years. We are the first point of contact for parents, the ones who get to create those all-important first impressions, to put in every strategy and the support each individual child needs.

The Chinese thinker and social philosopher Confucius observed, 'Choose a job you love and you will never work a day in your life.' I feel incredibly lucky to have found that job.

Aspirations

My aim is that every special child will arrive in a classroom set up and ready so that they feel supported, confident, loved and able to show what they can do. Parents need to feel secure and hopeful, knowing that their child is in the very best hands. I want teachers to feel that they have the training, the strategies and the knowledge to be able to be those 'best hands'. Children with special educational needs are amazing to teach and can achieve so much, but they must have the right structures and supports in place from the very start. They must be surrounded by people who believe in their individual 'can do's' and talk about their personal triumphs.

That is why I have written this book. I want to share some of the lessons I have learnt from our wonderful students. I want to provide quick tips and signposts to resources and further training so that other teachers can set special children up for success.

Teachers can completely change a child's life and the more dedication and heart they put into this 'service' the more these children will transform other lives. Our responsibility extends beyond the child. We can affect the parents, grandparents, siblings and all those *they* interact with. These positive ripples go on and on.

CHAPTER 1

First Impressions

The Difference First Impressions Can Make to a Child's School Experience

Early impressions are hard to eradicate from the mind. When once wool has been dyed purple, who can restore it to its previous whiteness?

St. Jerome

Those school inspectors might say a school has 'outstanding' qualities, but if a child's first experience of it is 'unsatisfactory' that's not *good* at all.

Imagine you are in a restaurant. The cutlery looks dirty and your glass is kind of cloudy. As you take in the dilapidated décor you are half expecting to see Gordon Ramsay and the crew of *Ramsay's Kitchen Nightmares* appear. When the food eventually arrives it looks like a cheap microwave meal. So, do you…

a) kick up a fuss, refuse to pay and ensure every other diner knows why

b) shuffle the food about a bit and leave quietly, but never eat there again, or

c) decide you hate restaurants and swear you will *never* set foot in one again?

The third option seems extreme, but to a child who's never experienced fine dining it might make most sense.

Apply this logic to your setting. Think of a child's first impression. Imagine a sound sensitive child arrives when it's most busy. Next they are expected to say goodbye to Mum, knowing that when she leaves they will be stranded. Fear and panic could quickly descend.

The child settles after a while, but they did not like the arrival or separation. In fact they may take this even further (as children can). They are not going to like school. Every teacher that follows could have a battle on their hands because of that first bad experience.

A good start

There are simple things you can do to ensure that children with SEN have a positive first experience of your setting:

1. Gather information about likes, dislikes, fears and comforters.

2. Suggest children bring in a favourite (non-breakable) toy from home.

3. Offer an initial taster visit when there are no other children around.

4. Stagger start times so sensitive children can avoid the masses.

5. Avoid shutting parents off at the door. Suggest they stay while the child settles.

6. Create quieter areas and access to outside space away from the throng.

7. Kneel down to the child's level when speaking – it's less intimidating.

8. Use stickers and rewards. Be overly positive and enthusiastic.

9. Use Makaton™ signs, visuals, simple language and a consistently calm voice.

10. Build the child's trust and show empathy for things they might find tricky.

Home visits

Before each child starts at our school we will visit them at home and spend time getting to know all about them and let them get to know us in their comfort zone. We will speak to parents and learn of their hopes and fears, anxieties and priorities and if they have support networks. We get to know about siblings, grandparents and other family so that if the child mentions them we know who they are. We learn so much about the child's story, their motivators, how they like their food (if they like food), their toileting routines, sleep routines and comforters. We use all this information to create a smoother, more personalised transition when they start school.

If the child is already attending another setting we will also visit them there to build a bigger picture and learn about how they interact with other children, what areas they are most drawn to, what activities make them happy and what might cause them anxiety.

Home visits are vital in helping us set our young people up to succeed when they start school.

I'd like to see every child have a home visit before they start school. Every child is special. They all have their little quirks, their own unique set of needs. They all deserve to start school feeling happy and secure.

Home visits are important for creating a good first impression for both the parents and the child.

Approaching the anxious child

Starting school can be daunting for any child. When children are tearful or seem anxious the natural instinct might be to cuddle them, to stay real close, to offer comfort and support, but when a child has sensory issues, anxieties or autism this type of contact could confuse and fuel their anxiety.

Case study: Ollie – a bead frame a day to keep tears at bay

Ollie had done a settle in day with his mum and we were confident that he was going to cope with the new setting really well. Transport and arriving at the same time as the other children were all new though. Ollie was a bit tearful and overwhelmed when he came into class. One of our learning support assistants sat by him, trying to offer comfort. Instinct told me that the little boy needed distraction, but it was best to do this in a quiet way. I went and sat nearby with some bricks and focused on building a big tower. I could see him starting to look. As the tower got bigger and more wobbly I saw that he had stopped crying. The tower got really tall and fell. 'Oh no!' I exclaimed and Ollie smiled. I started building again and quietly asked the assistant if she would go get the bead frame as this had been his favourite thing the day before. She placed it down beside him and he started to look at the beads, happily examining them and moving them about. After that he forgot his initial upset and was happy and settled.

Ollie didn't need cuddles and comfort, but distraction, calm, quiet, maybe some interaction (on his own terms), a familiar motivator and that oh so important element: time.

Case study: Ronnie – a tale of two settings
A nursery nightmare!

Ronnie was eyeing the entrance with trepidation amidst the bustle of children getting their coats and bags on pegs. A little girl was crying and protesting about going through the door, and her mum was trying to comfort and cajole her. Mrs Simms took the girl's hand and said in a matter of fact way, 'Those are crocodile tears. She will stop as soon as you leave.' She waved to an assistant, who led the now sobbing girl away. The mum left, but was visibly concerned.

Ronnie could see through a window that the girl was still crying. He took his coat back off the peg. 'I'm not going in,' he said with absolute conviction.

Ronnie's mum paused. She knew she was in for a battle and didn't want a big scene in front of the other parents. Ronnie was soon the only child in the cloakroom. He had put his coat on and his dinosaur rucksack was on his back. His arms were folded tightly and his hands were clenched in strong fist grips preventing Mum's efforts to get things back on the peg. Mrs Simms could see she had another little protester. 'Come on in. It's time to say good bye to Mummy now,' she said.

'No.' Ronnie was defiant. 'I don't like you. I'm going home.' Mum saw the flicker of annoyance in Mrs Simms' eyes. This was not a great start.

'Mum is going home,' Mrs Simms said firmly. 'Ronnie is staying at pre-school.' She opened the outside door and ushered Mum out.

Ronnie's eyes filled with tears.

From then on every morning there was a battle. Ronnie did not want to go to pre-school. He said 'Mrs Simms was stupid and she told lies'. In fact Ronnie was so unhappy that his mum eventually found him a placement in a different nursery.

A nursery full of dinosaurs!

Mrs May knew a lot about Ronnie before he arrived because she'd met with his parents and they'd had a long chat. She knew he loved dinosaurs and books. She was aware that the sandpit might be an issue, and that sharing toys could require some supervision. She was also aware that saying goodbye to Mum at the door had been a big problem in the past.

Mrs May had suggested Ronnie arrive on his first day half an hour later than the other children. That way, she explained, he wouldn't have to deal with the hustle and bustle. She suggested that Mum come in with him, stay for as long as she wanted and leave when she knew he was comfortable.

Ronnie and his mum arrived at the pre-school. They found his peg. Ronnie was chuffed to see the dinosaur next to his name. 'Look, Mummy. There's a T Rex,' he said with a smile.

Mum felt instant relief! Mrs May came out to greet them with a big, warm smile. She knelt down and introduced herself to Ronnie at his level. 'I've got more dinosaurs in there and I've been trying to find out the different names from this book. I want to make sure I don't put the herbivores with the carnivores.'

Ronnie smiled right back at her and was totally enthused, 'I can help you,' he offered. 'I know all about dinosaurs.' Mum followed, but actually felt like she could have left there and then. She watched for a while as Ronnie became engaged in his dinosaur heaven, naming them all and happily lining them up, leaning in for a closer look and flapping his hands in delight.

After a while Mrs May introduced another child to play alongside Ronnie with a set of plastic animals.

Mum had already prepped Ronnie that she would stay for a bit. Once he was busy having fun she might go home and then collect him before lunch. Ronnie saw that his mum was making an exit, but was far too absorbed in his dinosaurs to be bothered. Mum blew him a quick kiss and left. She could have hugged Mrs May.

As Mum left her eyes filled with tears. What a relief to know that her complex little man was in good hands!

Personalising the learning environment

Find out about individual interests on your initial home visit or speak to parents. Investigate what the child's personal motivators are before arrival. For example, if you know a child loves trains then add a little train to the name label by their peg, have a train set laid out and some train books or puzzles. Let them know that you find trains interesting too. Be impressed and enthusiastic about anything they choose to communicate. This could be reaming off an entire timetable or showing you which one they like best by looking or pointing. Use those interests to get the child's attention and it will help them to feel secure and happy. Personalising the learning environment is a really simple strategy and can significantly ease children's transitions.

Personalised peg labels[1]

What makes an inclusive setting?

✓ Visuals showing where the 'toilets' are and symbols or photos so that a child can ask to go.

✓ Photos showing the contents of boxes and cupboards and symbols or photos to make requests.

✓ Visual schedules set up for individual children.

✓ An area for sensory integration or for 'time out' to let off bounce.

✓ Photos by pegs, on schedules and individual schedules so that non-readers can achieve independence.

✓ A snack folder with symbols or photos so pre-verbal children can make choices.

---

1   *You can print free personalised pegs labels with personal motivators at senassist.com / labels.html*

✓ A lack of clutter (both visual and verbal).

✓ Clearly defined areas for play, for work, for choice, for snack and for active play.

✓ Sand timers and visual volume controls within easy reach.

✓ A loving, supportive atmosphere. A clear focus on the 'can dos'.

When Josephine Mele's grandson Nick was diagnosed with Asperger's Syndrome she set about researching and learning all she could to support him. When Nick was ten they co-wrote a fantastic article, 'The ABC's of Asperger's Syndrome'. They have kindly agreed for me to share excerpts from the article throughout this book.

Nick recalls starting pre-school:

> I couldn't wait to go to kindergarten. When I got there, I was surrounded by lots of kids I didn't know and by lots of noise. I felt like I couldn't breathe. My teacher thought I had a behavior problem and yelled at me every day until my grandma and my mom talked to the school principal. The principal must have talked to my teacher because she was nicer to me after that, and I started to like school again. (Mele 2012)

The author and artist Donna Williams, who is diagnosed with autism, shares her own life experiences and extensive knowledge to help others. In her book *Autism: An Inside-Out Approach* she describes her 'ideal educational environment' as:

> …one where the room had very little echo or reflective light, where the lighting was soft and glowing with upward projecting rather than downward projecting lighting. It would be one where the physical arrangements of things in the room was cognitively orderly and didn't alter and where everything in the room remained within routine defined areas. It would be an environment where only what was necessary to learning was on display and there were no unnecessary decorations or potential distractions. It would be one where nobody unexpected would enter without everyone getting a cue and processing time to expect change. It would be one where learning was through objects and nature and doing, not through having to rely on interpretation of written words or having to watch someone's constantly changing face or body; it would be an environment where the educators wore the same clothes

all the time (i.e. a uniform) so that they became visually similar and able to be relied upon. It would be an environment where the educator's voice was soft, so that you had to choose to tune in rather than being bombarded. The educator's intonation and tone of voice would remain the same so that auditorily they were perceived as consistently being the same person. (Williams 1996, pp.284–285)

I'd love for all teachers to read Williams' 'ideal educational environment' because it reveals so eloquently where the child might be coming from and why they might find their placement difficult to relax or learn in.

We put so many strategies in place in special needs schools. We insist on order, visuals and quiet and uncluttered classrooms with specified areas. There are reasons behind all of these things, there are reasons they make our students less anxious. When you read Williams' 'ideal' it just goes to confirm that all of these strategies are essential if a child is to stay on track.

Final thoughts

We must ensure that our special children are set up to succeed from the moment they walk through the classroom door. These children must start school feeling safe and secure. They will need accommodations – access to symbols, signs, information, empathy and support and maybe a dark tent, safe space or sensory bolt hole.

There are no second chances and no excuses for waiting. There are so many simple strategies and supports that all children can benefit from. Early Years teachers cannot wait for that diagnosis or a visit from a specialist advisory service. What if these things don't happen? What if when they do happen they happen wrong?

First impressions are so important – each child should rate a setting as 'outstanding' from the moment they walk through the door.

CHAPTER 2

Keeping Mum

Supporting, Listening to and Learning from Parents

My mother was the most beautiful woman I ever saw. All I am I owe to my mother. I attribute my success in life to the moral, intellectual and physical education I received from her.

George Washington

If we are to do the best for our children with SEN, we must always support, listen to and learn from their parents.

Mum bustles George into the cloakroom, removes his coat and puts it on his peg. Next she tugs off his boots and puts his shoes on. You say nothing, but feel a pinch of frustration. You have mentioned already that George could be a bit more independent. 'Given the time', you explained, 'he could do these things himself.' Mum's reaction was to roll her eyes and shrug off your 'advice'.

Later George is going out to play in the puddles. He stares at you blankly when asked to put on his boots – of course he does; at home this would be done for him! If only Mum would support you in building his independence instead of undoing all your good work.

Now let us shift the focus to how Mum might feel in this situation. What if Mum believes that your setting is undoing all *her* good work? What if she thinks her Jimmy is losing skills instead of gaining them, withdrawing rather than interacting, and regressing since he started with you? And what if, dare I suggest it, Mum is right?

Mum might not tell you how she feels, but before Jimmy joined you, his progress may have been her entire focus. She may know more than you about his SEN because she has researched them on the internet, read the books and consulted professionals, as well as other parents who have been there and done that. Parents do not wait for a diagnosis or statement of SEN to seek ways to help their child.

The following case studies come direct from a mum. Beth Heinemann has 13-year-old twin girls and a five-year-old boy, who is diagnosed with autism...

Case study: Freddie – first pre-school

Dear 'Mrs Can't',

Before Freddie turned three I'd learnt so much about autism. We'd started to use Makaton™ signs and PECS® for communication, and worked hard to teach him social skills. Before he started at your pre-school I asked for a meeting. You gave me a standard ten minutes, during which I filled in your standard 'About Me' form. You admitted to knowing nothing about autism...

You mentally grouped Freddie with two other boys on the spectrum – one diagnosed and one not. There was no extra support, and you referred to this 'situation' four times in front of me, saying, 'I have been stuck with three autistic kids in my setting with no extra help'.

Freddie was coping, though – not getting the best, but coping.

Next thing, you decided to physically group Freddie with the two other boys, who were not coping so well. They were *all* to arrive and leave through a different door to the other children and spend the first and last 20 minutes together in a room with you, doing 'IEP work'. Freddie started to regress. When I bathed him I noticed bruising caused by another child. I asked you to include him back with his peers and explained why, but you replied with, 'He can't do this. He can't do that...' I tried, in vain, to explain that he never would if you weren't willing to give him the opportunity to learn.

I felt I had no choice but to take Freddie out.

A lady from Early Years came and listened to me after that. She observed Freddie at your pre-school and got it... From then on Freddie was back with the main group. I felt at least he was getting play and social skills if not much else. It's heartbreaking to look back on that time and write this down; I would never settle for that now.

Case study: Freddie – second pre-school
Dear 'Mrs Can',

Before Freddie started with you, we had an amazing two-hour meeting where we discussed autism and Freddie... And you got it! Hooray! I could have cried. I think I did. You came to see Freddie in his home environment. You observed him for about 20 minutes, then started 'working with' him, getting him doing stuff I knew he could do but nobody else (outside the home) had achieved.

We had visits to nursery before Freddie started at *his* pace. You provided a booklet for Freddie with pictures of the staff and the different areas of the nursery, so I could visually prep him over the summer. While still waiting for Freddie's Statement, the school funded a full-time one-to-one for him, so he could have the best start possible.[1] Lots of meetings were held. I was always involved in the decision making and got to meet all the staff who would be working with Freddie.

---

1   *In the UK a child with SEN will now get an Education Health Care Plan (EHCP)*

Freddie's one-to-one had a basic knowledge of Makaton™, and you provided extra visuals for her to use with Freddie. You all used a lot of visuals anyway, which helped with inclusion.

Freddie has been extremely happy and successful with you from day one. Each day was clearly structured, and this helped greatly with his expectations and understanding. He conformed from the very start, doing everything that all the children were doing with no issues at all.

I got verbal feedback daily as Freddie still struggles with this type of communication. He also had a visual strip that he filled in showing what he had done throughout the day, so he could share this with me. You supported us through toilet training, drinking from an open cup, drinking water, extending speech, play, social skills, etc. etc. – everything really. Thank you!

P.S. When I saw the Christmas play and you had taught all the children the Makaton signs to go along with the songs, what a fantastic sight that was!

Ten tips for supporting parents

Here are ten simple things that you can do that can make all the difference:

1. Arrange home visits.

2. Provide visuals for home.

3. Give verbal feedback.

4. Use a home/school diary.

5. Have regular meetings.

6. Be positive – focus on the 'can dos'.

7. Share strategies.

8. Praise children, and parents, and show empathy.

9. Suggest respite.

10. Suggest support groups.

In the beginning...

Imagine that you are holding your newborn baby for the first time. You are checking those ten tiny fingers and toes, feeling that overwhelming love and instinct to protect... You are experiencing that rush of absolute, unconditional love. Your mind dreamily races ahead to a future filled with special moments – first words, first steps, first love, a wedding day...dream after dream and you will be there proudly protecting every step of the way. That baby is now your whole world.

Now imagine being told that due to a lack of oxygen at birth your perfect baby is: 'Severely disabled'.

She will probably never walk...

She will probably never feed herself...

She will probably never speak...

She will certainly be completely dependent on others for the rest of her life...

You hold that same beautiful baby and feel the same unconditional love, the same instincts to protect, but the future you thought you were anticipating is now full of fears.

Picture another scenario. You are sitting in that 'little room' with a pre-school teacher. Your three-year-old is in the next room (your only child, who took eight emotional years and three attempts at IVF to conceive). You can hear the mayhem in the classroom, his name being called in exasperation again and again. Your little boy is the one causing chaos. You brace yourself for what the teacher is going to say. In your heart you already know, but as long as they don't mention it then the problems could be down to your own worry. The teacher suggests calling in the educational psychologist and you suddenly feel as though you are sinking into quick sand.

Lauren Warner describes herself as 'a wife, writer and mama of four little ones'. She writes a blog called *Sipping Lemonade*. She's kindly allowed me to share this post in which she reflects on what she did not know before having a child with Down syndrome:

> Back before I had my four-year-old, daughter, Kate, I didn't know that Down syndrome had a capital 'D' and a lower case 's'.
>
> I didn't know that another name for Down syndrome is Trisomy 21 – or that it is caused by a third copy of the 21st

chromosome. I didn't even know how many chromosomes we had. Or that we had pairs.

I didn't know that some people have high tone and that others have low tone. Or that the heart has four chambers. (But then again, I've learned a lot about the heart in these past years – how it beats, how it works, how it grows and changes.)

And in 9th grade, I didn't know why tears welled in my eyes when I watched the young girl with Down syndrome dancing in my mom's Jazzercise class. I had no idea what to think about people with Down syndrome – after all, I didn't know any.

Years before I had any children, I didn't know why a friend confessed that she longed for a child with Down syndrome.

And before the rainy day we received a Down syndrome diagnosis with our second child, I didn't know what it felt like when everything you think you know, you suddenly don't. (Warner 2015)

Parenting is a constant rollercoaster and we never know what's round the corner. But parenting a child with SEN is an even more intense and hair-raising ride. No matter how brilliant the natural skill set, parents must have access to support and *their* first impression must be that their child will in the best hands.

Listening to parents: Jekyll and Hyde

Children can behave completely differently when in different settings. At school there are different demands, different anxieties and different ways of coping. If a parent tells you that they see a different child to the one you see at school don't doubt them. Instead think about why. Why doesn't Jimmy speak at school when Dad says he talks non-stop at home? Why is Billy so compliant when mum describes such challenges?

I'm going to hand over to another wonderful mum, who explains how holding it together during school can lead to meltdowns at home.

Michelle Myers offers a brilliant explanation for 'The Delayed Effect' in her blog *A Slice of Autism*. She's kindly allowed me to share it here:

THE DELAYED EFFECT

The delayed effect is a very common challenge facing many children on the Autistic Spectrum. Some children are able to contain their feelings all day at school, with the teacher blissfully unaware that there is a problem.

However the stress hormones are slowly building and building inside these kids. This creates a Jekyll and Hyde sort of situation that can put incredible pressure on families. Especially if the teacher doesn't understand or believe what the parents are telling them.

So let's think about it this way for a minute...

Imagine yourself as a bottle of pop. Your ingredients include: Autism, sensory processing difficulties, ADHD, and a hidden speech and language delay. The world's a confusing place and your difficulties are largely hidden to the wider world; not many people understand things from your perspective.

Your day...

Going to school is just one big worry for you...so give that bottle a shake!

You get to school and your teacher says 'let's start a new topic' What does that mean?... Give it a shake!

You don't understand what you have to do...shake it up!

You make a mistake...shake, shake, shake!

The lights in class are buzzing, it's annoying. Shake it a little more!

It's assembly. You have to sit still while your insides are wiggling and jiggling around. Shake it up!

The timetable changes and it's not maths like it should be, it's now music...and again!

The taxi gets stuck in traffic, you're late home, and the wrong radio station is on in the car... That's a few more shakes!

You get home and the lid blows off with the pressure!! That's the delayed effect! Its a real thing... Trust me.

The times over the years I have felt so confused and isolated when teachers would say to me 'Well that is a surprise we don't see any of that here at school.' Or I would hear 'Well he can behave for me, so maybe you're being too soft on him.'

I spent many a sleepless night wondering if it was me. Was it my parenting?

But I am his mum and my gut instinct is always right. I knew there was something my child was struggling with and all I had to do was really understand what his behaviour was telling me.

My child explodes at home with me because I am his safe place. I am predictable and calm and he can really be himself at home. At home he is fully accepted.

So this tells me that there are many things that can be done in order to reduce this build up of stress hormones for children like my son, by making them feel more safe and accepted for who they are.

And that means really embracing their individual needs. Not just trying to fit a round peg into a square hole. (Myers 2015)

I believe we learn most about the experiences of children with SEN and autism through learning from adults with SEN and autism. The autistic author, Daniel Tammet, recalls in his memoir, *Born on a Blue Day*:

I don't remember feeling lonely at the nursery, probably because I was so absorbed in my books and beads and circles. Slowly I think the feeling was creeping over me that I was different from the other children, but for some reason it didn't bother me. I didn't yet feel the desire for friends; I was happy enough playing by myself. (Tammet 2007, p.34)

Tammet explains how it was only when social demands were placed that he felt anxious and would refuse to join the throng. A child might seem deeply content playing by themselves, zoning out and avoiding social contact, but while doing this they are gradually building up an image that they are different, isolated, a loner. We as teachers must become the bridge to social interaction and contact. We can be trusted not to make unpredictable noise. We are more predictable. We must ensure that the child who removes themselves from the group is not left alone to developing and consolidating 'loner' as a self image. We go and sit by them. We don't place demands. We provide the interaction the child can cope with and gradually as we build their self-esteem and trust they may begin to join the group and feel less anxious.

Tammet's supervisors tried to gently persuade him, but he explains he was 'allowed to stand by one of the walls and watch the other children play' (Tammet 2007, p.5). He goes on:

> The moment I came home from the nursery I would always go upstairs to my room. Whenever I was feeling tired or upset I would crawl into the darkness under the bed and lie there. My parents learnt to tap quietly at the door before coming in to see how I was. (p.35)

Tammet's description of his nursery days must be familiar to so many adults with similar memories. Tammet was a little man, who would one day amaze everyone with his genius with numbers and languages, but he doesn't recall a teacher enjoying his interests and admiring his can's. He was happier left alone.

I've seen so many children who, left to their own devices, would believe themselves to be happier away from demands or interactions, who gradually discover that people can actually make things more fun. They start to seek interaction, to come and look for cuddles, tickles, dances or squeezes. They seek the feeling of being loved for their own uniqueness. Children who seem to prefer to stand away or zone out can be so playful, cheeky and interactive. They can smile and giggle and communicate. They simply require a different approach.

Let parents in

Invite parents into school to join activity mornings. Seeing you get covered in paint or flour while truly enjoying engaging with their little person can make such a difference to how they perceive you as a professional.

Parenting is one of the greatest learning curves and it may be that we need to teach parents a less traditional set of play skills. It is so much more powerful to show a parent how we interact with children than to tell them.

Inviting parents in to share play sessions builds their confidence in seeking advice or reassurance and can be a chance for them to meet with other parents building those all important support networks. These mornings can also provide ideas for home activities and a chance to see their child is happy and safe at school.

Parents' nights out

Once in a while we encourage the parents to take a night off and join us for a night out. These evenings are about getting to know each other, building relationships, encouraging playdates and strengthening the support network around each child. Parents at special schools often send their child in on school transport so they don't have those school gate chats.

Parents' nights out also allow parents to see us as fellow parents, who can experience some of the same challenges as they do at home. They get to know how much we care about their children's progress and want to support their families in any way we can. When I hear about the parents meeting up in the holidays, the triumphs they share, the way they support one another (and continue to do this as the children progress through school) I know that the work we do to encourage these parent friendships is so worthwhile.

Anxiety is catching

A child might not yet speak, a child might seem to be 'in their own world', but that same child can be so empathic. They can read how a parent feels and absorb it. If Mum feels anxious, they feel anxious. If Mum remains completely calm no matter what, this makes them to feel safer. Parents do not automatically know this from the start (although many will learn over time).

Marci Lebowitz is an occupational therapist and author. She writes a blog aimed at parents and explains, in her blog post *Tips for Calming Your Child*:

> Being calm at your child's times of need gives them a feeling of calm they can begin to mirror. Managing your own state as a parent influences your child's behavior as well as the emotional state of others around you. If we are out of control and frantic, other people will mirror this. If we can learn how to approach the situation of our child melting down in public calmly, and are able to calmly reassure others around us, everyone will sense that you know what you are doing, you are in control of the situation and

that they are safe. With this sense of control, it helps the autistic child move within the energy of others, and you can begin to relax when you and your supersensitive child are outside of the house. (Lebowitz 2015)

We must also help teach our parents to take care of themselves so that they can be the tower of strength and consistency their child will need. We encourage them to say 'Yes' to respite, explaining that when they get to go for a walk or a swim or sit in a café they are actually strengthening themselves, which benefits their child. Our parents will go on and on giving and giving, but they need us to tell them that they can only do this with some time to restore and recharge.

Miriam Gwynne is another wonderful mum. She writes a blog called *Faith Mummy*, about her journey parenting twins with SEN. She openly shares her worries and her triumphs in order to support other parents.

She's allowed me to share the following:

WHO SUPPORTS THE PARENTS?

We are the ones dealing with the challenging behaviour, the meltdowns, the endless screaming, the not sleeping, the sensory difficulties and the food refusals. We are the ones who do the personal care, fight to get the uniform on and battle to get them to school. When the holidays come we are left alone and everyone at the meeting carries on with their day.

We are the ones fighting with schools, dealing with transport issues, and filling in forms. We are the bottom line and the most important people in it all. Our opinions matter hugely, our insight is important and our knowledge crucial. We should be valued, respected and acknowledged. We are the true professionals, the best experts, and have the most invested in our child. But we also deal with the reality so much more than anyone else.

I love that so many people support my children. But I do wonder sometimes when I watch other families going through the same thing as I do, when I hear so many parents of children with SEN struggling with depression or crumbling with the stress of it all:

Who, in all this, is supporting the parents? (Gwynne 2015b)

We teachers are not only there to support and teach children. Parents are the child's support network for life. If we can support them with love, understanding and practical information we can signpost a happier journey.

Final thoughts

When a parent leaves their child in your care, they are handing over someone absolutely precious. That child is their everything and their happiness is their priority. Parents have to know you are doing everything to support, encourage and protect their child. We must build bridges by communicating, listening and learning. Parents will never forgive you or forget if they feel that you have got it wrong, because you will not only have failed their child but left them feeling guilty too. Strengthen parents. Support them. You have the children during the day, and plan for a year, maybe two… They are at the start of what could be an emotional roller coaster. They will carry the memory of your early support in their heart for life.

CHAPTER 3

Good Communication
Can Save You Time

Communication Boards, Books, Tick Lists, Emails, Phone Calls and More

We are never so defenceless against suffering as when we love.

Sigmund Freud

When a parent leaves their child in your care they are placing their heart in your hands. That little person in their oversized T-shirt that they are waving goodbye to and watching through the window is their whole world. No wonder they linger, no wonder they ask questions and want details...

Good communication with parents from the outset is essential. If that little voice in your head is saying 'that all sounds true, but I don't have time' remember that good communication can *save* you time.

Communication boards

A communication board displayed at the collection point gives parents something to look at while you search for that missing hat, saves you repeating the same speed summary of the day. It impresses, encourages and allows a parent to have a proper conversation with their child on the journey home. Without reading the board the conversation may be restricted to 'Did you have a good morning?' and a single word reply. Having a bigger picture of a child's day will encourage conversations and reduce separation anxiety. Have you ever noticed that the child who doesn't want to leave Mummy often has the mother who really doesn't want to leave their child? Maybe that Mum has a good reason. We don't know the history of how long they waited to have that child or their past experiences of childcare.

Children are naturally instinctive and will pick up on their parents' feelings when they leave them at the door. Do everything in your power to ensure those parental vibes are 100 per cent positive.

A communication board can be created during a tea break. At the start of the week write down your theme, letter or number focus and add information about daily activities such as making face cakes or painting fireworks pictures. You could add that tomorrow we will be making red play dough or hoping for nice weather so we can visit the park. This will help encourage more communication and help children who respond well to having a schedule.

If you can find the time to add photos or display the children's work the parents will love this. I would suggest you keep it random (don't do this every day or even on a set day). This way you won't set up an expectation that could lead to disappointment. Instead the parents get a lovely surprise when you have found the time to celebrate their children's achievements with a quick visual display.

Communication books

Communication books can also be a useful way to keep parents informed. These are really important if a child has little or no speech. Each child in my class has a little home/ school book and we try to write in them each day. I include photos when I can because they allow a child with limited understanding of spoken language to have a moment of 'conversation' about their day. Again it's better to keep these random because, no matter how good our intention, there is not time to do this every day.

Tick lists

Using tick lists can save time too. Fill in the times for naps and nappy changes. Tick a box for a wee or poo. Have a list of the foods offered and tick off if they have eaten. Parents like to know. Why? Up until they leave the child in your care they have known and possibly worried about every detail. It's quicker to tick a box than try to remember when asked at the door. Parents might not ask, but they do appreciate the information. If a child has or hasn't slept or eaten enough it can have an impact on the rest of their day and how they sleep at night.

Online learning journeys

Schools can now buy into some great online learning journeys, for example '2 Build a Profile' by 2simple.com and 'Tapestry' (see the 'Useful Websites' section at the end of the book). These offer a way of doing 'observations on the go'. You log in, then find the child's profile and take photos or log observations. You can also add notes, next steps and link this to assessment and you can log in from home to add to comments or assessment. Over time a profile is built, creating a learning journey for each child. Parents can share this with their child at home, which promotes communication. They can also make comments or 'like' the observations. I've seen this from a parent's perspective and have to say that our four-year-old regularly requests to look at the photos or herself and her friends. We have such lovely conversations and I am able to learn so many things about her day. As a teacher it has been a great way to ensure that our photographs have a context, a date and that the expectations, outcomes and next steps are clear. They also make us feel rather techie and up to date.

Filming

Video recordings can be a great way to allow parents a window into what you do at school; they can also allow a parent to see how you are working to develop communication, interaction and play. Not all parents know how to instigate play with children, but when a child is not demanding their attention or even resisting interaction it can be difficult for them to see a way forward. Seeing video of how staff interact with their child may open their eyes and inspire them to introduce more play at home.

Video can also allow you to get a snapshot of a child's progression and may even be great for training future staff (provided you obtain the necessary consents).

Websites

Websites – please don't wince... Adding and updating photos is easier than it sounds. Once you are past the fear factor and learn the basics this does not take much time. I love getting an email from my son's school to say the website has been updated. Children like seeing their pictures on the website. It makes them feel important and raises their self-esteem.

Prospective parents will also love getting a real window into your setting, when deciding if it is the right place for their child.

You will need to ensure you get written consent from parents or guardians to publish photos on the website. Once you get started you may even enjoy updating the website. Maybe you could add a blog, which could be viewed by other settings to get ideas.

Email lists

Have a list of parents' email addresses. This can be a good way to get emergency information out fast. Even if not every parent sees the 'Emergency closure' email you send at 10pm when you find out the boiler is broken, some of them will. This could help the working parents arrange childcare. You can't phone parents at 10pm, but email doesn't have the same rules. You could ask them for a quick reply if they see the email. One less call to make in the morning...

Telephone contact

Phoning parents is also a great way to build a trusting relationship and find out more about their child. If you've sent a note home asking for rain boots and a week later they haven't appeared, don't get frustrated. Instead give the child's parents a call. They may have lost the note, forgotten or have difficulty reading or translating your note. Most parents love getting a call from the teacher. It tells them that you care and allows them to speak openly, without the time restraints and other ears that can restrict communication at drop off and pick up times.

Home visits

Home visits are essential before a child starts school, but they must continue (if additional support is required). An additional home visit can really help parents put strategies, such as PECS®, schedules and routines in place, or give practical ideas or supports. Home visits can also help ensure a consistent approach to sensory issues, personal care, communication or eating. They allow us to remain up to date with motivators and changing circumstances. They let parents know that our support extends beyond the school day. We want their child to succeed in all areas. We care about their whole family. We can offer a listening ear, a strategy, a support. Perhaps even a lifeline...

Letters home

Letters at the start of each new term are also a great way to let parents know about your new topic, request supporting items such as baby photos and request voluntary contributions to snack time, soft tissues for runny noses or even volunteers to help.

Appearing in the local paper

Getting into the local paper really impresses the parents and grandparents and can give the children a real sense of pride. It's also excellent publicity and raises the profile of your setting. Have a look in your local paper to see the stories they include and get thinking about something your children could do. You can usually find the contact details of the journalists in the paper or on the website. Again written parental consent is essential.

Parents worry

All parents worry. From the moment we hold a newborn baby in our arms it starts. Are they too cold? We wrap them up then wonder if they are too hot. Are they feeding enough, feeding too much, sleeping enough? Are they meeting milestones? All of these are the usual parent worries. But throw in a potential diagnosis that they have a learning difference or disability and a whole additional set of concerns, and the uncertainties and worry can become overwhelming,

As Miriam Gwynne explains in her blog, *Faith Mummy*:

> I worry what he will find to do tomorrow. I worry that one day there will be no red school jumper in his size for him to wear. I worry how I will continue to lift him in and out the bath, in and out of car seats and his buggy as he continues to grow and get heavier by the day. I worry that he might never ever speak. I worry how people will look after him. I worry I might one day be changing nappies on a teenager or grown man. (Gwynne 2014)

It is our responsibility to be aware of these worries and support the parents. The anxiety a parent feels at drop off times will pass directly to the child and really impact on how they feel at school. Children look to parents to judge their safety and if a parent is nervous they will be as well.

Ten tips for communicating with parents

1. Display a communication board.

2. Display photos and children's work.

3. Use communication home/ school books.

4. Use tick charts to record basic information.

5. Update websites with photos.

6. Keep a list of parents' email addresses.

7. Pick up the phone and ask.

8. Send letters home at the start of a new term.

9. Do something special and invite the local press.

10. Invite them to join in or help.

Final thoughts

Elizabeth Stone once famously commented on what a momentous decision it is to have a child. She compared it to deciding to forever have your heart walk around outside your body. Communicating with parents builds trust. Try to answer questions before they need to ask them and when those kisses goodbye take a little too long or you'd prefer them not to watch your lesson through the window…remember that their child is more precious to them that anything in the world and the handover can be scarier for the parent than the child.

CHAPTER 4

Unlocking that Special Child

Observing, Investigating
and Getting Creative

*The whole world is a series of miracles, but we're so used to
them we call them ordinary things.*

Hans Christian Andersen

Have you ever come across the child who doesn't seem to be
motivated by *anything*? You have got out the dinosaurs, the books, the
paints, even the snacks and there has not been a flicker of interest. So
how are you supposed to engage them? How can you begin to get
them communicating or learning about 'appropriate' behaviours and
routines? Is there a set of magic keys to unlock these children?

Key 1: Observe

Note down everything the child does whether it be spinning in circles,
repeatedly flicking a bit of paper or fingering through soil. Do they
cover their ears, avoid touch or gravitate toward a certain area? Do
they show awareness of adults and/or any other children? Get another
member of staff to observe and then give their feedback. Is there any

repetitive behaviour? Is there anything (no matter how unusual) that seems to be catching their interest? If possible visit the child's home. They may change in a familiar environment.

Key 2: Investigate

Talk to the parent/carer of the child. Ask about the child's interests. What do they like to do at home? Do they show any interest in particular music television programme, toy or object?

Key 3: Create

Think outside the box but take it further. Every child is different – each one is a unique puzzle. Getting creative is the fun bit. Take time to brainstorm with other staff and try out different ideas. Don't be upset if things don't work – you are eliminating possibilities and constantly getting closer.

Case study: Billy, the display ripper

Billy's 'file' described him as non-verbal. He was not communicating in any functional way. I first encountered Billy as he was being shown around school with his parents. I noticed his mother had a tight hold of him at all times and there was panic in her eyes. What did she think he would do if she let him go?

The observation

We didn't have to do much observing. By the end of day one every display, every name label and bit of backing paper was ripped. My lovely, bright classroom looked like it had been attacked by a mini dinosaur. I say mini because the top part of the displays (out of Billy's reach) were intact.

My classroom assistant looked as if she'd been dragged through a hedge backwards and had given up following Billy's trail of destruction with the staple gun. On a normal day, we would have got on with the million jobs we always seem to have to do after school, but on this occasion we collapsed with cups of tea and looked at each other, shell shocked.

The investigation

So far, as we had observed, Billy liked to rip down our displays. We had also noticed that each time he did it he looked to us with twinkling eyes and a cheeky smile as though expecting praise. What was he getting from the behaviour? Were we reinforcing it by running around after him – was he wanting us to shout or even cry? I imagined what this would be like for his mum at home, or worse still on a visit to friends. Children who seek reactions through their behaviour may not be able to distinguish positive reactions from negative. So the first thing to do was to control our reactions.

Getting creative

We knew it was pointless putting the displays back as they were, so we chose a different tactic. We decided that all 'Billy level' displays would be laminated with Velcro on the back. This way if they were ripped off the wall they could not be ripped up and we'd just put them straight back. Our hope was that this would deny Billy the reaction he was seeking.

Billy arrived the next morning. When he got to his peg he ripped off the name label and looked up at my teaching assistant. It was intact (having been laminated) and she picked it up and attached it straight back to the wall. Next name label – same non-reaction. Billy went into the classroom and discovered the same thing. Ripping displays was not having the effect he was seeking. Observing Billy I felt a twinge of guilt, but what had clearly started as a sensory searching behaviour had become a reaction seeking one. We gave Billy a box of paper to rip up – no interest. Next we gave Billy a big box with layers of paper glued to the side of it and bingo – happy Billy ripping away, and each time he tore some off we praised him.

Billy learnt to ask for his 'Rip box' as we called it, using a photograph in his PECS® book. It kept him occupied and happy during transitions and was a great starting point for Intensive Interaction. He was getting his sensory need met in a positive and appropriate way.

Case study: Rhianna's rice of many colours

Rhianna had emerging speech. She would sometimes sing familiar theme tunes like 'Bob the Builder, can you fix it?', but never engaged in conversational speech. She would opt out of lessons in a quiet, but definite way and often get 'stuck' en route to different places. She spent the majority of her time in the corner of the classroom, in the corner of the playground, or in a corridor.

The observation

One thing that came out of watching Rhianna was how expert she was at opting out and how incredibly definite she was about it. Two things that did get a spark of interest were the interactive whiteboard and watching cereal being poured at snack time. She didn't want to touch it or eat it, but she was entranced by watching it pour. When the box was left unattended Rhianna was there with lightning speed pouring the contents all over the table.

The investigation

After a long chat with Rhianna's mum I found out that she liked watching things pour at home too. Everything had to be locked away high out of her reach to avoid it being poured. Rhianna's poor mum – I could only imagine...

Getting creative

We made a selection of sensory trays for Rhianna to explore – pasta, sand, glitter, rice and flour. Rice was the clear winner. The rice tray became a great starting point for Intensive Interaction. Rhianna would even ask for it using her PECS®. But rice was the only thing Rhianna would ask for and we wanted to extend her communication. She had mastered the sentence 'I want rice', but I wanted to see if she could extend this. Rhianna was motivated to get the rice, but never asked for anything else.

If only the rice could be different colours perhaps we could get her using symbols to request a specific colour. We dyed all the rice in rainbow colours and put it in the trays to dry out. Our experiment paid off – Rhianna clearly liked her new coloured rice. She didn't do what I'd hoped, which was to select a favourite colour and ask for it, but she did like watching us add one colour at a time. In time this did motivate Rhianna to extend her PECS® sentence to 'I want red, yellow, blue, green, orange, purple, rice.'

Case study: Lily's own little world

Lily was a beautiful little girl, who won our hearts from the moment she arrived. She was ever so quiet and ever so expert at opting out of engagement, interaction or communication. In her first days with us she slept a lot. When she was not sleeping she would sit on a bean bag and fixate on a magazine. Mostly she seemed happy, but there were times when she would have a little cry. This was usually followed by a sleep.

The observation

Lily would always gravitate towards one area of the room. She particularly liked our Peppa Pig magazine and would spend a long time flicking through then zooming in on certain pictures. Left to her own devices Lily would be completely happy. She could become upset at times when any demands were placed and she could be very assertive. As long as she could follow her own agenda and look at her magazines in peace she was quite content. But Lily wasn't learning to interact and if she continued to zone out in this way she would not learn to communicate or develop relationships.

The investigation

Lily had built up a great bank of ways to protect herself from demands or social interaction and was brilliant at getting her way. We spoke to Lily's dad, who was clearly very anxious about her not eating. We explained that we would get there over time, but we needed to build Lily's trust. I had a feeling that Lily might be very aware that her eating was causing her parents anxiety. When I explained that although Lily did not speak she could most probably understand all that was being said it seemed to be a bit of a revelation. I asked dad not to talk about any worries about eating or communication in front of her or make an issue about them.

Getting creative

Lily gradually became more aware and interested in us through a lot of one-to-one Intensive Interaction. Over time Lily has become more and more interactive and playful. She gives us great big smiles while we sing songs like 'Row, row the boat'. She loves dancing and spinning around with staff and gives us the most amazing smiles and cuddles. She will still find a quiet little corner at times, but now she will often come and take an adult to where she wants to play. She loves to bounce on the little trampoline holding your hands. She runs to us and gives us cuddles when she is happy. She rarely cries or sleeps in school. We are hearing her voice more often, even the occasional song. Looking back on how she started it is amazing how far she has come on.

Donna Williams is an artist, author and poet. She also has a diagnosis of autism. In her book *Autism: An Inside-Out Approach* she explains:

> If you suspect that a behaviour may be an adaption or compensation, then use your imagination to consider how you could expand upon such a strategy or compensation; how you could use it to build bridges to other skills. Do not think so much about what the person is doing, but about the particular skill being used in doing what they are doing. If they are lining things up, for example, and seem indifferent to what they are lining up, then focus on the lining up rather than on what they are lining up. Consider, for example, all the useful skills in life where a skill of lining things up can be put to good use. Gradually over time, introduce

new collections of objects to be lined up that progressively resemble the things for which there is a practical need to line them up or which occur lined up in the world, in general (i.e. bowling pins, toy railway tracks, queues of dolls or cars). (Williams 1996, p.282)

If as Williams suggests, rather than worrying about a child's tendency to line things up and not play in a way we see as 'appropriate', we praise them and suggest more things to line up, if we see their strengths and their potential, they will pick up on this. What a fantastic way to build a child's trust and show them how we believe in them and see their personal potential.

Williams continues:

If the skill is categorising, here are shelves to be tidied, clean folded laundry to be put away, cutlery to be put into sections, crockery to be put away. If the skill is disassembly or shredding, supply the sort of things that require disassembly or shredding (e.g. for recycling purposes).

If you successfully and gradually assist people who have a variety of these type of skills into using them for a whole range of practical purposes, then they may eventually be able to spend their time more constructively and develop more independence-related skills than they otherwise might have.

You could lead the horse to water and it will probably drink it. If you drag it there then it may be much less likely to. (Williams 1996, p.282)

Final thoughts

L.P. Jacks, an English educator, philosopher and Unitarian minister observed:

A master in the art of living draws no sharp distinction between his work and his play; his labor and his leisure; his mind and his body; his education and his recreation. He hardly knows which is which. He simply pursues his vision of excellence through whatever he is doing, and leaves others to determine whether he is working or playing. To himself, he always appears to be doing both. (Jacks 1932, p.1)

We must look at how a child is and see their individual potential. We must see their strengths and gifts and reveal the possibilities. There is always a positive. There is always a reason, a 'can do'...

You know that amazing feeling, that buzz, when you do a truly great session. If you could only bottle that feeling – I would compare it to flying. Well when you begin to fathom the puzzle of that special child, you will discover a whole new teaching euphoria.

CHAPTER 5

Colour-Coded Symbols

The purest and most thoughtful minds are those which love color the most.

John Ruskin, *The Stones of Venice*

Imagine you are in an unfamiliar place and need the toilet. You look around, but there is no sign. There are lots of people, but you can't communicate with them because they don't understand your language. This is getting urgent and you're starting to panic...

Children with listening and communication difficulties or those who have English as a second language face this situation every day and there are some simple ways we can avoid it.

Most settings now provide some visual symbol to indicate the whereabouts of the toilet. Most often it will be black and white. The child needs to be taught that this symbol represents 'toilet' and how to use it to communicate their need. They will learn this by repetitive use of the symbol. Each time they go to the toilet they take the symbol and match it to one that is the same in the toilet.

You can also experiment with using photographs of the toilet to match to the same photograph.

If they wear nappies make the symbol or photograph a nappy or the changing area. Some children might need to use an object of reference and take the actual nappy with them – use what works for the individual child.

Show a child the 'toilet' symbol, but do not expect them to process it at speed. They may take some time to shift their focus, then connect meaning, and then decide whether to act on that meaning. Children with SEN and autism will often require more time than other children. It can also help if you use an egg timer to physically give the child some time. You are not saying 'toilet right now', but 'toilet in one minute' – this may seem like a much more achievable and reasonable demand.

More

Children need a motivator to communicate. We may gradually build a bank of photographs, but there will be times when we just don't have a photograph or symbol and we don't want to lose the moment. Having a stock of 'more' symbols can help with this. For example a child likes bubbles being blown, but you don't have a symbol. Teach them to ask for 'more'. Make sure you say the word each time you use the symbol and quickly introduce the idea of using it for other motivators.

Snack can be a good time to start a child communicating with PECS®. Having a stock of 'more' symbols means that there is always a way to ask (even if there has not been time to go off, print and laminate a specific symbol). The more exchanges a child makes in the day the quicker they will progress. We must find ways to create these opportunities and if our 'to do' list makes it impossible to keep up with every new snack then find clever ways to allow the child to still make their exchanges.

Case study: Arlo asks for 'more'

Arlo was an energetic child. He loved food! He could swipe another child's food at lightning speed. Arlo did not have any speech so he could not tell us what he wanted. We quickly started him using PECS. Snack time was going to be the most motivating time. The beauty of the 'more' symbol was that we could use it for any food. We would give Arlo a little of it and he could lift the symbol to request 'more'. To teach Arlo this skill took two staff. The 'teacher' would have the motivating snacks and the 'support' would help him lift the symbol and place it in the 'teacher's' hand. Over time Arlo learnt to make these exchanges himself. We were not expecting Arlo to recognise the symbol yet. The symbol was a token he would exchange for what he wanted.

Over time Arlo learnt to travel across the room with his symbol to request a snack. In PECS® this is known as 'persistence and distance'.

Help

Children are very good at finding ways to get what they want without using speech. Maybe they will take your hand to open the snack cupboard or open a door. Again the 'help' symbol gives them the power to communicate when there is nothing ready prepared. In our classroom we have a 'help' symbol and an 'open the cupboard' on every cupboard. Toys are stored in boxes with lids. There is a 'help' symbol on these as well. Why is this? The more times we can encourage a child to use their method of communication the quicker they will progress.

One of our children likes to be pushed around in a little car. He has learnt to use the 'help' symbol to ask staff to push him. Every time he brings the symbols he hears the word 'help'. He has learnt that there is a reason for communication and that we teachers can be quite useful.

Finished

Hold up this symbol whenever an activity is finished. Use it at the end of snack, at tidy up time, at the end of session. You can also use it to request a challenging behaviour 'finish' without having to use lots of language. Sometimes language can be seen as rewarding challenging behaviour. Many children use behaviour to seek attention – they don't mind if the attention is negative.

So why colour code the symbols?

Some children will connect with the colour before the image. By colour coding the most basic symbols you include these children and help them to learn that different symbols have different uses.

Colour coding the background, as opposed to the actual symbol, is helpful so that the symbol can be seen clearly and provide a visual cue to the user.

When you need a symbol fast to suit an immediate need you quickly learn to find it by colour.

Even if a child can understand black and white symbols in calm moments, when they are at crisis point we need to give them the quickest way to communicate this.

These colour-coded symbols are free to print from the SEN Assist website.[1] They come in sheets of different sized symbols to suit the child and the situation:

---

1   www.senassist.com

Good waiting

This symbol was created for children who find waiting difficult. One of the best places to teach this symbol is in the car. The amber colour relates to traffic lights and there is the visual reference to the clock. Each time you stop at traffic lights or have to wait, show this symbol. When the waiting is over remove the symbol and praise the child if they have waited calmly.

As a baby our son would cry when we stopped at traffic lights and then, when we moved on, he would stop crying and look all smug. He thought his noise had made us start moving, so he would do it every time. This is how children learn that their negative behaviour can affect our actions.

I saw the power of this symbol when I arrived at the school ICT room with my class of children with autism and found another class still using it. My expectations were not good and I was expecting a few meltdowns. But no – they surprised us all. I showed them the 'good waiting' symbol and said 'waiting' very calmly and they did just that. This is a powerful symbol.

Good sitting, looking and listening

Sitting still and keeping hands down is difficult for a lot of children. Most will understand without a visual, but there are those who don't. This symbol shows them exactly what you want them to do. It also means you do not need to keep disrupting the group by telling the child to sit well.

This symbol is only for use if you are expecting the child to sit in a chair because children can be very literal. Individual carpet sample squares can work well to get the children to sit well at carpet time. You can get these for next to nothing or even free from nice carpet shops, when you explain their use.

Display 'good sitting', 'good looking' and 'good listening' somewhere prominent and teach all the children what they mean. You'll be surprised how quickly the children learn them.

Always use symbols to reinforce positive behaviour and show your expectations. Don't have images of negative behaviours such as 'no throwing' and 'no hitting' because they can easily be misread.

Colour coding

Having a clear order can help a child feel safe and in control We know that many children with autism have a tendency to want to create categories. We also know that they are often more drawn to colour and shapes. I have examined this in depth in *Colour Coding for Learners with Autism* (Devine 2014a) so will only touch on colour coding briefly here.

For the past two years our Early Years class has been trialling using colour codes. We have created clear categories for our symbols. Transition and schedule symbols are on purple or have a *purple* outline. This includes our schedule symbols, timetable symbols. The 'Now and Next' transition boards are purple as are our schedules and class timetable. If a child sees purple it explains where they should go. We have transition boards with a purple outline. The child takes the symbol from their schedule and places it on the transition board. We will have schedules set up to direct children within sessions. They have four colour symbols relating to four tables. The tables are not the actual colour, but the boards are. This provides a visual cue the child can relate to. We change the activities on the tables.

Our behaviour symbols are outlined in *orange*. They may get to the blue table and see an orange 'thumbs up' with 'good writing' on it. This shows the expectation. They will also have an orange token board and can collect a thumbs up token at each table. This can lead to a reward.

Our personal care symbols are outlined in *aqua* and work in a similar way.

These colour codes appeal to the category loving child, but are also a really useful way to organise a myriad of symbols and allow staff to quickly locate the one they need. This encourages staff to use them and to provide a place to put them all away.

We do not outline any PECS® symbols with a colour. This means that we can easily explain and differentiate for new staff and parents that only symbols or photos with no colour outline belong in PECS books. There is so often confusion between what is a PECS symbol and what is a schedule symbol. The colours make it all so much easier to explain.

This system has been so useful, consistent and clear that we are now aiming to roll it out across the school.

Nick (age ten), diagnosed with Asperger's Syndrome (who we have heard from previously) explains:

> I like my shirts and pants hung by similar colors so I can find the ones I want to wear. My desk is neat so I can find things quickly. I sort my toys into bins by color and size. I don't even like different foods touching each other on my plate. It seems wrong to me to have things crowding each other. I like everything in its own space. (Mele 2012)

Symbols on staff

The support staff in our Early Years class each wear their own set of colour-coded symbols. These may be on a lanyard along with their ID or on a key ring with elastic so that they can be accessed at speed. Useful symbols to have are 'good sitting' (with different ways of sitting), 'good walking', 'good waiting', 'good being quiet', 'good sharing', 'good tidying', 'toilet', 'more', 'help', 'finished', and a symbol for the class. You can also add some more behaviour symbols such as 'good lining up' and 'good work' (if they will be used often). Personal care symbols can be good additions: 'shoes on', 'shoes off', 'coat on', 'coat off' and so forth.

When making these up I asked staff to put the 'help' symbol at the front so that the child can quickly access it. They can ask for 'help' to open the door, the cupboard or a packet of crisps in their lunch box. We often find ourselves wearing these symbols when out and about. I personally think that the 'help' symbol is better on view than the 'toilet' or 'finished' symbols, which could send out unintentional visual messages.

If a child responds to objects of reference (OOR) then staff may wear a little apron or tabard with a pocket to store them. If the child is on a one-to-one program this can be a good visual reference as to which staff should be supporting the child.

Final thoughts

If you find that any symbols or strategies are helping a child in *your* setting, then pass them on to the next teacher. Give them to parents to use at home – the more consistent their use, the greater their power.

CHAPTER 6

Show Them the Way

Using Visuals –
Practical Ideas and Examples

Rather than love, than money, than fame, give me truth.
Henry David Thoreau, *Walden*

Imagine you are on a mission to walk on the moon. Every preparation has been made and you really want to do this, but the outfit provided does not remotely resemble the images you have seen of astronauts in space. You are already out of your comfort zone and this unexpected change is making you feel anxious. You consider resisting and abandoning the mission altogether. If only someone had shown you the suit earlier and explained modern changes to space gear, you would have felt so much more in control...

When a child arrives at school they are a million miles away from the comfort of their 'home planet'. The more accurate the visual information we can provide, the less anxiety *they* will encounter.

We might think we have this covered, but let's stop a second and look closely at the information we provide. Imagine not being able to read social rules and search the environment for clues as to what might be expected. Accurate information can help a child feel safe and in control, and enable them to take that leap of faith to unfamiliar territory.

Case study: Hassan's sausages

Hassan was a complex little man who could be fine one moment, but could physically attack another child or teacher the next. His trigger was not always clear, meaning his behaviour could be hard to predict. But there was one food that always seemed to trigger a lunchtime 'incident': sausages.

Hassan was a vegetarian, so when pork sausages were on the menu he could not have them. My first thought was for the kitchen to make some vegetarian sausages so that Hassan could still have some sausages, but due to oven space and chef's timings, this was not going to be possible. I decided not to pursue this with our cook as giving him sausages could potentially set him up to fail in the future – there would come a time when Hassan would not be able to get a meat-free alternative.

At the start of each day I would talk the children through our visual timetable. I was doing this when I had a lightning bolt moment – I suddenly noticed that the lunch symbol showed a plate of sausages and peas. I wondered if there could be a link between the symbol and the sausage meltdowns. Every day we showed Hassan an image of a plate of sausages, and then when he went to the lunch hall, he was served something else. On the one day when we seemed to have got it right, when our symbol matched the menu, we told Hassan, 'No sausages'. Could this be the reason for the meltdowns?

I changed the symbol to one that showed sandwiches. The next day Hassan went into the lunch hall and tried to take a sandwich from a child who was eating their packed lunch. Next I changed the timetable symbol to show three different options for lunch. As we went through the timetable I explained that there could be different things for lunch.

Hassan had his own visual 'Now and Next' schedule. The shorter schedules were used to break things down so that if he could not process the entire day's activity, he could see what he would be doing next. We added the new lunch symbol, talking it through in simple terms each day using the same language, so it would become recorded information. The day arrived when sausages were on the menu again. It was fantastic to see Hassan get through that lunchtime without a meltdown. Hassan had needed accurate visual information and our original symbol had been confusing. We had seen 'lunch' because we could read and process the word, but he had seen 'sausages'.

I began to go through every symbol that we used with the class, ensuring they would make sense to a literal, visual learner.

Case study: Ernie, a talkative child with a throwing issue

Ernie was a very talkative child. At playtime he would ask to have a ball, but he would always end up lobbing it on the roof or over a fence. After he had thrown the ball far, far up and away he would say 'I'm sorry' and expect that an adult would go and retrieve it. He would keep on asking and asking, as if throwing the ball was the whole point of playtime.

If there was no ball to throw, Ernie would look around for something else – a book, some building bricks or a jumper. This could cause distress to other children, who did not like having their items thrown. It also meant that we started to avoid having balls and objects out at playtime, which was unfair on the other children.

Ernie was happy and occupied if I went on the other side of the fence and we spent playtime throwing a ball up high over the fence back and forth.

I noticed that our playtime symbol showed a child throwing a ball up in the air. This was the only activity shown for playtime. Looking at the visual timetable the playtime symbols really stood out. Could it be that each day Ernie had been looking at the visual timetable and seeing playtime as 'throw a ball up high' time? Could this misperception have formed the basis of a habit? Ernie had started off wanting to throw because he thought this was the right thing. Perhaps one day, when there was no ball, he had thrown another child's toy and got a rewarding reaction.

Children with autism spectrum conditions can enjoy mixing things up and getting reactions. They might not mind if the reaction is positive or negative.

I developed a symbol that would show the different activities children might do at playtime to avoid another child seeing 'playtime' as 'throw time'.

If a child is not following your expectations, then explain in simple language or show them by using an accurate visual. It is so important to get the right information across in a way that is clear to *every* child.

Visuals can help *every* child

Here are five ways to improve your communication for everyone:

- Use photo labels to show box and drawer contents.

- Have a visual choice board with an 'I want _____' sentence strip.

- Have a 'wash hands' visual schedule above the sink.

- Send home a visual suggesting a practice dress up in uniform or PE kit.

- Have an interactive 'clothes for different weathers' visual on display.

Visuals can help all children, not only those with a diagnosis of SEN. They should be in place from the moment a child walks through the door. Every child should have access to a way of understanding your requests, knowing your expectations and communicating basic needs.

Teachers must constantly look around the environment and imagine themselves into those small shoes. Are these visuals in place? Could the child who speaks a different language understand when you tell him to do 'good sharing'? Will the child who takes time to process language be able to jump into line with the rest of the group? We must always set these children up to succeed. Visuals can allow a child to show that they can. This will impact on self-esteem, which has a knock-on effect for the child's future. In a previous book, *Literacy for Visual Learners,* I discussed more of the many reasons why symbols should be used in all settings (Devine 2016). I also highlighted some wonderful work going on in Scotland. It is a fantastic example.

Exciting innovations in Scotland

Fife Assessment Centre for Communication through Technology (FACCT), whose service supports clients for whom speech is not the main means of communication, developed in service training, 'Symbolising the Environment: A Whole School Approach', which developed into a Fife-wide project within the education service.[1] Eleven schools initially signed up – one nursery, eight primary schools and two additional support units attached to mainstream secondary schools. To ensure a consistent approach schools were provided with training in how to create and use symbol resources. Each setting was supplied with a symbol pack. The chosen symbol software package used to create the resources was Mayer-Johnson's 'Boardmaker'. This was used already in Fife by other agencies such as Speech and Language Therapy.

Benarty Primary School in Lochgelly took part in the project. Before introducing the symbols they ensured that everyone involved with the students would have training in the reason for the symbols and how to use them. This included teachers, support staff, parents and staff not involved directly in teaching and learning. They reported that any sceptics were soon turned around once they saw how the use of symbols enhanced the learning environment. The school also noticed

---

1   See *www.educationscotland.gov.uk/resources/practice/s/symbolsproject/introduction.asp*

that by using symbols with *all* students they removed the stigma attached to them.[2]

The work being done in Fife is an exciting starting point towards this being rolled out in all schools. I believe the next step should be to take this on nationally and then internationally. Every child can benefit from access to symbols; they should not need an EHCP. What about the children who will never receive a diagnosis of SEN at school? What about the many, many children whose language is not spoken by anyone at school?

Beyond a tick box

Using visuals is an accepted strategy, but all too often the visuals are not used consistently. Putting up the schedules might seem like another 'to do', but if teachers could only see through the child's eyes and feel how they feel when unexpected change occurs then they would ensure the visuals were constant.

I recall seeing a little boy with autism in a mainstream reception class. It was sports day. He was looking at the visual timetable and I could feel his confusion as he looked around and nothing was as it should be. The timetable had not been changed from the day before. Why? When I asked the teacher she was quite blasé about it; the reason she'd not changed the timetable from the day before was that it was sports day and everything would be different. It seemed so unacceptable, so cruel, and opened my eyes to what is happening in so many classrooms to so many children.

Teacher, consultant and trainer Lynne McCan who writes a blog *Reach Out ASC* explains:

> I see far too many visual timetables as wallpaper, and by that I mean, they are pretty pictures on the wall – but then sometimes the pictures are not even that day's schedule and the child hasn't been taught to manage the timetable themselves. It's often then I hear 'Oh, we tried a visual timetable, but it didn't work,' or 'They

---

2   See *www.educationscotland.gov.uk/resources/practice/s/symbolsproject/benarty. asp?strReferringChannel=resources&strReferringPageID=tcm:4-652592-64*

don't need a visual timetable, they've grown out of it,' – but the pupil still has poor independence and organisation skills.

Visual timetables grow with the child. I have one – It's a full term calendar on one sheet that I write in all my school visits, INSET sessions and meetings. It's visual and I'd be very anxious (not to mention totally lost) without it. Diaries and lists provide a similar visual aid to my life and how it is organised (or not!). If we want our pupils with ASC to develop good organisation skills, a visual timetable can be a great start. And whether you use photos, symbols or for older children, written lists, the format can develop as the child does. (McCan 2016)

The visual timetable and individual schedule are not there to tick a box; they are there because the information can help the child feel safe, secure and in control. Maybe the teacher won't see the meltdown – maybe it will happen later at home or maybe the meltdown will be internal – but maybe that is worse.

Final thoughts

Nobody likes to step out of their comfort zone into the unknown. We feel less anxious when we know what to expect. We like to be prepared with the right clothes and the right equipment. So next time you ask little Johnny to put on waterproofs at playtime and his eyes show alarm, stop and think about how you have prepared him. Take time to look at every visual in the most literal way. Remember that to some children your reasonable requests could cause the same warning alarm bells as being asked to step out of a space rocket without wearing a protective suit. Zoom in on the visuals and the misleading ones will jump out at you. As Wayne Dyer (2008) once said, 'Change the way you look at things and the things you look at change.'

CHAPTER 7

What's Next?

Seeing from All Angles – Understanding the Reasons Behind Behaviours

Life can only be understood backwards; but it must be lived forwards.

Søren Kierkegaard

Different days can be extremely disconcerting to children, particularly those with SEN, but a calendar can help explain and reassure. Showing children what it is planned will happen tomorrow, next week and beyond can help to reduce their anxieties.

Imagine that your tomorrow is now a total mystery. Suddenly you have no idea what might happen beyond today. You could be set to do exactly the same thing as you are currently; but then again you could be going to the funfair or heading off to sit in the dentist's chair.

How would you feel if you had to get by without access to a diary or calendar? Planning systems help us to think ahead and sort out our schedules. We write down future appointments so we don't miss them. We look to the weeks ahead and know if we need to organise childcare, pay a bill, send a birthday card or go to the dentist. Planned activities don't pop up unexpectedly because we have seen them on our calendar.

Children may not understand our scribbles on the calendar, but it can still be important for them to plan beyond today. Access to information gives children a greater sense of control. They may be able to communicate and conquer fears that might not otherwise be addressed before a dreaded day arrives. We can plan ahead, putting systems such as Social Stories™ in place to support and set the child up to succeed.[1]

We're all familiar with advent calendars, one of the child-friendly visual systems that have been created to help count down to Christmas. Children understand that each time they open a door the big day gets closer, long before they can count or read. Similarly, we can create our own child-friendly visual calendars and use pictures to highlight important events or future changes to our routines. By doing this we respect children's need to know and prepare them for future change.

Case study: Danny – calendar count downs

Danny, who has Asperger's Syndrome, was fascinated by calendars, diaries and schedules, and would ask staff repeatedly about upcoming events. He didn't only need to know, but seemed to need to hear it over and over again. His repetitive asking was becoming distracting and we needed to find a way to show Danny what was going to happen in advance without the constant need to talk it through with him.

Our solution was to create a large laminated version of the calendar on the wall with enough space on each day to draw a little visual that Danny could understand without reading. If we planned an outing that was weather dependent, we would split the calendar square in two; one side would show sunshine and a visual of the park, the other would show a rain cloud and books representing the library.

---

1   See *www.thegraycenter.org/social-stories* for more information

As the month progressed we would tick off the days, and Danny was able to use the calendar to count down. When he interrupted story time to ask about what was going to happen on Friday, staff could suggest he had a look at the calendar. What had begun as a genuine need to know had also become a way to disrupt and gain attention. The calendar allowed us to give him the information he wanted without redirecting our attention from the other children.

This system was so successful that Danny's mum started to use it with him at home. She put a large calendar on the wall in their downstairs toilet and found that Danny was using it to count down to special dates, which allowed him to voice concerns and fears ahead of time. This seemed to help avoid some of his unpredictable meltdowns, as they became less frequent.

Adapting the calendar so that Danny could understand was a small change, but one that made a huge amount of difference at home and school.

Case study: Ginny – dress-up day distress

Ginny, who has autism, had a history of anxiety associated with dress-up days. She absolutely refused to wear 'different' clothes. Ginny liked to wear the same pink T-shirt and tracksuit bottoms every day. When Ginny's mum tried to convince her to wear a spotty T-shirt or pyjamas to school instead, she knew before she began that there was no chance of success. The issue, however, was that when Ginny got to school she couldn't cope with seeing other children dressed 'wrong' either. She would try to remove the offensive clothes by force to make things right, which could cause the other children distress.

The school insisted on having charity dress-up days and most children seemed to enjoy them. Ginny did not have to dress up, but she did need to learn to deal with others doing so. We added visual images to the class calendar of a stick person wearing coloured tops and blue trousers. On the dress-up day (which in this instance was spots for Children in Need day) we showed a spotty outfit. The following days were back to the tops and trousers. We talked through the calendar each day and ticked off days as they passed so Ginny could see the dress-up day getting closer.

Finally, the day arrived. Ginny came to school in her usual pink 'uniform'. She had a spotty T-shirt in her bag and point blank refused to change, but she did allow the other children to wear their different clothes without the drama we had come to expect. Ginny kept looking to the calendar during the day to reassure herself that tomorrow things would be back to normal. This spotty madness was for one day only, and the familiar would soon return!

Different days can be extremely disconcerting to children, particularly those with SEN, but a calendar can help explain and reassure.

Ten tips for visual calendars

Here are some simple ideas to help your children prepare for anything:

1. Display the visual calendar somewhere prominent, so that it can be seen at all times.

2. Draw simple stick figures so children who do not yet read can understand upcoming events.

3. Tick off the days as they pass.

4. Split days with a line and show both options if activities are weather dependent.

5. Talk through future events regularly so that children can make sense of the visual.

6. Show that things can change last minute even if they are on the calendar.

7. Model the correct reaction when you have to change plans.

8. Use Social Stories™ to break down and explain events and expectations.

9. Give a copy of the monthly calendar to a child's parents or carers.

10. Encourage the use of a visual calendar at home if it helps at nursery.

Josephine Mele started to research autism when her grandson Nick was diagnosed with Asperger's Syndrome. When it comes to knowing what is next she explains:

> Setting times for meals, getting dressed, leaving the house, doing homework, and going to bed are vital elements of a daily schedule. Routines are absolutely necessary and serious meltdowns can be triggered by major or minor changes in the schedule and by changing rules (even if they're to the child's advantage). Set a plan and have everyone in the family stick to it.

Her grandson, Nick, aged ten, added his own explanation:

> I'm happiest when I know what's going to happen next. On Sunday I get to write on a whiteboard what's going to happen for the week. I don't like surprises or being told something will happen in 10 minutes. I like to know the rules and follow them. My teacher has a lot of rules in our classroom and I like it that way. Sometimes kids make fun of me or call me names when I tell them they are breaking a school rule. (Mele 2012)

What about when change happens?
Teaching a child with autism
to handle a 'whoops!'

It's raining and that lovely day at the beach that's been on the calendar 'forever' suddenly isn't happening.

A change of plan seems logical, but may be difficult for the child to accept. They like to know and expect you to stick to the plan. Why can't we go to the beach in the pouring rain? Beach is on the calendar.

We use visuals such as calendars, schedules and 'Now and Next' boards because knowing what's ahead creates a sense of order and allows the child time to process.

On the flipside changing set plans can create mistrust and anxiety, leading to shut downs or meltdowns.

So what do we do? We know the potential reaction so we try to avoid the situation, but then change happens...

The day comes when we need to collect a sibling who's poorly when we were about to watch a DVD or there's a phone call we must take.

'Whoops' symbol[2]

Preparation is everything!

- Be more aware of your own routines and try to mix them up a bit. Do not sit in the same place every mealtime or lay out the clothes in the exact same order.

- Avoid always going the same route, as this creates the idea that there is only one right way.

- Read a Social Story™ about when the phone rings or the traffic lights are broken and role play good reactions.

---

2   *Available to download free from JKP*

- If a scheduled activity relies on dry weather then show on the calendar that rain will mean a change of plan. It's on the calendar so it's 'okay'.

Holding up a 'whoops!' symbol (shown above) alerts the child that change is in the air. It allows them time to process and prepare to control reactions.

Choose a time to test out using the 'whoops!' symbol:

'Whoops! We have no vanilla ice cream. We only have chocolate.' Change is easier to cope with when it is good change.

Have another adult or sibling model a good reaction:

'Oh dear! I am sad that there is no vanilla ice cream. I was looking forward to it. Oh well, I will have chocolate instead.' Praise the 'model' for their good reaction. The child with autism will be watching and learning.

Next time try a less rewarding 'whoops!' Ask a friend to stage that unexpected call or visit. By role playing a change situation we create a stepping stone. Practising when the situation is not 'real' removes the pressure.

Change Toolkit

Be prepared for times when change happens by putting together a 'change toolkit'. When you are calm, controlled and prepared the child will feel less anxious.

- A whiteboard and dry wipe pen to write or draw the new schedule.

- A visual timer such as a time tracker or egg timer.

- A motivating activity (colouring, books, LEGO®, play dough) or fidget toy.

- Some sort of food (cereal or raisins) and a drink.

- A set of Social Stories™ (when the phone rings Mummy needs to speak, when a visitor comes to the house, when we have to go out in the car, when we have to take a different route).

- An emergency occupier – iPad, or android tablet or game (make sure it's charged).

- A visual of a reward for after – (going to the shop or park, baking a cake) and a token board (if used).

- Symbols for 'whoops!' 'good waiting', 'good sitting', 'good listening', 'good looking' and 'good standing in line'.

- A visual volume control (see page 149).

- Bundles of praise, patience and empathy.

Communication with parents

Michelle Myers writes a blog *A Slice of Autism*. She used the 'Slice of Autism' Facebook page to explain why it is so essential to communicate small changes direct to parents:

> Despite being very structured places the school day can throw up lots of unpredictable changes for pupils such as staff illness, meetings that teachers need to attend, the hall being out of action, wet play, early lunch due to a trip etc. etc. the list is endless. And this is particularly true in primary schools.
>
> These small changes can throw up all sorts of anxiety for children on the spectrum, so no matter how small or insignificant the change may seem to us it's always vital to give advanced warning to pupils so they have time to process the change and address any issues it may cause.
>
> This could be in a home school book if you know the day before (many children don't remember if being told verbally and can't process the info once at home so panic… but if it's written down it helps alleviate stress at home). (Myers 2016)

Final thoughts

If something helps us to get by as adults, then we should find a way to create a child-friendly version. Visual calendars can help children plan ahead and mentally prepare. They can also prompt a 'discussion' and help alleviate some of the anxieties associated with 'different' days.

CHAPTER 8

Be a Supermodel!

Teaching Children Through Using Staff and Other Children as Positive Role Models

Education is the kindling of a flame, not the filling of a vessel.

Socrates

Showing can be far more effective than telling. We just need to practise our modelling skills...

It's story time. Maisy puts up her hand and announces loudly, 'I need a wee!' As she skips off merrily six more eager little hands shoot up...

We all know that children copy – sometimes without thinking. This can have a negative impact, but it can also be turned around to reinforce positives and promote independence. Some children find it difficult to process language and can miss a large percentage of what people say. If a child has the ability to follow instructions when they are visual rather than verbal, and we do not provide visuals, are we meeting their individual needs?

One of the most effective ways to cater for visual learners is to have other children and support staff model what to do, as the following case studies illustrate.

Case study: Help for Henry

Henry's dependence on adult approval was holding him back. He was constantly waiting for prompts. Leaving him to figure it out did not work. If he couldn't get reassurance and help he would burst into tears. If I asked the class to copy simple pictures, Henry needed to be told which colour pen to use. He would sit pen in hand until someone told him to remove the lid. He would not apply pen to paper until he was given another personal instruction. Each small step required a prompt. It wasn't that he couldn't do the task, but the thought of proceeding without constant approval and reassurance seemed overwhelming.

We needed to find a way to get Henry doing things for himself and break the habit of always asking for help in a way that would not cause distress.

I began by showing the class how to complete a very simple task within a structured 'Attention Autism' session. The tasks were well within the abilities of the group – things like making a play dough head with peg features and adding dry spaghetti for hair. I handed out a little kit so each child could create an identical 'Mini Make'. A member of staff also got a kit so that they could sit and work alongside the other children. The adult spoke aloud their thoughts and actions so that if a child did not know what to do, they could copy rather than ask. This worked so well with Henry and it was amazing what a contrast we saw between a normal art activity and these 'Mini Make' activities.

Building on this, each time I gave Henry's group something to do, I gave a member of support staff an identical task. Henry had someone to follow and knew he was on the right track. His requests for help and reassurance reduced.

Henry became more independent and his self-esteem improved because he had been given a structure to support his needs.

You can find more information on Attention Autism in the 'Useful Websites' section at the end of the book.

Case study: Carly's sensory cooking

Cooking provides so many learning opportunities for children. I always begin sessions by modelling what the children need to do, then the children have a go themselves, following a set of simple visual instructions.

Carly was a sensory seeking child, and it was a struggle to model what to do while having to guard the ingredients. She was lightning fast and would pour flour everywhere or dive her hand into the margarine and scoop out a handful. This sensory need was overriding everything, and no one was benefiting from my usual cooking demonstrations.

So, what to do? I did not want to stop cooking and I knew if I could get Carly to watch the demonstration she could get a lot out of cooking. Before my next session I set up the class camera and did the cooking 'Nigella Lawson style' without my class. I went through each step showing clearly what to do. It felt odd, but strangely liberating.

When the cooking session started I kept the ingredients out of sight and started the video, doing my demonstration as I would have liked to. The video had the children's attention and there was no grabbing or pouring. They all remained in their seats. The session had a much smoother start and without Carly distracting them, the other children saw the demonstration as intended.

Carly still got her sensory fun with the flour when it was available, but at least through the use of video modelling she had seen some cooking. In time we even saw Carly copy some of the steps on the video.

Video modelling can be really effective if a child is distracted by a sensory element or doesn't like teacher talk. Using video not only helped Carly but freed up the other children to learn to cook without being showered in chaos.

Ten tips for modelling

Help your staff become supermodels…

1. Model being the perfect child so the group leader can praise you: 'Great sitting, Lisa.'

2. Model problem solving when given a task: 'I can't open it. Ah – I need to pull here.'

3. Rather than tell a child to do something, model an action and explain the reasoning: 'It's cold. I'm going to put on my coat.'

4. Model using communication aids for pre-verbal children. Hand over a picture of raisins at snack and say, 'I want raisins, please.'

5. Show good reactions to not getting a turn. The group leader can praise you: 'Lisa, you were so good about not having a turn today.'

6. Listen attentively and react positively to activities and stories – enthusiasm is contagious!

7. Try different activities and foods so children can see that trying new things is okay.

8. Model what to do when stuck by trying or saying, 'I need help, please.'

9. Model waiting for a turn so the group leader can praise you: 'Good waiting.'

10. Model sharing anxieties and showing how the children can conquer them with adult support.

Modelling opportunities

The following are situations when children can learn valuable lessons by example:

- at dressing-up time

- when washing hands

- during physical activities

- during art activities

- while finding equipment or resources

- when tidying up

- while transitioning between activities

- at snack time

- when turn taking

- when it is necessary to be a 'good loser'.

Models for staff training

I love it that all of our staff have induction training when they start working at our school. This is so important and gives them a basic understanding of some of the things they will see in school. But staff will not always have the confidence to start using these strategies and they will soon be forgotten if they are not continually reinforced by other staff modelling them.

We recently had Intensive Interaction training for all of our school staff, which was wonderful. We have a large team in Early Years as we have a lot of children with diverse needs. After the first day of training one of our newer members of staff commented, 'A lot of this is what we already do.' This is exactly as it should be when staff train. They see what they have already seen in class, but learn the theory behind it.

Children learn from children
Case study: Darcy, and a child who hits

A few months ago our daughter Darcy came home from pre-school saying that 'Billy' had hit her and often hurt her. The hurting had happened quite a few times despite him being told 'No' by teachers.

I asked Darcy why she thought Billy might have hit her.

She thought about it a bit, but could not think of a reason. 'Is Billy bad?' she asked.

Instinct told me that Darcy was best placed to help Billy learn.

'Billy is *not* bad,' I said. 'Maybe he wants you to play with him and does not know how to ask. Some children need to learn how to make friends in pre-school. Maybe Billy is hitting because he likes you and he does not know how to show it. Maybe Billy needs a friend.'

I suggested that Darcy could help Billy learn to be a friend. She could show and tell him the sorts of things that friends do.

We did not speak about it again.

Months later we were doing some gardening and Darcy said, 'Billy is my friend now. He doesn't hurt me any more.'

'That's great!' I replied and then I remembered our previous conversation. 'How did you make friends?'

'I told him be nice, do what I do – play and no hurting,' said Darcy.

I hugged Darcy and told her that she had made me very proud.

Darcy had helped little Billy with a social hurdle, simply and brilliantly and in a way that a grown up never could. Billy now has a friend, a role model and great potential to make more friends. Darcy could have changed his whole school experience.

I've heard parents and professionals observing a child who hurts say: 'One day another child will hit him back.' But what would being hit back really achieve? Maybe it would teach the child a 'lesson', but would it be the right lesson?

Behaviour is so often a form of communication. We must always look for the roots. We must help our children to understand the roots and become role models.

If a child hits or kicks or knocks over brick towers then they do not need punishments. They need support and clear role models. They need directions and the chance to show they *can*. They need this to happen in the right way before behaviour habits begin to form.

The child who has been hurt may be best placed to turn things around.

Plant the seed. Children learn best from other children.

The conversation I had with Darcy made me very proud and reinforced my belief that children are our best teachers.

Ten tips for handling hitting

1. Be aware of triggers such as hunger, tiredness and boredom and avoid them.

2. Be aware of things that create anxiety such as noises, lighting and crowds.

3. Use visuals to forewarn children of changes to the typical schedule.

4. Support children with small group structures if they are not ready to mingle with the masses.

5. Take the time to role play and teach play skills, pointing out good role models.

6. Use Social Stories™ to explain expectations in a clear and consistent way.

7. Use Comic Strip Conversations™ to clarify why incidents have happened.

8. Explain the behaviours and promote a helping attitude to avoid social isolation.

9. Invite parents in. Strengthen and support them with strategies for home.

10. Use clear praise attached to 'good' visuals when the child gets things right.

See more at my *SEN Assist* blog site, under the title 'Helping that Special Child who Hits' (Devine 2015c).

Final thoughts

Josh Billings famously said, 'To bring up a child in the way he should go, travel that way yourself once in a while' (Billings 1871). Children learn by what they see, and they are always looking to us adults for examples. We must train our support staff to be the next top models. Children copy, and if they see someone else getting praise for doing the right thing they may follow. We can never make assumptions about what children *know*. By modelling we could build a child's self-esteem and scaffold their success.

CHAPTER 9

Toilet Training

People don't care how much you know until they know how much you care.

Theodore Roosevelt

Toilet training can be tricky with any child, but we must be extra supportive when a child has special educational needs.

Children are arriving wrapped up in winter coats, and parents are busily changing boots for indoor shoes with lights (of course).

Then there is little Billy. His clothes are worn, outgrown and ragged. As other children play and chat Billy tries to pull Mum back towards the door. Billy will be starting 'big school' in a few months and (shock, horror) he is still wearing nappies.

Mum feels those sideways glances. She imagines what those other parents are thinking – 'Billy should be wearing a coat. Billy should be settled. Billy should be toilet trained by now…'

Other parents are getting little kisses and waves. How Billy's mum would love to experience a goodbye like this… She feels their judgements and makes a quick exit. She can't tell the other mums about the chewed sleeves, the sensory issues, the anxieties or the autism diagnosis.

When a child like Billy walks through the door we must support, encourage and be extra proactive. Not only will the child need additional support to meet milestones, but parents need our emotional support and care. Dressing, feeding, washing, toilet training can all be huge issues.

Toilet training can be a hurdle for any parent, but when a child has special educational needs toilet training can seem a lonely, frustrating uphill struggle.

Toilet ready?

Not all children are ready to toilet train during pre-school years. A child may have a developmental delay or not show awareness that they need a nappy change. Their age may be right, but we know that children learn things at different ages and stages. If you don't think the child is toilet ready then let parents know because they could be wasting effort and causing unnecessary anxieties, which will create barriers when the child *is* ready.

Penina Pearl Rybak is a speech-language pathologist educational consultant and founder of Socially Speaking™. She published this checklist of indicators for toilet training readiness, included here from Socially Speaking™ Toileting Protocol, with permission:

CHILD'S READINESS INDICATORS –
PREREQUISITES FOR TOILET TRAINING:

1. Joint Attention and rapport, so that positive reinforcement is meaningful.

2. Communicative Intent, so that child can ask for toilet and/ or indicate wetness.

3. Understanding Causality (cause and effect, contingencies), so that child can make a connection between his action(s) and your reaction(s).

4. Body Awareness so that child feels when he/she is wet and knows from where.

5. Understanding Part-Whole Relationships, so that child can follow the steps and make sense of the toileting process and the vocabulary involved.

6. Physical Agility, so that child can walk to toilet, climb up, and sit upright to use it, without any medical condition barring physiological/anatomical ability such as low muscle tone (hypotonia), spastic muscles, or poor motor planning and coordination resulting in difficulty walking (reduced ambulation) and chest i.e. thoracic rotation (sitting upright using the abdominal 'core' muscles).

My own experience is that it is possible to toilet train children with some of the physical disabilities listed in point 6 above, but this should be done with the guidance of a physiotherapist.

Toilet anxieties

It may be that the child will use the toilet at home, but not at school. If that's the case, investigate. Changes in routine and place and sensitivity to smells and sounds can all cause huge anxieties for the child with SEN. We must be aware and try to accommodate and adapt.

Common toilet fears include:

- hand driers
- flushing
- falling in
- discomfort
- change of routine
- different setting
- germs
- smells

- toilet paper
- being there forever.

Ten tips for toilet training

1. Have small comfortable seats.
2. Use a step or foot rest.
3. Schedule regular toilet times.
4. Show empathy for anxieties.
5. Use visuals charts to schedule stages.
6. Use books, charts or timers.
7. Wait until the child seems ready.
8. Be specific about expectations.
9. Use rewards and motivators.
10. Share strategies and successes.

Toilet kit

It can be useful to create a toilet kit specific to the child. Have their photo on it so that they can recognise it as their own. Consider including the following things:

- multiple changes of clothes
- pull ups or nappies
- individual motivators and rewards
- a timer or chart to extend sitting
- a visual schedule made using photographs or symbols
- charts to record successes
- a portable fold up toilet seat.

Make an identical kit for home and any other setting (such as respite).

Be consistent

When toilet training it is so important for parents and professionals to agree on timing and strategies. This will make the process much quicker, less frustrating for the adults and aid the child's understanding and feelings of security.

Case study: Visuals for Vinny

Vinny had started out in a mainstream setting. He loved all the visuals we had in place. He did have some anxieties about separating from his mum, made some unpredictable noises and needed a little time to learn our routines.

Vinny was very good about having his nappy changed, but resisted when we suggested that he try sitting on the toilet. We didn't push this. We continued with the nappy changing, building trust and saw his confidence increase.

The first term went by. We saw so much progress in other areas. We knew that we wanted to try to toilet train Vinny, but we needed to tread carefully and kept good communication up with Mum. We felt that it would be better if we followed her lead.

Once we knew that Vinny had started to sit on the toilet at home we tried again. This time he was willing and even helped pull his trousers down. He liked looking at our visual toileting schedule on the wall and pointing to the different stages – pull trousers down, sitting, stand up, trousers and pants up.

He did not seem to get that he needed to sit a while so we started off showing him an egg timer, but for hygiene reasons this was not ideal...

Vinny loved numbers so I put a big 100 number poster by the toilet. He really enjoyed us counting to 100 while he sat. He knew how long he would need to sit and understood the routine. He would sit while we counted and pointed to the numbers. We would use different voices and speeds, which made him giggle. Vinny was sitting longer and also learning. Perfect!

Case study: Charlie – toilet seat terrors

Charlie had been great at learning to do wees on the toilet. He had a cousin who was six months older and having seen him do a wee on the toilet decided he would too. Instant success!

Doing poos took a while longer as this seemed to cause real anxiety. He knew when he needed to poo and would go and hide under the table. Getting past this had taken reassurance, time and the promise of a big reward.

When Charlie started pre-school his mum noticed that he was always bursting to go to the toilet by the time they got home. After he had an accident on the doorstep she questioned him.

'Do you use the toilets in school Charlie?'

'No,' said Charlie, matter of factly. Further questioning revealed a reason we would not have predicted. The toilets in school did not have lids. Charlie had learned to always put the seat down before he flushed. The flush noise had always pained him and he had developed anxieties about germs. So Charlie had decided not to use the school toilets. No matter how desperate he got he would rather wait until he got home.

Charlie was able to explain what the problem was and we could use Social Stories™ to help him understand and get past his anxieties. But what if Charlie did not have the communication skills to explain his anxieties? Imagine having to go through the whole school day without using the toilet and not being able to explain.

Playing detective

Temple Grandin is one of our most well known adults with autism. She has written numerous books on autism and even had a Hollywood film made about her life. In her teaching tips she highlights why a child with autism might use the toilet at home, but refuse at school:

> A common problem is that a child may be able to use the toilet correctly at home but refuses to use it at school. This may be due to a failure to recognize the toilet. Hilde de Clereq from Belgium discovered that an

autistic child may use a small non-relevant detail to recognize an object such as a toilet. It takes detective work to find that detail. In one case a boy would only use the toilet at home that had a black seat. His parents and teacher were able to get him to use the toilet at school by covering its white seat with black tape. The tape was then gradually removed and toilets with white seats were now recognized as toilets. (Grandin 2002)

The author Donna Williams explains that trouble choosing the toilet rather than the sink:

> can be a visual-perceptual thing where they are only part of the information; i.e. enamel receptacles into which fluid goes. It can also be a category thing where the person has formed the idea that all these things are interchangeable with basically similar things. (Williams 1996, p.311)

Williams also explains how she had trouble with distinguishing toilet paper and the towel:

> A white towel hung on a ring between the bath and toilet, next to the toilet roll holder was an invitation to trouble. Both things were obviously for the same purpose of wiping, both were white, but the towel was softer. Naturally, and without apology I chose the towel in place of toilet paper. (Williams 1996, p.311)

When children do things we may view as 'inappropriate' then it is important to try to find out why and help them learn how to follow our expectations. The towel and toilet paper issue could have been solved by having a coloured towel or a visual above each showing the intended use.

Smearing

Some children will choose to put their hands in their nappies and explore their own excrement. They may take this further and sprinkle or smear it on walls. This may begin as innocent sensory exploration, but can become a most unwelcome and distressing habit. The important thing to work out is the reason for the smearing. Is it sensory? Is it wanting something to do while they sit on the toilet? Is it a way of communicating they need changing? Is it the reaction they have come to expect after they do it? When children are likely to put their hands in their nappy or smear we must be on heightened alert and provide alternatives. Having brown play dough or paint may not seem an attractive prospect, but compare the alternative. With the right support children can learn to change these habits.

Every child is different and there is no one answer. We must ask and if a child cannot or will not tell us then we investigate, play detective and find a creative solution.

Avoiding accidents

So you have reached the point where the child is using the toilet successfully, they usually understand when they need to go and will transition there without reminder. But then there are times when the child becomes so involved in an activity that they forget and have an accident. This is not unique to children with SEN. *All* children can do this. Maybe they are at a birthday party or playing on the tablet. I've always told our children that I have a special radar that bleeps when they need to go to the toilet. In truth it's that tell tale wiggle or the time that has past or will pass until the next opportunity. But saying it's my radar means it's not me they need to argue with so they agree to go.

Tips to avoid accidents

- Make a toilet visit part of the routine start to activities.

- Make a rule about regular toilet breaks.

- Use a visual reminder and timer (if needed).

- Be aware – look out for the physical signs.

- Have a reward system with tokens for visits.

Increase independence

As we start toilet training we will be very hands on with helping the child with clothing, wiping and washing hands, but the aim is that they will do all these things independently. We also need to ensure they learn to do them properly. The child will need to learn these things in a stepped way. Visual schedules can help show the stages. Build hand washing in as a routine from the start. Give hand over hand assistance at first, but let this fade so that the child gradually becomes more independent.

A washing hands visual schedule (Devine 2014a)

A note about wiping

Wiping can cause huge anxiety for some children and we must be empathic about this. Social Stories™ and Comic Strip Conversations™ can help explain the rationale behind the child taking ownership of their personal care. They can also increase our awareness of the reasoning behind the anxiety, which will allow us to clear up misconceptions and reduce associated fears. We must be patient and not make this too huge an issue, but we must also be firm and consistent with our expectations.

Should teachers be toilet training?

I've thrown this question in because it is one still asked by teachers. The simple answer is 'Yes!' If a child is not meeting milestones, which will affect their future independence, then these skills should be a priority. Children will start school still in nappies and this may be because they have not reached the point where they are ready to learn to use the toilet. Children progress at different stages. We should never judge the parents or make assumptions. Our job is always to support, to move the child forwards, to show what they *can* do.

In 2015 I read an article by the *Guardian's* 'Secret Teacher', who wrote that 'We are teachers, not supernannies. We care about your children but some jobs just aren't in our remit – and toilet training is one of them.'

I was outraged by the lack of care shown in this article and responded on behalf of parents and children and the many professionals who understand that we cannot compartmentalise a teacher's job. We must teach what children need to know.

Here's an extract from my own *SEN Assist* blog, entitled 'Dear Secret Teacher':

> the other day my class team went into joyful celebration when a four year old with autism did a wee on the toilet at school for the first time. Maybe you would say, 'that's because I teach in a special needs school?' Maybe you would say that 'special' child would not belong in your mainstream class? But then maybe with the right structures, the right supports and a little empathy that special child could learn to cope in a mainstream setting... In Early Years it's our job to support ALL areas of development. These include eating, drinking, speaking, listening, co operating, dressing AND toileting. Teachers are not 'super nannies', but neither are most parents. Having children is a lottery, but finding the right teacher, who can support children based on their individual needs, should not be. (Devine 2015d)

A mother describes her experience toilet training her son Sam

Tina Bailey is a mother to two boys. She writes a blog called *Mother Geek* and often relates her experiences of bringing up her son Sam, who has autism. This is from her article called 'Autism Toilet Training':

> Sam was four in June. He has Autism and is still non-verbal for the most part. Until very recently, he showed no interest in

using the toilet. Last week, this changed! He kept going into the bathroom to look at the toilet, repeatedly took off his nappy, and sat on the toilet a few times. I decided to try to get him using the toilet.

Sam's lack of speech means he can't simply 'Tell' us he needs to use the toilet. We have to read his body language, take him there a lot, and we are also showing him a flash card of a toilet when we ask him, in the hope that in time he will use the flash card to tell us he needs to go.

The first few days involved a lot of accidents, lots of time spent on the toilet without using it, and lots of patience. Yesterday morning, Sam refused point blank to wear a pull up or nappy to go to nursery, so I sent him in wearing his underpants. I picked him up two hours later, and they told me he had done two small wee's on the toilet and had one accident. I was so proud of him! Sam was squealing with excitement when I praised him, and actually said 'Weeeee' – yet another step in the right direction!

Yesterday afternoon, he had a couple of wet accidents at home, but when he needed to do a poo, he shouted, 'MUM' – I recognised his 'poo stance' straight away, and popped him on the toilet. I won't go into detail, but it's sufficient to say, Sam did exactly what he needed to! He was so excited (as was I)! There was lots of praise, cuddles and cheering once he was cleaned up!

We are definitely making progress, and I am so proud of Sam! Every child's toilet training journey is different, but I think that having buckets of patience, and waiting for them to be ready are the two biggest tips I can offer. (Bailey 2015)

Final thoughts

We must go out of our way to support parents particularly when we know that their child has an invisible learning difference. Those sideways glances at drop off times can really sting. Look out for 'issues' (whatever they might be) and make the time to be that friendly listening ear a lonely parent needs. Do not judge or make assumptions. Supporting and strengthening the parent will help set that 'special' child up to succeed.

CHAPTER 10

Flower Power

Seeing Through a Child's Eyes and Finding Roots

'Just living is not enough,' said the butterfly, 'one must have sunshine, freedom, and a little flower.'

Hans Christian Andersen,
The Complete Fairy Tales

Children with SEN often stand out; they might not be motivated by the usual rewards or bothered by reprimands.

There's a dandelion growing in your garden. What will your response to it be?

a)   the quick fix – remove the flower head

b)   the long-term solution – get a spade and dig up its roots

c)   acceptance – learn to love dandelions.

Dandelions will not stick to neat flowerbeds. They spring up in the middle of the grass. To green-fingered neighbours they stand out, making us look like we are not caring for our gardens properly. Our children with SEN often stand out too. They may present unusual or disruptive behaviours. They might not be motivated by the usual rewards or bothered by reprimands.

Let us take the example, a child with 'playing' at the sand tray. You observe the child repeatedly lifting sand and watching it pour through his fingers. He does this again and again; he does not play or move on as other children do. When the other children transition to the carpet for story-time this child stays put as if his feet are glued to the floor.

This sand tray play is an opportunity to develop communication by using techniques based on 'Intensive Interaction' (see the 'Useful Resources' section for more information). Get alongside the child and mirror how he plays. Become a fellow investigator. In time, the child may start to interact, which is the start of communication and cooperative play. We accept and learn with the child on his terms.

Maybe the child shows disruptive behaviour at the sandpit such as throwing sand in other children's eyes. Provide visuals showing the right way to play with sand. Praise children getting it right. We work with the child to teach him an alternative, acceptable way to interact with other children and get good 'reactions'. Remember that children who seek reactions may not distinguish between positive and negative reactions. A 'Johnny, stop!' could seem as rewarding to them as a 'Well done, Johnny!'

Perhaps the child tries to control the sandpit, showing distress when others join him. Set another sand tray nearby, allowing other children to play, and providing opportunities to praise those behaviours you want to see.

Case study: Bessie, the tipper

If there was a basket of toys, a box of puzzles or a tray of pencils in view, Bessie would launch herself towards it and tip it up. The classroom was set up to avoid temptation. No pencil pots were left out, no boxes of scrap paper... Everything was up high or locked away. But this was not fair on the other children. The tipping caused them distress, and not being able to go and get things was removing opportunities for them to develop their independence.

A pattern had developed: Bessie would tip, and staff would insist she tidy up. She would tidy up with the staff and when done, they would tell her she was a 'good girl'. What was she getting out of this? Was she enjoying the cooperative tidy up time or the 'good girl' praise?

I asked staff to give Bessie lots of over the top 'good girl' comments for the other things she did well, but then, when she tipped, to show no reaction. We gently moved Bessie away and tidied up, without commenting. I spoke to Bessie's mum so she could get on board with the new strategy too.

At first the tipping continued, but over time, we found that we were getting more relaxed about leaving things out. The tipping became more occasional, and by the time I came to write the end of year reports, it had stopped altogether.

Case study: 'Shoeless Sam'

Sam always arrived at school without his shoes on. With visual symbols and patience we would get him to wear shoes, but it took a long time. I knew there must be a root cause and that the best place to start helping Sam with this shoe issue was to ask his parents.

Mum said that the 'shoe issue' had only started since Sam had started coming to school on transport. So what was their morning routine?

Once Sam was dressed he would sit snuggled up with Mum watching kids' TV until transport arrived. When Mum saw the school bus, she would give Sam his shoes and turn off the TV. Sam would refuse to put them on and, after a battle, he would end up getting onto his transport without them. Mum would hand the shoes over to the escort.

I wondered if Sam was associating putting his shoes on with the TV being turned off and him getting on the school bus. Seeing the shoes signified an end to his lovely snuggly TV time with Mum. We had noticed at school that Sam needed time to process. If we showed him a symbol, he would take about four minutes to process and act on it. Once we knew this about Sam it had helped, in so many ways. We'd show him the toothbrush symbol five minutes before brushing teeth and he would brush his teeth, but if he was shown it and then immediately expected to do it, he would not.

I suggested that Mum change the morning routine and add some visuals. We created a visual schedule, allowing five minutes warning with a 'Now and Next' schedule showing 'TV' then 'Shoes on' before the TV went off. The TV would go off and then Mum would show Sam the 'shoes on' symbol again. Sam's shoes were by the door.

The morning after we put this all in place, Sam arrived with his shoes on. All he'd needed was a change to his routine, removing the association, a visual schedule and time to process.

Finding the root

To find out what children achieve through their behaviour, we need to observe their actions. Ask yourself, are they:

- attention seeking
- wanting a reaction
- investigating
- copying
- trying to play
- opting out
- showing fear
- experiencing sensory discomfort
- making an association
- trying to communicate?

By understanding this, we can work out how to respond appropriately.

I include Miriam Gwynne's wonderful blog post about her daughter, who has autism, called 'My Best Friends… The Beautiful Flowers' which she has kindly allowed me to share here (Gwynne 2015a).

Sometimes I just don't want to know about my daughter's day at school. It seems contrary to all good parenting advice but when I asked my six-year-old whether she had any friends the other day she told me she spends her outside social time at school talking to and looking at the 'beautiful flowers'. I just can't bear to hear any more.

I know the school well. I know the names of every single child in her class. I even volunteer within the school for several hours a week. I talk to the Head on first name terms.

My daughter is not being bullied. She is just unable to play with the other children. Her social skills are limited. She takes what the other children say in a very literal way. She is vulnerable. Her interests are far different to the others of her age and ability. She is socially isolated and happy in her own world. She is surrounded by children who know and understand popular culture, current television characters and have physical skills she has yet to even attempt. She has only one current interest which not one other child in the class have even heard of. She is a little girl with autism in a world of mainstream children.

Her perception of what goes on in school is so different from the other children. Where others listen to a story she will home in on that one child who is biting their nails and tell me at home how biting your nails is not good and that child should have been told to stop. It is only when I deduce that the children were sitting on the carpet that I figure she was perhaps having a class story. Her tales of school are all about what children did to break the rules, whose name was taken down the tree today (a behavioural chart used in the class) and who touched her and when (she hates being touched!).

Try as I may she cannot grasp that the world can be seen another way. Her autism prevents her from seeing things from other people's viewpoints. And this is impacting on so much now. Even in the simplest tasks like reading. When I asked her the other night why she still had the same few words home to practise when I was confident in her ability to know those words she said, 'I read them to you Mummy so why do I have to read them to the teacher too?' It was a genuine question. In her mind she knows them. She knows that and I know that so why would her teacher not know the same thing? She is genuinely 'blind' to the fact the teacher will not know she knows them without her reading them to the teacher. The same way she thinks I know exactly what goes on in school because she does so why would I not too?

This is happening to so many children. 'Inclusion' is the way to go apparently. It is a very delicate balance between what is right for my child (and many like her) academically while balancing the child's social and emotional wellbeing. School is like a mini real world where she will be misunderstood, become confused at things others find easy and just interpret everything in a different way.

She is the proverbial round peg in a square hole. It is about allowing her to be her, allowing her to be autistic but balancing that against her mental wellbeing and self-esteem when she seems so different. It is a very difficult balance and one that needs very careful monitoring.

So today as I walked my beautiful daughter home from school, with trepidation, I once again asked her how her day had been. 'Oh Mummy, wait until I tell you what happened to my friends today…' It was beautiful to hear her happy, animated and excited and talking about that elusive thing we call 'friends'.

Has someone lost a tooth, had a birthday, had a new baby brother or sister, or even asked her to play I silently wondered.

'My friends, the beautiful flowers, opened up for the first time today and now they look even more beautiful!'

Maybe I have it all wrong. There is an area in her playground full of greenery, shrubs and flowers. But the one flower my daughter noticed was the one that was different. Because it was more beautiful, more noticeable and something very special indeed.

I think today she just told me the most beautiful thing about school I ever heard.

Final thoughts

I once told our son that the flowers I loved most were dandelions. He could pick me as many of them as he liked, but only them. He happily picked the dandelions and I knew no one would mind. The funny thing is that over time, as he proudly presented me with fistfuls of dandelions and I put them in vases on the windowsill, I came to see them as lovely, sunny flowers.

Take time to get to know that special child in your care, see through their eyes, love what they love and learn together. Set the child up to succeed, raise their self-esteem and see how they can flower. And remember, as somebody unrecorded by history once said, 'the difference between a flower and a weed is a judgement.'

CHAPTER 11

If You're Good...

A Positive Approach to Behaviour
and Using Rewards

In the best, the friendliest and simplest relations flattery or praise is necessary, just as grease is necessary to keep wheels turning.

Leo Tolstoy, *War and Peace*

A positive approach can tackle challenging behaviours – the trick is to offer children the right rewards. We all like rewards, whether it's a simple 'Well done', a 'Thank you' or even (if we're being really spoiled) a bunch of flowers. Working for rewards motivates and provides structure. I once saw a little boy raise his hand to his mum, but he hesitated and stopped himself, deciding not to hit. Mum was about to tell him off because he had raised his hand, but I quickly praised him. The boy had controlled his hitting instinct – this was huge progress.

It is important to address unwanted behaviours one at a time. Don't mention unwanted behaviours by saying things like 'no hitting', but instead praise the child in question for having 'kind hands'.

Case study: Billy – what a difference a snack makes

Billy was four years old. His mum was at breaking point! If he had 100 per cent adult focus he could be an angel, but without it he would tear through the house.

We created a chart to use between home and nursery. Billy got a sticker for every hour that he managed to 'be good'. We decided to focus first on him controlling physical behaviours such as hitting. The charts were kept in view at all times, and we tried to ensure that Billy got his stickers. Billy seemed very motivated by the sticker system.

The hourly stickers were transferred to a weekly chart to highlight time patterns when behaviour went off track. Billy would often miss the 11am sticker. We started to introduce a snack at 10:30am to see if the behaviour was hunger related. The weekly chart revealed that a snack made a huge difference.

Billy loved his stickers, but as with many reward systems we needed to stay a step ahead to retain motivation. We created a mini 'shop' so that Billy could trade his perfect chart for a prize at the end of each day. The prizes were mini dinosaurs and cars bought at the pound shop and wrapped in tin foil (to save time). Some might say a system like this could spoil the child, but what it did was teach Billy to control his behaviour. In time the rewards were unnecessary, and we all knew that if Billy had a rumbling tummy we had best fill the gap before the 'Billyraptor' emerged...

Case study: Barney – creating positives

Barney, who has autism, was five years old. His behaviour had become so explosive that he was often taught in a separate room. When he was with other children, he always found a way to mix things up...

For example, at the sand tray he would start off well, but within a minute a handful of sand would be thrown in another child's face. He moved chairs as other children went to sit. Papers were scattered, paintings defaced, junk models squashed and drawings ripped up. He had an ability to create absolute havoc in seconds and seemed to enjoy watching the aftermath.

But being taught in a separate room was not going to help Barney long term. He needed to learn to control these urges and join the group. I examined the visual supports in place. In his individual room there was a sign that explained all the unwanted behaviours. There was a long list of 'no throwing', 'no kicking', 'no spitting', and so on for Barney to look at when he was in his separate room. There was nothing positive about these signs. Seeing these negatives each day was more likely to encourage 'expected' behaviours and remind him of them, so I removed this visual.

To replace it, we took photographs of all the good things Barney could do – from sharing a tricycle at playtime and waiting for his snack, to turn taking on the computer, listening to a story and sitting nicely. We created a really positive visual that Barney enjoyed sharing with staff. Time and again he received praise for these past achievements. I heard staff saying 'What good turn taking Barney,' while looking at the visual, and saw Barney beam in response. These comments were the rays of sunshine he needed. The dark cloud of negatives shifted, and sharing all the things he could do so well helped paint a positive self image.

We also introduced token boards with rewards during sessions. Barney would select a motivating reward and place it on his board. Once he had five tokens he could have his reward. This could be time on the computer or holding a guinea pig. At first our expectation was that Barney would stay on track for ten minutes, earning tokens to get his reward. Over time we stretched this out. Turning negatives into positives helped Barney realise he could have more fun without mixing things up.

When fun things finish

When a child is engaged in a fun activity the last thing they want is to be told it's 'finished'. Toddlers begin by asserting themselves. Dad tells them it's time to leave the park and suddenly they are met with defiance, tears and tantrums. Dad knows they have been there a long time, that it is about to rain or maybe it's time to collect big brother from school, but all the toddler is thinking is, 'This is fun. I like it here. I want to play here more.' They don't see beyond this. They are the centre of their own world. Parents soon learnt that a five-minute warning can help, that a count down can help and that the promise of a reward or motivator can really help. In time the toddler grows up and learns to understand Dad's reasons.

But children with SEN hit milestones at different times, may not process the language or may not agree that their fun must finish.

One Sunday evening I took our three children to the local softplay. I observed a little boy, who was quietly walking around fixating on his two little fingers. Our children were playing a game which involved using these round softplay cushions with letters and numbers on them from the baby area. Darcy (four) came up and told me that a little boy had taken her number cushion from her. We watched him go and put it back in the baby area. Darcy wanted it for her game. I told her to wait. We watched as the boy went off and was no longer looking and she went and got it back. Later he took it from her again and did the same thing. He did not take it in an aggressive way. I explained to Darcy that the boy knew that the number cushion belonged in the baby area. He was helping the staff and looking out for the babies. It was getting near chucking out time and there were few children left.

I commented to the child's mother on how her little boy loved the number cushions. 'He has autism,' she explained. I told her that I was a special needs teacher and thought he had handled himself really well because it must be frustrating seeing children taking things to the 'wrong place'. We had a nice chat. I saw her speak to her son. She gained his attention and told him, 'Five minutes', showing him 'five' with her hand.

The next thing the boy disappeared. Mum went off searching. I spotted him at the top of the slide hiding and let her know. She went up after him and he was quietly resisting. I went and got one of the number cushions from the baby area and held it up so he could see, then placed it at the bottom of the slide and went back to help my kids with getting shoes and coats on. The boy came down the slide and took the cushion back to the baby area. His mum thanked me and went to help him with shoes.

Watch the child and the motivator will become apparent. Watch the parent and see if there is a way that you can offer practical help or support.

Ten tips for using tokens

How to turn rewards into positive behaviour:

1. *Motivate the individual* – if the child likes a character, colour or topic, use it to style the token board.[1]

2. *Set them up to succeed* – we must judge how long we can stretch out between tokens by the child's ability to wait for a reward.

3. *Be positive* – be over-the-top enthusiastic when the child gets each token; let them know you are really happy with them.

4. *Be consistent* – if it's working at nursery, share the system with home.

5. *Have a reward board* – this way the child can select their individual reward.

6. *Reinforce learning* – token boards can be a great way to teach concepts such as time or money.

7. *Share their success* – let them see you telling other people how happy you are when they succeed.

8. *Take control* – children like to know adults are in control; it makes them feel safe. Don't allow them to take control of getting tokens and rewarding themselves.

---

1   *Time-based token charts and behaviour records are free to print at www.senassist.com/resources. html*

9. *Look for patterns and adapt* – are certain times of the day more challenging? Are there any possible triggers such as hunger, noise or lack of attention?[2]

10. *Keep it fresh* – a token system using stickers might lose its magic after a few weeks. Be ready to up the ante and make the rewards more exciting, or get creative with a whole new system.

'Thumbs up' tokens

Token boards with a reward can be a good strategy to help a child stay on task during a lesson, but children are very quick to work out how to get past them. The child may learn that they always get their tokens and reward. I've seen staff suddenly give all tokens for minor things at the end of a lesson because they know that not getting the expected reward may result in a meltdown.

I developed token boards that show the activity. The child and support assistant know exactly what each token is for. The child has a schedule showing they will need to complete work on four tables. At each table there is a corresponding token 'thumbs up' showing the expectation. They may be doing 'sorting' at one table 'matching' at another, 'writing' and then some 'cutting'. When the lesson ends the child will need to have five tokens to access a reward box. The contract is visual and very clear.

Final thoughts

Don't worry that using rewards will spoil the child. Children learn to control their behaviour in stages; help them to manage this and in time you can reduce rewards. Highlight when a child succeeds and they will surprise themselves with their ability to stay on track.

---

2   *ABC charts can be used for more detailed behaviour analysis. By charting the Antecedent (what happened before the behaviour), Behaviour and Consequence, triggers and patterns may emerge. These are available to print free online at ow.ly/otxIt*

CHAPTER 12

I Can't Wait!

Teaching Waiting Skills

The strongest of all warriors are these two – Time and Patience.

Leo Tolstoy, *War and Peace*

Learning to be patient can be a challenge for all children but especially those with SEN. We cannot always predict when our attention will have to be diverted, but we can think ahead and see if there are ways to help a child wait.

The traffic is at a standstill and stretches for miles into the distance. There is no apparent reason. You can do nothing but be patient. In another car someone is repeatedly beeping their horn, getting hot, bothered and frustrated. Maybe they are trying to get to the airport to catch a flight, to a job interview or perhaps, like you, they are on their way home. And it's not just traffic. The English people's apparent need to devise endless queuing systems is a source of amusement to those from other countries – think bus stops, shops, cash points... Things get faster every day as technology tries to serve our need for all things to be 'instant' but, as much as we might wish it didn't, real life still involves waiting.

For children, especially those with SEN, it takes time to learn to understand clocks, calendars, queues, road signs and traffic systems. On top of this, to them time seems to move slower – think how long the summer holidays seemed when you were little, or the eternity that seemed to pass between birthdays. The idea of 'appropriate distance' in different social contexts can also be a mystery. Most adults know not to stand right behind someone at the cash point as they type in their pin number, and to wait for people to exit the train before we get on. But we are not born knowing these things; we learn them over time.

Some of the rules described above we pick up naturally along the way, but others we are taught. I remember as a child, for example, being taught about waiting for people to get off the bus. Helping children to gain an understanding of them can be accomplished in a number of ways.

How to teach waiting skills

Try the following activities to help children to practise having patience:

- Plant sunflower seeds or broad beans and monitor their growth.

- Buy unripe pears or peaches. Taste them before and after they ripen.

- Use toy cars to show a traffic jam. Discuss why traffic jams happen.

- Teach road safety and experience waiting at real traffic lights.

- Make bread. Knead it, wait for it to rise, wait for it to bake, then enjoy!

Use waiting visuals

Recognisable images can be used to indicate the need for, and recognise, good waiting skills:

- timers – for example, egg timers, oven timers, traffic light timers, and time tracker timers

- clocks

- count downs

- schedules

- 'good waiting' visuals[1]

- visual calendars

- count down on your fingers

- hold up numbers so the child learns to wait for '1'

- use visuals for 'good waiting', 'good sharing' or 'good turn taking'

- praise other children for their 'good waiting'.

Waiting is an important skill and not having this can be the root of many other behaviours.

Tameika Meadows is an ABA therapist and writes a blog *I Love ABA*. She highlights the importance of teaching a child to wait in a post titled 'Learning to Wait'. She suggests some examples:

WHAT DIFFICULTY WITH WAITING CAN LOOK LIKE

Whenever the teacher tells the class to line up to go outside, Doug gets very excited. Doug loves playing outside. Doug gets so excited and impatient while waiting in line that he regularly pushes other kids down, and steps on their feet.

Iyanna is at the mall with her dad. Iyanna makes the sign 'eat' to her dad to signify she is hungry. Her dad tells her they are leaving the mall in 15 minutes, and she can eat then. Iyanna begins to cry, and a few minutes later bolts away from her dad and runs to the food court where she starts eating leftover food off of tables.

Tyrone's daycare teacher just bought a new trampoline for all the children to play with. Tyrone has fun all morning jumping on the trampoline by himself. After lunch, another child tries to climb onto the trampoline with Tyrone. The daycare teacher says only one child can jump at a time and tells Tyrone to get down.

---

1   *You can w one for free at tinyurl.com/NTgoodwait*

Tyrone watches the other child jump for a few seconds, and then he screams and pushes the other child off the trampoline.

Meadows continues:

A child who doesn't know how to wait may become aggressive, defiant, and may eventually have a meltdown. Most people just see the behavior as the problem and try things such as blocking the aggression, telling the child to stop pushing, or putting the child in Time Out for throwing chairs. The problem with that approach is that in all of these situations the behavior was the by-product of a skill deficit. These children did not know how to wait. When put in situations where they didn't get a desired item or activity 'right now' they engaged in problem behaviors. In order to effectively terminate these problem behaviors you have to target the skill deficit, not just the outcome behavior. (Meadows 2012)

Be alert!

No matter how well your waiting skills teaching goes, there will be hiccups along the way. Watch out for the following impatience flashpoints which can occur in your setting and in children's homes:

- slow internet connections
- scratched DVDs
- commercial breaks
- transition times
- another child's birthday
- any queues
- traffic jams
- phone calls
- supermarkets
- other busy places.

Case study: Milly – telephone trials

Milly was a happy child as long as she had 100 per cent adult attention 100 per cent of the time. She loved to play, to cook and explore. Milly's mum had learnt to adapt to 'Milly time'. The housework and paperwork waited until Milly was in bed. Mum devoted herself to making play dough, baking and arts and crafts. The majority of the time this worked well.

The time Mum needed support was when the phone rang unexpectedly and it was one of those calls she *had* to take. As soon as her attention was diverted, Milly would flip. She would start with making lots of noise. If that didn't work she would find something naughty or dangerous to do. She did anything she could to get her mum's attention back. Mum would come off the phone flustered and cross. Their tranquil, happy 'Milly time' had been interrupted and it was a challenge to get the day back on track.

What if Mum knew there was going to be a call or a visit? She would put on a favourite DVD or the Cbeebies website and Milly was usually happy.

So we came up with a plan. We made a simple Social Story™ explaining to Milly that if the phone rang and her mum needed to talk, Mum would put on a DVD. We practised in a role-play situation with a set up phone call. Mum kept the story by the phone and the DVD ready to go. The idea worked. In time, Milly learnt to go and find something else to do without needing a Social Story™ or DVD.

We cannot always predict when our attention will have to be diverted, but we can think ahead and see if there are ways to help a child wait.

A 'when' is better than a 'no'

A tantrum starts because a little girl wants her dad to buy a magazine. Dad says, 'Not today...' but as the protest increases and reasoning is not working Dad picks up a magazine, gives it to the child and says 'You can have this one – now shush.'

Child wants something – child is told no – child has tantrum – child gets something.

The child has learnt that tantrums work. What will they do the next time? What if the dad is feeling stronger or the no has to be a no? He'd better be ready for a monster tantrum because the child will think they have to turn the volume up – after all it worked once…

The best way around this is to avoid the situation. Set rules – don't give them a 'no' or a 'never', but try to think of a concrete 'when'.

Tell them you will get a magazine when they are poorly. This way they know that at some point they will get a magazine. They have a concrete 'When' to focus on.

Case study: Alfie – ice cream Fridays

Alfie was a very bright, bouncy boy who liked ice cream *a lot*. Children may love that tell-tale music and the sight of the ice cream van stopping at the park, but adults don't always share their enthusiasm. In this case, Alfie's mum had stopped taking him to the park after school because she didn't know what to do about his ice cream van behaviour. She felt she had two choices:

(1) to not go to the park

(2) to give in and buy Alfie an ice cream every day.

Why couldn't she just tell Alfie 'No'? Because 'No' resulted in an aggressive verbal onslaught, anger and even hitting. Mum found this embarrassing and didn't like other parents seeing Alfie like this.

The park was important to Alfie after school. He could let off a lot of steam playing football. Socially and physically Alfie benefited from his visits.

I suggested to Mum that she try a new tack and use a 'when' rather than a 'no'. We decided to choose one day a week when (if the van came) Alfie could get an ice cream. We chose Fridays so the ice cream could be seen as an end of week treat.

Mum highlighted ice cream Fridays on the calendar to give Alfie a visual. They talked it through and on the Monday went to the park. Alfie did try to pressure Mum when the van arrived, but Mum was firm. Each day it got easier and on the Friday Alfie got his ice cream. Replacing the 'no' with a 'when' meant Alfie learnt to wait.

Dos and don'ts

Use the following strategies to prevent problems from emerging and escalating:

Try

- having a 'good waiting' bag of motivating toys
- having a planned alternative activity for when you have to take a call
- having access to a selection of healthy snacks to appease rumbling tummies
- using Social Stories™ and Comic Strip Conversations™ to explain and prepare
- praising and rewarding children when they manage to do 'good waiting'.

Avoid

- visiting the likes of supermarkets, shops and cafés at busier times
- 'quick fix' sweet treats – sugar may intensify behaviours
- times when children may be hungry or tired
- using too much language – a visual may be easier to process
- leaving wrapped treats or presents in view (avoid temptation).

On the flip side

I always find it touching how our little learner, who seems so desperately impatient about waiting, can be so very patient when it comes to waiting for us to position our physically disabled class mates in their standing frames or when they spend longer over lunch. They notice when these children lose a shoe, they try to help with feeding. They instinctively understand when waiting is because of someone else's need. They are also lovely with animals. They do not crowd our pat dog. As they get older they learn to be calm and wait at horse riding.

Josephine Mele observes:

> Kids on the autism spectrum have no patience when they want something, but they seem to have more patience with babies, animals, people with special needs, and older adults than other kids do. They are more communicative with these groups than they are with their peers. They don't see them as different and they give help freely. They are open-hearted, well-intentioned, and kind with those they trust. (Mele 2012)

Final thoughts

If we dislike waiting, imagine how it feels for a child. When teaching the 'art' of waiting we must be patient. We adults can use clocks, calendars and that loading bar on the computer to manage our waiting. Try to find a visual that the child can understand and reward them when they manage a calm 'wait'.

CHAPTER 13

Choice Time

Helping Children Who Find It Difficult to Make Choices

I must have a prodigious amount of mind; it takes me as much as a week, sometimes, to make it up!

Mark Twain

Presenting expectations clearly gives every child the opportunity to make a choice. When a child won't choose, it is often because they need more direct instruction or some visual structure.

A scarf catches your eye. It's love at first sight. You are justifying the purchase in your mind as you check the price. Now you notice it's available in multiple colours – all of which are lovely. Do you...

a) stick to your original choice and take your new scarf to the cashier

b) buy the scarf in every available colour to go with different outfits, or

c) try each one in front of the mirror, hum and ha because you like them all, and finally leave the shop empty handed?

Whether it's what to wear, what to eat or what to watch on TV, the simple act of making choices can be difficult for all of us. Added options and thinking time sometimes make choosing even harder. Some adults simplify the equation by removing choice: they have a minimal wardrobe, and reorder the same food online each week. They make a lifestyle decision not to waste time and energy on choosing. Why? Are they being lazy in opting not to choose, or are they being more efficient?

There are a number of famous adults who eliminated choice:

- Steve Jobs, founder of Apple, had a signature look of jeans and black turtle necks. He had over 100!

- Mark Zuckerberg, founder of Facebook, has over 20 grey T-shirts.

- Albert Einstein was famous for wearing the same grey suits and no socks.

- Barack Obama wears only navy or black suits to save having to think about what to wear.

Transfer this issue to our typical nursery setting. We put out a host of exciting activities in different areas and give the children 'choice time'. Most children take to this incredibly well. They understand the unspoken rule that they must make multiple choices. They travel from the sand tray to the dress-up corner without issue. They choose and they transition.

But think of the child who chooses the cars every day and won't move on. They might not play with the toys in a typical way either. Alarm bells may begin to ring. You wonder what the future will hold for that child. Well, stop a second and spare a thought for Einstein, Steve Jobs and Zuckerberg. I wonder how they behaved at pre-school during choice time!

Case study: 'Sand tray Sam'

Sam's nursery assistants were forever trying to move him on from the sand tray. None of the other children got 'stuck' on one activity like Sam seemed to. Once he was there he became engrossed in watching sand pour through his fingers. He repeated this action again and again, and did not seem to hear the people around him.

The staff had tried removing the sand tray. Sam did not object as they had expected. When there was no sand he simply spent all of his time at the water tray instead. He did not seem to get the unspoken rule – that 'choice time' wasn't really 'choice time' at all. When the teacher said 'choice time' what she really meant was 'move around the different activities spending between 10 and 15 minutes in each area encountering a variety of learning opportunities. Oh, and play in a conventional way, interacting with your peers...'

To address the situation, I created a choice board for Sam. I laminated symbols showing different activities. The activities on the tables changed often and I knew I would not keep up with them, so I marked the tables with coloured flags and made symbols to match. I got a ten minute timer to use in case Sam needed an extra visual reminder that time at choice stations was limited. As Sam transitioned to an area he would remove the symbol from the board and post it in a box. He could still 'choose' a symbol, but once he'd tried something he would have to wait until he had had a go at all the other activities before returning to what would be his first choice.

Adding this visual structure helped Sam and the staff supporting him so much.

Case study: Little Lily's 'nuthin' days

Lily was a very talkative little girl, but when her mum would ask her what she'd done in school she drew a blank.

'What did you do at school, Lily?' Mum would say.

Lily would pause as if recollecting the day in detail, but then reply, 'Nuthin.'

I suggested to Lily's mum that she try rephrasing the question. Rather than ask in her usual way, instead she should say: 'Lily, tell me three things you did at nursery today.'

The next day Lily's mum arrived with a big smile. She said she'd changed the question and asked for three things. Lily had paused to think about her day as usual, but instead of the usual 'Nuthin' she told her mum about how she'd had a shiny green apple and a cracker at snack, and how she spread butter on the cracker herself. She ate the cracker and Mrs Moore had said that she was a good girl for sitting so well. She then told her mum all about the *We're Going on A Bear Hunt* story she had heard (Rosen 1989), and how Annie had her hair in bunches and she had wanted to touch it, but she knew she wasn't supposed to, so she sat on her hands. Finally, she told Mum that a boy had cried and it had made such a terrible noise she had wanted to leave and went to the toilet until Mrs Moore came and told her he had stopped.

Lily's mum was so happy to have found a way to gain insights into Lily's day. Lily had not been able to tell her mum *everything* about nursery as there were too many things that happened. Providing structure to the question had allowed Lily to answer and give details.

The author and consultant Linda Hodgdon has written a fantastic blog about the techniques to teach children choice making. She suggests:

USE VISUAL CHOICES

Visually show the student what is available. When working with very young children, lower skilled students or students who are just emerging in the development of choice-making skills, the initial teaching may be more effective when using real objects. Objects, pictures or written words are appropriate for students who understand them easily. Use whatever form the student will understand.

BEGIN BY PRESENTING TWO CHOICES

Place the choices in front of the student. Ask the student, 'Do you want an apple or banana?' When you name each item, move it toward the child or hold it out a bit to emphasise what you are presenting.

ENCOURAGE THE CHILD TO INDICATE HIS CHOICE

Decide what forms of communication you would like the student to use to make his choice. The goal is to encourage whatever combination of forms of communication the student with autism is capable of using. To reach that goal you need to encourage:

- touching or pointing to his choice

- handing you a picture of his choice

- combining his gestures or pictures with vocalizations or words.

Hodgdon also highlights the importance of teaching children to make choices in more than one way to set them up for success in 'real life':

> When teaching students to indicate their choices, gradually teach the student to use a variety of forms to make that request or choice. If you only teach one form, it will be more difficult to generalize that skill into real life situations where you may not have as much control over the environment. (Hodgdon 2016)

Kenneth Hall was diagnosed with Asperger Syndrome when he was eight and wrote an insightful book about his experiences when he was ten. When it comes to making decisions he explains:

> Sometimes I find it very difficult making decisions. Then I might toss a coin – heads one choice; tails the other. Sometimes the coin gives me the wrong answer and I say 'best of three' or 'best of five'. It's funny how sometimes I don't really know what decision I want till after the coin has been tossed. (Hall 2001, p.43)

Sometimes we may offer a child a choice and they simply cannot choose. Maybe they like both options, maybe making a decision hurts their head or interferes with other thoughts or focuses, maybe they have not been given the time to process that they need to choose before the choice is taken from them. Knowing these things helps us understand why choice may not be made.

Things that help

Here are five simple ideas to help children choose:

1. Create a choice board to give the child a visual to show they need to try all the activities on offer.

2. Use timers at different choice areas or have a timer that goes off every 15 minutes to indicate that it's time to move on.

3. Limit choices. Show the child fewer options and let them select one.

4. Praise them when they do choose, and support them when they can't.

5. Demonstrate what to do in different areas so children feel more secure in trying something new.

Final thoughts

If you are not getting the response you had hoped for from a child, rewind and reassess. Think about how you have presented your expectation. When a child won't choose, it is often because they need more direct instruction or some visual structure to help them.

And remember, the child who finds it difficult to make a choice could be the one with the most potential to one day make a discovery.

CHAPTER 14

Good Sitting

Supporting the Child
Who Cannot Sit Still

I am not absentminded. It is the presence of mind that makes me unaware of everything else.

G.K. Chesterton

What made those children of Hamlin follow the Pied Piper? He did not call out to them or cajole them. He played *their* music.

When our little ones wriggle, squiggle, fiddle or point blank refuse to come and sit at circle time they are not being badly behaved. We naturally want them all to join the group, but being forceful or directive is not our best tactic. Shift the focus and find their music. Think Pied Piper tactics: enchant them with sounds or sights that spark their interest so that they cannot resist being included with the rest of the group.

Case study: Attention Gigi!
Sitting issue
We were ready to start our 'Attention Autism' session. All the children were sitting on their beanbags ready except Gigi. My

support assistant had showed her the 'Box' symbol on her 'Now and Next' visual schedule, but she refused to move.

'I'm going to start now,' I said 'We want to see what's in the box.'

I drew a simple schedule on our dry wipe board.

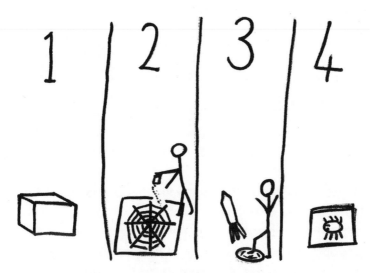

An 'Attention Autism' style visual schedule

'Attention Autism' or 'box' was a session that we did every day at the same time. Gigi was new and still learning our routines. It was up to me to make the box and activities so exciting that Gigi wanted to come and see. She could have all the time she needed, but not all the attention. Our session would continue regardless.

Sitting solution

'I've got something in my box...' we sang together. I looked in the box and found a favourite with all the children (a singing, dancing Elmo from Sesame Street). 'Yay! Elmo!' Elmo started to dance. The other children leant in to look. The support staff joined in with delighted giggles. I knew that Gigi was watching. I knew she wanted to come closer to get a better view.

We continued the session. Next I produced a singing, dancing 'Bob the Builder'. I was blocking the action on purpose, so Gigi had to move around towards the group to get a better look. Pretty soon she had manoeuvred herself to a spot where she could see, but still escape. She leant against my assistant and watched the session. She was really engaged and had chosen to come and sit because she wanted to see.

Outcomes

Gigi soon learnt the set routine of this session. She would sit beautifully and watch intently. She knew that our 'box' session after lunch would be familiar, structured, fun, exciting and worth sitting for.

Case Study: Barney, the bouncer

Sitting issues

Barney was sitting at the table with a support assistant right next to him. I noticed that every so often he would make a move to get up. The assistant was so on the ball and would show him a 'good sitting' visual and say in a nice, but firm voice 'Good sitting, Barney'. This was working and did keep Barney in his seat, but something niggled. My instinct was that Barney had a sensory need to get up and have a bounce and by focusing so much attention on not bouncing he could not fully attend.

Sitting solution

I took the opportunity (with a small group) to see what Barney would do if he was in an engaging session, but free to get up. I discussed this with the support assistant and asked her to do an observation for me. After about five minutes Barney got up. He hesitated because he was used to having a 'good sitting' prompt, I said, 'If Barney needs to bounce for a minute then that's okay.' I got a one minute egg timer and turned it over. Barney clocked the timer and smiled brightly before he bounced off to a corner. I continued with the session, but was really pleased when Barney came back and sat. Another five minutes and Barney was up again and then back again.

Outcomes

Barney wasn't being naughty. He had a sensory need to have a bounce and although he had learnt to control this with prompts I was sure that by focusing his attention on not bouncing he was missing out on so much learning. From then on Barney was allowed to get up and bounce when he needed to. He was also given more access to bounce times and a sensory diet involving lots more opportunity for movement.

The bouncing in lessons reduced and his happiness, ability to sit and potential to learn improved.

Autism, information processing and movement

The author and artist Judy Endow explains:

> Most children are able to better concentrate on the task at hand if they have still bodies.
>
> For autistic children the opposite can be true for a variety of reasons. For some, processing information – this includes thinking – can only happen when physical movement of the body occurs. Thinking is neurological movement of ideas and facts in the brain. Autistic wiring means that sometimes it takes physical body movement to spur on the neurological thinking movement necessary to allow academic completion of tasks.
>
> Many autistic children employ a repetitive movement such as flapping of the hands. We now know that hand-flapping can be a tool to keep the sensory system of autistics better regulated. Many report the calming effects actually allow them to be part of the world around them. Others report that hand-flapping allows excess emotion to be drained out of the body which avoids shut down from overwhelming physical sensations that intense emotions can bring to an autistic body.
>
> Whether regulating, calming or avoiding shutdown, hand-flapping or another repetitive movement (sometimes called stims) for many autistic students is their ticket to be able to concentrate on the task at hand. Having a quiet body or quiet hands, while helpful for typical students, is often counterproductive for autistics when it comes to hearing instruction or concentrating on academic tasks during the school day. (Endow 2015)

Promoting understanding

What about the other children in the class? Is it fair to make allowances for one child? Won't it be distracting to them if one child is allowed to get up and take movement breaks? Will they all want to do it?

Children are often more understanding and adaptive than adults give them credit for. Over the years I have seen how mainstream groups of children will go out of their way to try to help that one child who finds things more challenging. They don't mind the accommodations we make and will accept that one child needs 'movement breaks' or access to sensory integration equipment without question.

But if children do ask questions then the best way to explain is to use an analogy they will relate to.

Mum Mary McLaughlin, author of the blog *Mom-Not Otherwise Specified* has written a wonderful piece called 'Shake Your Sillies Out' about how she answered a group of mainstream children's questions about her son, Bud. The blog is full of brilliant analogies to use with children and I'd recommend reading it.

Some of the children asked about why her son needed 'movement breaks' and she explained it as follows:

> 'So, here's a question: Did you ever sit for a long time in the same position, and then when you stood up again your foot felt kind of funny?'
>
> 'YES!' came the cries and giggles from around the room.
>
> 'It gets tingly,' said Nathan, 'but it doesn't really hurt.'
>
> 'Sometimes it does,' said Brandon. 'Sometimes it feels like a porcupine.' The other kids chimed in with their experiences of limbs that had fallen asleep.
>
> 'That's right,' I said. 'It's all pins-and-needles, right? So, what do you do when that happens? Show me what you do when your foot feels all tingly.'
>
> The kids started shaking their feet and tapping and stomping on the floor, and I shook, tapped and stomped along with them. 'And then,' I said, speaking up over the stomping, 'what if the tingling gets worse? What if your whole LEG gets tingly?' They shook and stomped faster and harder.

'And THEN,' I said, even louder, 'what if your whole BODY feels all pins-and-needles?' They laughed as I stood up and shook all over, trying to work out my imaginary pins and needles. 'And THEN,' I said, still stomping and shaking and wiggling, 'what if somebody came along and asked you to do MATH?'

The class erupted in laughter, and I sat back down.

'I think that's how it feels for Bud when he has to sit in the same place for a long time,' I said. 'So, when that happens, what do you think he needs to do?'

'Take a movement break!' they answered.

'That's right,' I said. 'He needs to get up and move or run around in circles for a while until his body feels normal again, and then he can sit down and do his work.' (McLaughlin 2010a)

Chris Ulmer is a special needs teacher. In 2015 a video of him complimenting his class went viral. With the help of students with SEN he has created a blog and Facebook page with hundreds of videos. He says that his aim is: 'to spread love, empathy and acceptance (yes acceptance, awareness is not good enough) for individuals with special needs' (Ulmer 2015a).

In one of these posts he meets 'Jack' ('an articulate 8-year-old diagnosed with autism'). While bouncing with Jack he asks him about it.

Jack: 'I could stop if I wanted to. It's a great way to get my energy out so I don't stop. But guess what! They don't allow me jumping in school.'

Mr Chris: 'How's that make you feel?'

Jack: 'Having very much extra energy and nothing to do with it makes me slightly bad behaved.'

Mr Chris: 'Would it make you better in school if you could get up and go like this?' (Jumps and flaps his arms.)

Jack: 'If I could do that it would make me so slightly better.' (Ulmer 2015b)

Josephine Mele shared how her grandson, who is diagnosed with Asperger's Syndrome reflects on sitting. Nick (age ten) explained:

Sitting for a long time is hard for me, and my body needs to move around. When I was in kindergarten, my legs hurt if we sat on the floor for sharing circle. My teacher got me a special wiggle pillow (it's filled with air that lets me shift my weight without standing up) that made it easier for me to sit longer. Now that I'm older I don't need it anymore. I went to see a play and the special effects were so interesting I could sit through the whole show without having to get up. (Mele 2012)

Sitting was hard for Nick, but he has come to realise that when something is engaging enough the sitting is no longer such an issue. The teacher was not forceful, but empathic. She found a way to help him sit. She understood that he found it really difficult.

But movement breaks are not enough

Angela Hanscom, a paediatric occupational therapist and the founder of TimberNook, a nature-based development programme designed to foster creativity and independent play outdoors in New England, explains in her blog post 'Why Children Fidget' that children must access a lot more physical activity and outdoor play in order to improve attention:

A perfect stranger pours her heart out to me over the phone. She complains that her 6-year-old son is unable to sit still in the classroom. The school wants to test him for ADHD (attention deficit and hyperactivity disorder). *This sounds familiar*, I think to myself. As a pediatric occupational therapist, I've noticed that this is a fairly common problem today.

The mother goes on to explain how her son comes home *every* day with a yellow smiley face. The rest of his class goes home with green smiley faces for good behavior. Every day this child is reminded that his behavior is unacceptable, simply because he can't sit still for long periods of time.

The mother starts crying. 'He is starting to say things like, "I hate myself" and "I'm no good at anything".' This young boy's self-esteem is plummeting all because he needs to move more often.

Over the past decade, more and more children are being coded as having attention issues and possibly ADHD. A local elementary teacher tells me that at least eight of her 22 students have trouble paying attention on a *good* day. At the same time, children are expected to sit for longer periods of time. In fact, even kindergarteners are being asked to sit for 30 minutes during circle time at some schools.

The problem: children are constantly in an upright position these days. It is rare to find children rolling down hills, climbing trees, and spinning in circles just for fun. Merry-go-rounds and teeter-totters are a thing of the past. Recess times have shortened due to increasing educational demands, and children rarely play outdoors due to parental fears, liability issues, and the hectic schedules of modern-day society. Let's face it: Children are not nearly moving enough, and it is really starting to become a problem. (Hanscom 2015)

Cited in an article in the *Washington Post*, Hanscom explains:

In order to create actual changes to the sensory system that results in improved attention over time, children NEED to experience what we call 'rapid vestibular (balance) input' on a daily basis. In other words, they need to go upside down, spin in circles, and roll down hills. They need authentic play experiences that get them moving in all different directions in order to stimulate the little hair cells found in the vestibular complex (located in the inner ear). If children do this on a regular basis and for a significant amount of time, then (and only then) will they experience the necessary changes needed to effectively develop the balance system—leading to better attention and learning in the classroom. (Strauss 2014)

Seating in our special class

Our little class was not yet ready for the formality of sitting in chairs. Some of them liked our bean bags, but there were not enough for everyone and they did tend to end up lying down in unusual ways rather than sitting.

One of the children had a specialised 'Pea Pod' seat, which looked like a bean bag, but was moulded to support their posture. I wanted to find bean bag chairs to meet my slouching squigglers halfway and make the seating arrangement for circle times more inclusive for the child in the 'Pea Pod'.

I searched the internet and found a set of 'Reading Pod' bean bag seats. They looked ideal and we decided they could be the perfect solution.

The children took to the 'Reading Pod' seats brilliantly. We had met halfway. They had their comfortable bean bags and we had them siting in a slightly more structured way. We had also found a stepping stone towards sitting on chairs.

Ten tips for sitting success

1. Trial carpet spots, cushions, bean bags or swings.

2. Use timers to show how long the sitting will be.

3. Use visual schedules to break down and explain expectations.

4. Add in some movement opportunities or fidget toys.

5. Use 'good sitting' symbols showing the specific sitting.

6. Praise children getting it right by name: 'Good sitting, Billy.'

7. Avoid giving attention to children who do not sit. Carry on.

8. Make sitting sessions consistent, visual and attention grabbing.

9. Highlight positive role models (other children and staff).

10. Think about the whys and prepare to compromise and meet halfway.

Final thoughts

Roman Polanski once observed, 'Cinema should make you forget you are sitting in a theater' (quoted in Merchey 2004, p.33). What makes us go and see a new film? What makes us stay?

When you plan a group sitting session think theatre, think audience and think comfort. Think about their need for vestibular input and add more opportunity for this during the day: not just a two minute bounce, but an extended time to meet their physical needs.

If a child does not choose to sit when you say 'Story time', rethink and restructure. Fill a box with exciting toys and become their Pied Piper.

CHAPTER 15

Against the Clock

How Using Timers Can Enable a Special Child to Stay on Track

A man who dares to waste one hour of time has not discovered the value of life.

Charles Darwin,
The Life and Letters of Charles Darwin

Showing the passage of time in a visual way will help your special children stay on track. There will always be children who find routines intolerable; they need to see and process what your expectations will be.

We use our Sat Navs, phones or watches to see time passing when we travel. We like to know how long we will be stuck in the car, the train or bus. Our early learners are not yet able to read clocks, but they can learn time gaps between routines. They know that there's a set distance between snack, lunch and nap. Many children will accept not knowing all the details; they'll accept that they might have ten minutes at the sand tray, or they might have half an hour. They are happy, content and pretty flexible.

Then there are those children who find the Early Years experience more difficult. Maybe they cling to Mum at the door, maybe they refuse to sit for story time, maybe they lash out, run off or get 'stuck' at one activity. These children *can* learn to manage their anxiety – they may even learn to join in – but they will need a visual way to see and understand your session structure and know that time is passing.

For this role, sand timers are brilliant. They clearly show time pass and seeing the sand fall through the timer can provide comfort and distraction for children. Sand timers are usually colour-coded and children can learn to link the colour with the amount of time. In Early Years settings it's a good idea to limit the timers used – I'd suggest having a one- or two-minute timer and a five- or ten-minute one. You can use timer symbols on the visual schedule too.

Case study: Shakira's short swims

Pool problems

We knew Shakira liked to go swimming with her parents, but something about the school pool made her anxious. She needed time, so for the first few sessions Shakira got changed but stayed on the side of the pool, playing with the watering cans and watching. By the second session she'd had a little paddle but resisted going further into the water. After a few sessions I sensed that Shakira wanted to go in the water. We needed to get past this phase before being on the side became routine.

Addressing anxiety

When Shakira went to her visual schedule and took the swimming symbol off, I said, 'Swimming. Today Shakira is going to go *in* the swimming pool.' Her little glance up showed me that she had heard. I wanted her to be able to process this before it happened.

I took Shakira into the pool first so that there was no noise from other children. I sat behind her on the step and said, 'We are going in the water.' I counted down from five and then we got in the water together. When the other children arrived, Shakira was floating about happily. After five minutes another child started to make noise and I could sense Shakira's anxiety building. She wanted to get out. I asked my teaching assistant to show Shakira the one-minute timer. As it was turned over, I said, 'One more minute swimming, Shakira.' She watched the sand run through the timer. The watching calmed her and when the sand had run through, I said, 'Shakira can get out now. We will stay in the swimming pool for ten more minutes. Well done, Shakira, for swimming today.'

Sand solutions

Using the sand timer helped show Shakira how long was left and control her initial instinct, which was fight or flight. Keeping the swim session going for the rest of the children showed Shakira that even if she wanted to get out of the pool the session would continue.

Case study: Elliot's extremely long day

Establishing routine

Elliot had come to our setting from a mainstream nursery. It was immediately clear how much he appreciated having visual structure. We had an individual visual timetable set up for him and he very quickly realised that the information on the schedule related to his daily routine.

A change of schedule

Elliot's previous placement had been a half day. After lunch, Elliot would take the symbols off the schedule and get his coat. When I explained that this would not change things, he would become upset, but he slowly learnt to accept the longer day.

Unfortunately, one of the children in the class was collected 15 minutes early, at which point Elliot would become upset again. It was horrible taking a tearful little boy to Mum when otherwise he'd had a happy day.

Working together

I phoned Elliot's mum and after a long conversation we decided together that it would be best for Elliot to finish his long school day 15 minutes early so that he could end on a positive. We would review this in time, but for now it made sense to compromise. This worked brilliantly and it was lovely to send a happy Elliot home to a much less anxious Mum. That 15 minute compromise made such a difference.

Keeping track

Timers can help your special children by:

- reducing the need for teacher talk
- showing your expectations visually
- allowing a child to mentally prepare
- breaking your expectations down into steps
- enabling you to compromise in a controlled way
- providing a focus when a child is anxious
- helping to build confidence and trust
- acting as a tool for negotiation
- maintaining a sense of order
- reducing children's fight/flight responses.

What if we gave the child with autism a magic remote control?

Buttons would allow children with autism to have control of their school day. They could 'fast forward', 'pause' and change the volume at will. No one would question them.

Would they 'fast forward' that time before registration, when it is too noisy, unstructured and socially confusing?

Would they 'fast forward' registration all together? Is it fun?

What about maths, story time, spelling, handwriting, P.E.? Would any of these subjects escape that button?

What about lunchtime – the noisy canteen, the disgusting smells, the social minefield?

Never mind 'fast forward' – would the child with autism just press the 'skip day' button and be back at home, safe in their comfort zone?

What if you had a magic remote control?

Imagine stepping onto a crowed underground train and being able to fast forward the journey. Bliss!

Make journeys faster

Inventors are always trying to make transport faster, smoother and more comfortable, but until they develop teleportation for commuters we *must* spend time getting from 'a' to 'b'.

Most commuters are not looking out of the window admiring the views or engaging in social chat. Their attention is fixed on their mobile phone, laptop or newspaper. Or maybe they are taking the time to catch up on sleep. Distraction helps the journey go faster.

On the underground we use a visual map to count down the stops. Knowing where we are headed – where we are 'now' and where we will be 'next' – is comforting. The map helps us to prepare so that we can get off at the right stop. We can mentally prepare our walk to the door, pressing the button, getting past obstacles. The knowing and preparing eases our anxieties.

That map helps us stay on the train until we reach our destination. The destination (even if it is work) is our motivator.

Underground maps have a similar function to the child's schedule

The child's schedule helps them get things right, eases anxiety and helps *them* stay on track.

Underground maps also visually depict the time between stops. The length of the line between stops correlates with the distance and time between stops. This helps us gauge our journey and work out how long we have left.

Timetable Line

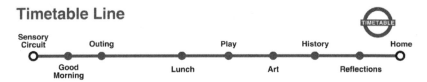

Timetable line (Devine 2014a)

Time[1]

Timers provide a visual for how much longer a favourable or unfavourable activity will last.

Sometimes timers can bear the brunt of frustration. They may even be broken in attempts to thwart time.

By adding visual time symbols to the schedule which link with timers we give the child additional information. We show 'goodbye' will be ten minutes, but lunch will be half an hour.

A timetable with egg timer symbols breaking down the length of time between activities (Devine 2014a)

---

1   *Symbols, schedules and timer symbols are all included in the resource CD that comes with* Colour Coding for Learners with Autism: A Resource Book for Creating Meaning Through Colour at Home and School *(Devine 2014a). See more at: http://senassist.com/ blog/#sthash.IwaxFZJ9.dpuf (Devine 2015f)*

A time timer and 'Now' and 'Next' schedule with time timer symbols (Devine 2014a)

Knowing helps the child feel less anxious.

Knowing helps the child prepare.

Knowing breaks the school day journey down, making it all seem less interminable.

Lost in technology

Oh, and when the child with autism tries to lose themselves in technology to help their school day pass quicker, think back to those commuters.

Making a 'no tech' rule on trains would be impossible and unfair. The way to get commuters looking out of the window is to provide an exciting view. The way to get them communicating is to provide them with a good reason and motivation.

We cannot provide that magic remote, but we *can* provide the visual structures to make school days seem more manageable.

Once we relate to *why* the school day can be challenging, we see why having good visual supports is such a necessity.

Final thoughts

The majority of children may run to the carpet when you say 'story time' and leave the sand tray to sit down for a snack, but there will always be children who find routines intolerable. They need to see and process what your expectations will be. They need time to process and decide if they can join in. Don't try to change such children, but do try to see through their eyes and add the structures and supports they need.

Finally, don't wait! Having visual schedules and timers ready before that special child arrives will improve their journey no end. As Benjamin Franklin once observed, 'Lost time is never found again.'

CHAPTER 16

The Relationship with Technology

How to Use that Love of Technology

All the world is made of faith, and trust, and pixie dust.

J.M. Barrie, *Peter Pan*

Technology is motivating for most children, but to those with SEN and autism it's more. The computer can become a safe place – it's predictable, it's got every motivator on the planet and it's a world behind a screen that can involve and include.

Once they find this safe haven is it any wonder that the child with autism wants to be there every minute of the day? They might *seem* to become manageable and happy rather than 'bouncing between the walls', but we must look at what they are actually achieving on the computer.

Taking control of IT use

We must ask ourselves whether the child's use of IT is including or isolating, educating or babysitting. Children with autism benefit from structure. If left to their own devices they might be on the computer all day and do nothing but click between YouTube videos or sound files. So should we stop them? No, but we must take control early on and structure their time. This way we will help them to develop a healthy relationship with IT.

Temple Grandin (author and professor, herself autistic) believes that without 'the gifts of autism' there would probably be no NASA or IT industry and most autism experts would agree. Bill Gates, founder of Microsoft (widely believed to have Asperger's Syndrome) demonstrates the possibilities if the computer 'obsession' is correctly managed.

There is also a 'dark side' to this relationship

The computer can reduce social interaction, nurture obsessive behaviour or even misdirect skills towards illegal computer hacking.

The case of hacker Gary Mckinnon, who faced extradition rings warning bells. His mother Janis Sharpe reflects:

> When Gary was nine, we bought a primitive Atari. He would beg me not to send him out to play so he could use it. We wanted him to mix more but we didn't want to deny him the information, pleasure and security computers gave him. They were an outlet for him to be himself, and that boosted his self-esteem. (Rhodes 2012)

So what should we do?

Richard Mills, director of research at the charity Research Autism, believes the answer is complicated: 'The computer age totally changes the world of autism. Things are instant, and they are unregulated. We see tremendous advantages to this if it is properly managed – and huge pitfalls if it isn't' (Rhodes 2012).

I would strongly recommend that you don't allow yourself to be railroaded into using the iPad too early. We constantly hear of the miracle that is the iPad. Truth be told we'd all quite like one, for fun, entertainment and if nothing else, the 'cool factor'. The power of advertising!

So what if your child was showing little or no sign of speech? What if you started reading about the amazing communication Apps now being developed? Wouldn't you want your child to access these as soon as possible? Of course you would…

'Just wait!' I want to literally shout to parents and Early Years practitioners. Consult a speech therapist before introducing the iPad to a pre-verbal child. The new Apps are fantastic; they *do* help some children find a voice and are particularly motivating to those with autism. But they are a tool to hold back. If introduced too early, I believe that iPad communication Apps could stop some children from *ever* learning to speak.

So why don't I believe early use of the iPad is 'appropriate'? We've seen the extensive media coverage. Isn't this the twenty-first century miracle tool we've all been waiting for?

I would suggest waiting for the following reasons:

- Many iPad communication Apps speak *for* the child and could take away the point of speaking. Look at it from the child's point of view – why do I need to speak when the iPad will do it for me?

- Communication Apps should not be used until a child has a good grasp of PECS®. They should be a way of *extending* the child's vocabulary of useable symbols.

- A child must learn the importance of a communication partner and this is better introduced through picture exchange (there is no point in them going and tapping the toilet symbol to tell you they want the toilet. They need to learn to actively gain your attention and *show* you the symbol). Communication must be two way to work.

- Children could learn to use the iPad for fun and games, which might reduce motivation to use it as an assistive communication tool, if needed later on.

Instead of making use of communication apps on the iPad we should be doing the following:

✓ Develop knowledge and use of sign language such as Makaton™ starting with a few simple signs used at home and in the nursery setting.

✓ Use photographs and symbols and encourage children to bring the symbol and attempt to say the words. An ideal time to start this is at snack time. Try to get on a PECS® course to learn more. You do not have to be a speech therapist to help a child learn communication skills.

✓ Model speech clearly at every opportunity and give the child the spoken labels for things.

✓ Reduce the number of words used to let the child learn important words (simply say 'snack time' rather than 'Come on children it's time to have a snack now').

✓ Try to link spoken instructions with symbols or photographs.

✓ Use vestibular stimulation, such as swinging on a swing, while teaching speech.

✓ Use microphones, voice recording and singing (any device or activity that might motivate a child to communicate).

✓ Get *all* who have contact with the child on board (the more consistent the intervention the more effective it will be).

Let's not rush in with the iPad too early. Speech therapists can introduce the iPad later on, *if* appropriate. But they can only realise its *true* potential if the timing is right.

Ten tips for developing a healthy relationship with IT

1. Have the computer in a communal area.

2. Have 'computer time' so it becomes *one* of many daily activities.

3. Establish the idea of turn taking early on.

4. Encourage a range of different activities on the computer.

5. As skills develop use a work system to structure computer time.

6. Give typing a function by making their name the computer login.

7. Avoid programs or Apps that speak for the child unless they are recommended by a speech therapist.

8. Try 'switch' programs for teaching cause and effect.

9. Try adapting the keyboard or getting a one button mouse.

10. Use visual count downs and stick to the 'rules'.

Final thoughts

Children are so often drawn to technology. Their skills in this area may be incredibly advanced. We must ensure that we support children to have a healthy, positive relationship with technology. On the one hand, computer use could become obsessive and isolating, on the other the child may be developing skills which could lead to future employment, greater independence and fulfilment. If a child is obsessing with technology it's important to limit its availability in a fair way and add in some structure. If you have a little 'techie' in your care, share reasoning and support strategies with parents too. That early interest in technology can quickly snowball and we must guide this. The earlier the child gets support and structure the more likely it is that they will be able to use their skills in a way that will enhance their life.

CHAPTER 17

Volume Control

Ways to Help the Sound Sensitive Child
Survive and Thrive at School

Kindness is a language which the deaf can hear and the blind can see.

Mark Twain

Close your eyes and try to tune in to every sound around you. Become aware of each little creak, electronic buzz or echo. What if someone turned the volume up and up on all those little sounds until it was unbearable? What if it got so loud that you had to cover your ears? Imagine it was your least favourite noise, for example, nails screeching down a blackboard. You cover your eyes, your ears; you may even rock to comfort yourself. No one else seems bothered. They are all acting normal. Can't they hear it? Why won't they stop it?

Okay – point made. Sound sensitive children do suffer genuine physical pain. When they cover their ears they are not being 'overly sensitive'; they are acting out of self preservation and blocking out noise that hurts.

I recently spoke to Scott James (an adult with Asperger's Syndrome, who found fame through the *X Factor*). He said he would not get on a bus if there were a baby on board, because if it cried the sound would hurt. He compared the pain to being stabbed. Knowing that the baby *could* cry would stop him going on the bus. Of course, Scott can choose not to go on a bus, but what about a pre-verbal child? How might they communicate the fact that they do not want to step foot in your setting?

How can you help the sound sensitive child?

When you're caring for a sound sensitive child, there are a few steps you can take that will help a lot:

- Suggest the child arrives before the crowds and transitions at quiet times.

- Have headphones available to muffle sounds.

- Have a listening station with MP3 players to block out sounds.

- Create a visual volume control to use when it gets too loud (see page 149).

- Use a traffic light system for children's noise levels.

- Switch off hand driers and have towels as an alternative.

- Have a quiet area where one or two children can escape.

- Avoid maintenance work, drilling and so on during their sessions.

- Agree and tell them you don't like it either. Can you compromise?

- Reward and praise them as they overcome hurdles.

Case study: Harry and the hand drier

Each year, the children in my class visit a charity fun day. It was during one such occasion that Harry started to do that recognisable 'little boy dance', so I took him to the toilets. Harry was always good as gold about going to the toilet at school, so I did not anticipate a problem. However, when Harry got to the toilets, he looked in then turned to leave. I *knew* he needed to go, and I didn't want an accident – Harry was so reliable that we had not packed any spare pants or trousers.

'Harry, toilet,' I said firmly as he pulled my hand to go.

'No toilet!' was his high-pitched reply. 'No toilet!' This time he tried to pull me away.

The toilets were empty and quiet. I saw Harry eyeing the hand drier and knew he was frightened. 'Harry, no one will use the hand drier.' He was not convinced. 'I will guard the hand drier.' He was considering… 'I will turn it off and guard it. No one will get past me.'

Harry processed this and then went tentatively towards the toilet. He popped his head back out after going in to check I was doing my guard duty. I did my best, most serious guard impression. It was enough. I felt privileged that Harry trusted me. He knew that once I gave him my word I would have guarded that hand drier with my life.

Case study: Nel, who never showed

Nel had never made it to class. She would cuddle her knees in a corner by the school reception. She kept her hands over her ears and head down until home time and would have a violent protest if anyone tried to move her further, hitting out, scratching and attempting to bite. We had to get past this.

I'd noticed Nel wore an MP3 player for her journey to school. I looked at the issues and asked Nel's mother if she could trial keeping the MP3 player. Nel's mother reasoned, 'No other children have MP3 players in school, and she would not be able to hear the lessons.'

I explained that the other children were getting to class. The way things were she would never hear the lessons. We needed to compromise.

We decided to trial letting Nel keep her MP3 player. I waited until all the children had gone in from their taxis so it was quieter. Nel's mum did not ask for the MP3 player. I took Nel a different route to class, avoiding the reception by going around the outside of the school building. Nel seemed pleasantly surprised to still have her MP3 player, and ended up in class. She caused a bit of havoc and refused to go out at playtime, but she managed to get to class the 'Nel way' from then on.

At the start Nel had the MP3 player on at all time, drowning out unwanted noise, but we made steps forwards. As the term went on I noticed that although Nel was wearing the headphones the music was often switched off. Nel was coping with our day because she had her MP3 player there as a crutch. If it all got too much she could avoid class noise. Gradually, we built trust and reduced the need for headphones. By the end of the year Nel was able to keep the MP3 player in her bag and just use it at playtime, lunch and on transport.

Nel needed those headphones to get to class as another child might want to bring their teddy.

'Ouch!': The top ten noisy offenders

- hand or hair driers
- toilets flushing
- dogs barking
- babies crying
- vacuum cleaners
- any alarm
- fireworks
- people shouting
- clocks ticking
- the hum of fluorescent lights.

Visual volume controls

Teach the children to use a visual volume control, such as that pictured, so that they can communicate how bad *they* find the noise too. You might say, 'Oh dear! The volume is now on black. That is too loud!' then move the arrow down and say 'I like it here'.[1]

A visual volume control

Children with sensory issues are a bundle of contradictions. Often the most noise sensitive child is the one who can make the most noise. A visual volume control can really help. They can show when others are too loud. Your can do the same with them. Have a visual volume control available in class and model using it on different occasions. Allow the child to have fun with it, but do take care that they are not creating their own little game of 'control the teacher'.

The five point scale

The five point scale can be a good way to gauge how bad a sound is to a child. We might not realise that the continual hum of the classroom lights is the equivalent to nails down a chalk board to a child. Giving

---

1   *You can print out a visual volume control free from senassist.com/resources.html*

them a visual way to explain this help them communicate and us to understand.

The five point scale

Nick explains how the sensory perception linked to his Asperger's Syndrome can cause him pain:

> The noise in a group, like the lunchroom, playground, and the classroom, can get too loud for my brain. I might cover my ears and put my head down to make it quieter so I can think. (Mele 2012)

Highlighting the contradictory nature of the child with autism, Nick also states:

> Sometimes I make noises like a cat or dog; spin my pencil, or kick the furniture while I'm thinking. I have no idea I'm doing this until someone tells me to stop. Sometimes I blurt things out; my brain just needed to say things right then and it didn't ask for my permission. (Mele 2012)

We must take care that we know the children who might make noise without intention, who might speak thoughts aloud or get 'stuck' repeating an enjoyable sound over and over. Tell the child quietly that they are making a noise and ask them to stop if necessary, but do so in a kind, respectful way. We must not tell a child off for doing something they are completely unaware of. That is injustice and injustice is completely intolerable.

Supply teachers, trainee teachers and staff cover

We get to know the children in our care. We know their little quirks, their anxieties, their triggers. Teachers have to be out of class at times. This may be planning time, meetings, training or illness. We must ensure we have structures and supports in place so that we set those who cover up to succeed. There may be children who are not on any radar, but you know them. Create a little synopsis of your class. Do not have it on display (for obvious reasons), but have it saved somewhere so that a supply teacher or lunchtime supervisor can get a quick picture. This could make such a difference to how the child copes with the change.

When our boys have difficult days at school it is so often associated with a supply teacher or trainee taking the class.

Case study: Our son and a supply teacher

One day our son came out of his infant school with red eyes from crying. He was beyond himself and too upset to explain. He was completely furious and also frustrated with himself for losing control. What could have happened? It took a while to find out. Eventually we learnt that the class had had a supply teacher. She had told him off for talking. He said he was not talking. The injustice! Next she had told him off saying that he was doing it again *and* she had written his name on the board. He was mortified.

That evening I wrote a note to his teacher. She phoned the next day and said that she had never seen him upset like this in school. I knew that this was because she got him. She understood that he would speak aloud without even realising it. This was him working out an answer, concentrating. He was not misbehaving, or disrupting. After three years in the same class his peers would probably know this as well. So when the supply teacher singled him out, told him off and wrote his name up she was publicly humiliating him and he saw total injustice. It was like being sent to the gallows innocent with no trial. That's why he reacted. That's why he was so upset.

His lovely teacher said that she knew what had happened. She had spoken to him and evened things out. He knew he was not in trouble. She also said she'd heard enough about the supply teacher from him and his class mates to meet with the head and together they had agreed that no matter how short staffed they were that teacher would never again cover classes in their school.

Speak up!

I'm so happy that our sons both had such a fantastic teacher at infant school. Mrs Stocchetti (who is now a headteacher) got to know every child in her class, cared deeply about them and would go out of her way to support them and if necessary fight their corner. Years since teaching them she can pick out that brilliant piece of writing or amazing moment. How I wish that every teacher our children encounter could be like this.

When I was a trainee teacher there was another teacher in school. She was brilliant with the children, organised and had the highest standards. Her teaching assistant followed her lead. She was a great example. This teacher was less popular in staff meetings where she would continually speak up, demanding everyone have the same dedication. She rightly expected everyone to give their all. I had a lot of respect for this teacher. I felt lucky to observe her in action both in and out of class.

There was also another brilliant teacher at the school. Her dedication was the same, but her approach was softer. She had a very happy team, her standards were high, her lessons well prepared and the atmosphere in class was loving and respectful. She was more humble in meetings, but would speak up when needed. These teachers set a high bench mark and helped me understand the type of teacher I wanted to be. Speaking up and having beyond high standards can be a bit unpopular with other staff, but this is our responsibility. It is important to explain the reasons behind strategies and praise all efforts. In my experience if your motivation is the best interests of the child then you know you are on the right track.

Teachers should never shout!

Children need to know you are consistent and even so do not shout. The only time a teacher should shout is if a child is in danger. Children with learning differences and sensory issues will be thrown into anxious panic if a teacher shouts.

I recall a little girl whose mainstream inclusion placement started failing. Why? She explained that the teacher spoke, 'too complicatey and she would often shout'. The teacher would shout at the children who were breaking rules. This little girl was not disobeying, but the shouting felt like a personal attack. Shouting not only causes pain, but makes the teacher look like she has no control, which makes the child feel insecure. Raised voices can cause anxiety resulting in a shutdown or meltdown. A leader who lacks self control is not a leader.

Minimise chat

Teachers like to talk, but sometimes talking can be the worst thing we can do. If a child is anxious they may not be able to process language. You think you are talking sense, but they are just hearing noise which is adding to their discomfort. I once taught a boy whose anxieties when demands were placed could very quickly spiral into a chair-throwing meltdown. The thing that helped most at these times was to go and sit down nearby. I would not speak at all until he spoke to me. I'd simply be there, trusting that he would find his calm and knowing that our relationship would be intact. Somehow that helped.

Having a whiteboard ready so that you can draw pictorial representations of expectations at these times can really help. Maybe you have a child who loves swimming, but at the last minute swimming is cancelled when another class put the pool out of use. You've used the 'Whoops!' symbol and the other children are okay, but for one child this change is catastrophic. You have completely destroyed their whole day. Speaking and explaining won't help, but drawing what you are going to do on a whiteboard holding it nearby will allow him time to process. We cannot always stick to a schedule and children must learn this, but we must respect that the learning can be an ordeal. They need time.

Final thoughts

You might expect a sound sensitive child to be silent, but they often also *cause* the most noise. They might be very vocal, repeating sounds, echoing, flicking switches on and off or slamming doors. There is nothing straight forward about these children – they are a complex, often contradictory puzzle. But by observing, listening and building trust you may secure foundations for their future inclusion.

CHAPTER 18

Space Invaders

Increasing Awareness
of Personal Space

It had long since come to my attention that people of accomplishment rarely sat back and let things happen to them. They went out and happened to things.

Leonardo da Vinci

As adults we understand how close is too close when it comes to physical proximity, but children, especially those with SEN, may need support to grasp the concept.

You are in a bubble. It contains fresh, unpolluted air and a specially adapted environment. Not everyone can see your bubble. The fine wall is only visible if it catches the light in a certain way. Oh, and the slightest little touch will cause it to pop. You can only guess what the consequences would be...

We all have our bubble. There's an invisible line that we don't like people to pass. If someone gets too close we will naturally take a step back. But it's more complicated than that – our bubbles have layers, like an onion. We expect people to know which layer applies to them, but this can cause confusion. We anticipate that a stranger will know to stand further back than a close friend. Our best friend can walk in and give us a huge hug without bursting our bubble, but if someone we didn't know did this our reaction would be different. Personal space might be instinctive to the majority of us as adults, but many children (particularly those with Autism Spectrum conditions) will not have the inbuilt ability to define those space boundaries. So it's up to us to help them learn.

There are many ways to teach children about personal space. We could go out in the playground and draw a chalk 'bubble' around each of them, or give them each a plastic hoop. We could use pictures of different situations with a coloured circle representing personal space. But the earlier we address the issue of personal space the better, because it may not go away. We cannot assume this is a simply natural instinct that will kick in over time.

Teach personal space

Try the following strategies to help children learn about personal space:

- Use spots on the floor to teach children how to line up or find a space.
- Use carpet squares so the children have a physical 'personal area' on the floor.
- Use coloured tape or hoops to define personal space visually.
- Refer to visual symbols for good lining up, walking or sitting.
- Use role play and Social Stories™ to explain terms like 'find a space'.
- Structure transitions so a child always has something to do.
- Model what to do and use support staff to help.
- Display photographs that model correct spacing.
- Use visual rewards and offer praise when children get it right.
- Wait until *every* child is in their space before moving on.

Case study: Finding a space for Will

Once a day I would ask all the children in my class to 'find a space'. This was working fine, but I noticed that Will always chose exactly the same space. I wondered what would happen if another child was in his space. Would Will realise and go somewhere else, or had he learnt to 'go and stand on that scratch mark in the far corner of the room'?

Because I had observed what Will was doing I'd prepared a 'just in case' Social Story™ about finding a space. I prepped Will's one-to-one learning support assistant so she knew to get the story if it was needed.

A few sessions later, I watched little Rosie unwittingly beat Will to his special corner of the sports hall. We watched Will run to the corner and pretty much stand on Rosie. My lovely LSA was there in a flash, story in hand. She took Will's hand and led him to the bench. Together they sat and read the story. I saw her point to the other children standing waiting. While she was reading I praised individuals for keeping their personal space and explained to the group. Will got up from the bench and tentatively found a new space. From then on Will read the story before the request and found a different space each time.

Social Stories™

As the 'Bella' case study demonstrates, Social Stories™, developed by Carol Gray, can be a great way to explain and tackle issues with personal space.

Gary J. Heffner, creator of The Autism Home Page suggests:

> Use a Social Story to explain the reasons for personal space and personal safety (e.g., 'Sometimes I stand too close to other people. When I do this, the other person may get mad at me because I am too close. The other person may think I am trying to hurt them. I will try to stand one arm length away from people when I talk to them unless it is my Mom, Dad, or grandparent'). (Heffner 2016)

Carol Gray has put together a series of useful videos and sample Social Stories™ – these are particularly useful if you're helping a child with ASC decode social situations.

Case study: A new spot for Bella

Bella loved being first. It was the most important thing. She would rush through activities, wolf down her lunch, slap on her paints. The focus was all about being first. I was concerned that Bella or another child might get hurt in the rush to always be at the front of the line at the door. We needed to create some structure fast...

We began by defining space for lining up by using floor spots. A chart on the wall showed the children what colour spot to stand on. I had laminated the children's photos so we could swap them each day. On the first day I purposefully put Bella first. Of course she thoroughly approved of my new system. I made a great issue of rewarding children further back in the line with praise, tokens and stickers. We waited until all the children were in line, ready to go. This meant our class was not first out to play that day. Bella noticed this, but she was used to us not being first class out.

Next day I moved the photos so Bella was third in line. She clocked this the moment she walked in through the door. 'I'm red today?' she asked, to be sure we had not changed the photos by mistake. 'It will change every day Bella. That is fair,' I explained. Bella amazed us all and totally accepted our new system. I didn't even need the Social Story™ I'd prepared! Sometimes all a child needs is some consistent visual structure.

Problems and solutions

Tricky times for children who struggle with the concept of personal space include:

- transitions
- playtime

- carpet time

- lining up

- choice time

- in the car

- on the sofa

- on the trampoline

- during party games

- waiting in queues.

To support their learning, I recommend *Tobin Learns to Make Friends* (Murrell 2001) – the story of a little train learning to make new friends.

Eye contact

Eye contact or lack of it can be a cause for concern. There is something disconcerting about talking to someone who never looks you in the eye. It can also be unnerving if someone holds eye contact too intensely. There is a balance and a skill to eye contact and it will not always be natural.

In the past educators would be quite directive about getting children to look them in the eye, believing that if they were not looking they could not be listening or attending.

In recent years there has been a shift. The modern educator now knows that they need to gain a child's attention, to make them want to look. Most will know that to be more directive or forceful could be counterproductive. The child may look, but the looking may make them extremely uncomfortable or anxious. The looking may require so much concentration that the listening or attending becomes impossible. Author Judy Endow explains:

> For many autistic children looking at people speaking to them is problematic. Many autistic people will tell you eye contact is painful. Even when it is not downright painful, eye contact can be a problem for many autistics in that the information picked up is too intense, which can then trigger shut down.

Whether painful or too intense, eye contact with an adult speaking to an autistic child will not insure that child's undivided attention. In fact, demanding eye contact of an autistic will most likely be counter-productive to your goal of having them take in the information you are saying to them. (Endow 2015)

Nick (a ten-year-old boy with Asperger's Syndrome) explains:

just because I'm not looking at your face doesn't mean I'm not paying attention or listening. Looking in someone's eyes seems really weird and uncomfortable to me. Sometimes when I look in a person's eyes I have trouble concentrating on what she is saying. (Mele 2012)

Research into eye contact

It is important to realise that when a child does not make eye contact it may be due to a physical difference in their central cortex rather than a social deficit (as often assumed).

A research paper published in 2013 in the European Journal of Neuroscience offers evidence supporting 'atypical cortical representation'. The results of the research that visual processing of central stimuli did not differ between the participants with a diagnosis of autism and those without, but there were clear differences in response to stimuli presented in the periphery.[1]

Social circles

The psychologist Tony Attwood devised an effective way to explain relationships and social interactions. He suggests taking a big piece of paper and drawing a series of concentric circles with the child at the centre. Their close family are in the next circle, then other close family and friends. Using this visual we can explain:

A handshake may be an appropriate greeting for the doctor, but not the expected greeting for the grandma. The child may really like and admire his/her teachers, but greeting them with a big hug or kiss each morning would not be an age-appropriate thing for a seven-year-old

---

1   See 'Atypical cortical representation of peripheral visual space in children with an autism spectrum disorder', European Journal of Neuroscience. Available at http://www.ncbi.nlm.nih.gov/pmc/articles/PMC4587666

to do. An alternate affectionate but verbal greeting can be suggested. (Attwood 2007, p.76)

Stranger danger

We must try to teach the children the difference between 'safer' strangers – police, shop assistants, flight attendants – and non-safe strangers. Teach the child about not accepting sweets and getting in unknown people's cars. Teach the child how to get the attention of others if they are worried or anxious. A pre-verbal child can still make a lot of noise if they are anxious.

Use role play, puppets, dolls, teddies or even toy cars. Keep things light hearted, but get the message across. Find ways to show the child how to tell an adult about concerns without having to use speech.

Observe the child at play. Children often echo what they see, hear or experience. If something they are doing causes little alarm bells do not keep this to yourself. Know the child protection policy. Share your concerns with the appropriate colleague. The child may be echoing what they have seen on television they may be echoing real life...

Final thoughts

Not every child is born with an awareness of personal space. Up until they start nursery it may not have been an issue. Being at home with a parent is different to having to negotiate a group. The parent may have been a personal climbing frame, a swing bar and a seat, and children need to learn that climbing on other adults or even children is not acceptable.

When it comes to eye contact we must be aware of how difficult and distracting it can be to some children. We must listen to the explanations from adults, who have been through school and still find eye contact difficult. We must understand that a lack of eye contact could be physical rather than social.

There will be moments when it seems frustrating that one child can't seem to line up, sit still or stay in one place. Children are naturally wriggly and some will only learn about personal space with the right structure and support. If we make learning about personal space visual and motivating, they have a greater chance of success.

CHAPTER 19

The Sixth Sense
(Proprioception)

Is that Bouncy Child Still Learning
Where Their Body is in Space?

There are no facts, only interpretations.

Friedrich Nietzsche

The true sixth sense

Close your eyes and raise your arms above your head. Can you get your thumbs to touch? Imagine if you couldn't even get your hands to meet. What if through lacking this sense you misjudged when lifting your tea and collided with other staff?

We know the five senses, sight, sound, smell, taste and touch, but there is a sixth sense we sometimes take for granted, which our bodies use to gain information about the world. This sense is 'knowing where our body is in space' (whether we are upside down, leaning, standing upright or falling). It is known as the 'sense of proprioception'. How topsy turvy and confusing the world could seem without this sense.

Paul Ingraham, a writer, massage therapist and assistant editor for ScienceBasedMedicine.org explains:

Proprioception is a *large* sense. It produces a tremendous amount of data, as much or more than all the other senses combined. So although it is a silent sense, it is a very important one.

Just knowing that it exists is significant self-knowledge.

The nerves that generate proprioception are embedded in the tissues of our musculoskeletal system: in muscles, tendons, ligaments, joint capsules and cartilage. They send information to the brain about how much tension or pressure is being applied to them, and how quickly it's changing.

The brain uses this information to figure out:

- how hard your quadriceps are contracting

- how bent or twisted your knee is

- how long a step you've taken

- the size of something held in your arms by their position

- the effort needed to lift a glass of water without throwing it into your face.

But proprioception is much crazier than that.

You might expect the brain to be able to figure out the position of the eye based on what you are looking at. But that's not how it works. You actually know the direction and focus of your gaze because you know the position of your eyeball, and the effort it took to change the shape of your lens. Without those nerves in the muscles in the eye balls, we would be able to see, but we wouldn't know where any of it was. Try to imagine that! You would in effect be virtually blind. (Ingraham 2013)

Developing this sixth sense

Babies begin to develop the sense of proprioception from birth, using their hands to reach and clutch and exploring with their mouths. Often they sleep better when securely swaddled. We help this sense develop with baby massage, 'tummy time', encouraging them to reach out and experience motion through bouncing, swinging, sliding and turning.

But what if that connection in the brain does not develop? If a child seems to lacks the sense of proprioception we must investigate, build trust and support their differing needs.

Getting equipped!

The following are useful in establishing the sense of proprioception:

- balance beams
- steps
- trampolines
- large therapy balls
- weighted balls
- weighted blankets
- swings and slides
- different floor textures
- softplay
- dark dens.

Build occupational therapy activities into the daily routine

With the best intentions amidst all that is going on at school including occupational therapy activities can get sidelined as less important, but these activities can make such a huge difference to the child.

It may be worthwhile building a little time into the start of morning or afternoon sessions (or both) where all the children do some of the activities. The session can be a great starter and will become familiar and enjoyable to all children, but particularly those needing a sensory diet and routine.

You can also build breathing exercises into the end of this session. This can be a great way to build a support strategy for when a child becomes anxious. Children cannot learn to breathe when they have reached crisis. This must be taught when they are happy and in the right frame of mind to learn.

Steph Reed, who is a dedicated teacher of children with autism has put this into practice in her classroom with great success. She has allowed me to share this excerpt from her blog *ASDteacher.com*:

OUR CLASS 'EXERCISE' SESSION

As well as the pupils' individualised sensory diet activities, my class also take part in 'exercise' where we all do short physical activities which also provide sensory input as well as some calming activities just before starting our morning and afternoon lessons. The activities have been tailored to the class with a couple of the activities being specifically for individual pupils but also benefit other pupils in the class. The activities are quite physical as well so they get the pupils moving before they start their work. More importantly, they all really enjoy it!

We do the same activities every day and therefore the exercise activities are familiar to the pupils and over time this has enabled the pupils to take part in the predictable activities independently.

Each activity is done for approximately one minute. When one activity has finished, I will count down from five to one and then say '_____ has finished' while moving the corresponding symbol to the red 'finished' side of the board. You can use symbols, photos, pictures or objects – any kind of visual that your pupils can relate to and understand. Have fun! (Reed 2015a)

Weighted blankets, sleeping bags and hugs

Josephine Mele wrote a much shared article explaining Asperger's through an ABC. She explains:

A weighted vest, heavy blanket, sleeping bag, or strong bear hug can calm down an overactive brain. Full-length body contact is soothing and calming. The movie *Temple Grandin* is about a woman with autism who achieves a PhD in animal science and becomes a professor and an inventor. While in college, Grandin invented a squeezing machine to calm herself down when she was stressed out. (Mele 2012)

Mele's grandson Nick shares his personal experience:

> Sometimes I need to pile pillows and blankets on top of myself to stay calm. A friend has a vest with weights in it that he uses when he feels out of control. Sometimes squeezing my mom real tight helps me to feel comfortable and safe. (Mele 2012)

Case study: Ali's new 'Squease'

On the go!

Ali was constantly on the go. He was little whirlwind running, climbing and leaping about. There were a lot of near misses and he needed one-to-one support at all times. The only times that Ali seemed to be still was when he was in a buggy. He did not need a buggy as he was physically very able, but if there was one in class he would rush and climb into it and seemed to be comforted by the support. Sitting in a buggy was not ideal, but if this was a sensory need we wanted to try to find a way to support it.

Individual support

We tried using a swing in the classroom and he did like this, but it did not have the buggy effect. We started to investigate if there was a type of seat that would give the same feedback as a buggy. The problem was that he seemed to want to be on the move and have the feeling of the buggy. As time went on we found that Ali liked our little car. He liked to be pushed around in it. He started to come and take our hands to get us to push him. He was persistent about it. I gave him a large 'help' symbol and he learnt to exchange it to get staff to push the car. This was great as it was a step forwards with developing communication through PECS®.

Outcomes

We knew that Ali would eventually outgrow the car and wanted to find another way for him to have the deep pressure and movement he craved. We decided to trial a pressure vest. The first time I put the 'Squease' vest on Ali we noticed he was calmer. He sat on my knee for about 15 minutes, he went and sat on the floor amidst the group of children and stayed there for five minutes. We had never seen him do this before. He walked down the corridor; he seemed less anxious and more able to focus on where he was and less bombarded by his surroundings. Could a bit of deep pressure do this? We continued our trial and as we observed Ali we noticed that he was calmer. Mum mentioned that he was calmer at home. Being aware and helping meet Ali's sensory needs makes such a difference.

Squease vests

I found out about Squease vests because I was searching the internet, hoping that there was something like that available. Once I started to look into the website I found testimonials from highly respected adults with a diagnosis of special educational needs. I also looked at the testimonials of parents and first hand experiences. We are still in the early stages of testing our Squease vest, but I do feel confident enough to include it as a being well worth investigating if a child seeks deep pressure and seems to have difficulty with proprioception.

The following case study is shared with the kind consent of Keano's mother.[1]

Case study: Keano and his deep pressure vest

Keano has trouble with sensory processing, ADHD and trauma. He lacked confidence and would withdraw or shut down when insecure. His mother had noticed how he would calm when experiencing the deep pressure of a hug sitting on her lap or up against her. A doctor suggested trialling a deep pressure Squease vest.

The family soon started to notice differences. On a car journey Keano's elder brother commented about how quiet

---

1   See the Squease website for the full testimonial: www.squeasewear.com/en/testimonials/keano-6

Keano was, when he would usually rock back on forth. 'Mom, is this because of the little vest?' he asked. At school Keano's teacher commented on his focus and improved patience with drawing. Keano's mum remained sceptical, but then that night when Keano was going to have a bath he didn't want to take the vest off. And then that night for the first time ever Keano (wearing his vest to bed) went to sleep for a full twelve hours, which was a completely new thing. He continued to have better sleeps wearing the vest.

Over time Keano's mother noticed his self confidence improve. His ADHD medicine was reduced and he needed fewer puffs on his asthma inhaler.

Keano continues to use the vest at school when he is working on individual assignments and at times when there is less routine and structure such as Easter and Christmas. At home he uses the vest for family dinners, birthdays, rest moments and when it is time to go to sleep. Keano compares his vest to a 'cool' police vest.

The next case study is shared with the kind consent of Nancy, an occupational therapist, and Theo, a child she worked with.[2]

Case study: Nancy and Theo

Theo was an 11-year-old boy with mild muscle disease. He was easily distracted and could lack concentration and act impulsively. His occupational therapist, Nancy, noticed how well he responded to therapeutic brushing during their sessions. She noticed that the deep pressure and touch seemed to 'give him peace'.

Nancy trialled a deep pressure Squease vest with Theo and seeing positive results in therapy sessions Theo started to take the vest to school. He would put it on himself and choose when to use it. He would inflate it during language classes or after his playtime break to help him calm down.

---

2   See the Squease website for the full testimonial: www.squeasewear.com/en/testimonials/theo

Nancy states that she cannot be sure all these positive changes are due to the vest, but is sure that he is now calmer and more able to focus.

Tacpac®

We have been using Tacpac® for many years in our school. It is a multi-sensory process and combines music and touch. We started using Tacpac® as an approach in our class for students with profound and multiple learning difficulties (PMLD).

In our Early Years/Reception class we cater for all abilities. We will have children with severe physical difficulties and also very active 'bouncy' children. We started out borrowing the Tacpac® boxes for our PMLD children. The boxes are numbered and in each box there is a CD and a laminated list of activities. There are also separate bags, which each contain six everyday objects which are easy to get hold of, such as feathers, pastry brushes, spatulas or pieces of fur. The CD structures the session with musical cues and clear instructions. One object is used at a time, touching the student in a set way in time to the music. The music has been specifically composed to match the objects and the objects are used as follows:

> The receiving partner hears what they see and what they feel on their skin: sensory alignment – and sensory reinforcement for seeing, hearing and touching.
>
> Through linking what becomes familiar music with objects, actions and people in a pattern of different activities, the partners communicate with each other.[3]

Between objects there is always a pause. This pause is hugely important for students with delayed processing or those who find change difficult. The session will take place in an uncluttered, quiet space and always lasts about half an hour. This routine becomes familiar and the structure promotes a sense of calm.

---

3   From *www.tacpac.co.uk/TP-about.htm; see this for more details*

Case study: Using Tacpac® with a mixed group

We decided to start using our Tacpac® as a group session including our very active children and our children with severe physical disabilities. It has been quite amazing to see how some of our very active children will settle in these sessions. A child with autism, who usually climbs on everything and rarely stays still, is able to sit for the entire half hour. He loves the session and the structure and he is incredibly calm. There are wonderful moments in these sessions where staff make connections with the children. One of the children refused for the brush to be used on his legs and directed it to his hair. This showed me that he had connected brushes with hair. Another student giggles and puts out his feet to be tickled; another reaches out to hold and explore the feather then directs it towards the member of staff and smiles. These are little communication moments, so important and so easily missed. These sessions build the students trust and reveal so many 'can dos'. They are a great session to include parents in because they can give them a really lovely structure to work to and share with their child at home.

I love our Tacpac® sessions; the structure and the music create a wonderful atmosphere. We have some lovely, sometimes unexpected moments. We discover things about our individual students, through things they like and dislike, how they think and how they respond. Sometimes as we are doing these sessions, people who are being shown around school might peep through the window of our 'little stars room' and see us tapping children with brushes or wooden spoons. At first glance these sessions look unusual, but then at first glance many of our most successful strategies and interventions will.

There is a wonderful case study on the Tacpac® website written by Jackie Osborne, who is a teaching assistant at The Loyne School, which caters for pupils with severe learning difficulties (SLD), PMLD and autism.[4]

---

4   See www.tacpac.co.uk/articles.htm

The Loyne School teamed up with Ryelands Primary School. Ryelands selected six of their mainstream 11-year-olds. These children seemed to have lower self-esteem and some also had issues with behaviour. The Loyne students were ages five and six with PMLD or SLD. The Ryelands pupils were to act as the 'givers' in Tacpac® sessions, whilst students from The Loyne would be the 'receivers'. The idea was to develop positive relationships and experiences and raise the children's self-esteem in the process.

Osborne explains how over weeks the children developed communication and interaction and how the Ryelands children learnt about pre-verbal communication and patience and discovered their own 'can dos' by helping others. It is lovely that after the project finished many of The Ryelands students continued to pop in to see the students at The Loyne.

I wonder what long-term affects this 'Building Bridges Project' had on those Ryelands children. With the curriculum being so geared towards academic progression it is important to keep in mind the importance of projects like this created to develop the 'whole person' and send them out into the world more open minded, more patient and less likely to judge.

Case study: Sol's softplay
On the go!

Sol was a very busy boy. He was always on the go. On our first home visit he zoomed into the room and just missed banging into a low level TV unit. The fact that he stopped suggested that he did know to avoid it. When I asked his mum she said that they had had a trip to hospital when he had bumped his head on it and since then he would stop, knowing that the TV unit could hurt. So focusing on the 'cans' as we always do, we knew that Sol must have some awareness of his own safety and an ability to recall past 'hurts'. When Sol was in the classroom he explored by climbing on the furniture and jumping off the radiators. We made sure he had lots of access to activity and created an individual sensory diet filled with activities to meet his needs. He had trampoline time, swimming, softplay, outside play and access to our sensory circuits.

Individual support

For one of our weekly activities we would go on an outing to a local softplay centre. We expected that it would be perfect for Sol. What better place than a huge softplay area to actively explore without anything hard to get hurt on? So when we arrived at softplay and Sol point blank refused to get out of the buggy we were surprised. Sol seemed genuinely terrified and we realised that we would need to take smaller steps. We started by taking the buggy into the softplay. Sol loved the trampoline in our classroom so we moved the buggy near the softplay trampoline. Over time we were able to coax him out to have a go. These bounces started out short, but became longer each visit.

Outcomes

As time went on Sol became braver. He still took time to process the surroundings after arrival, but he was less anxious and more curious. We never forced him, but always encouraged him. It took months and months of softplay outings, but by the end of the year Sol was climbing all the way to the top of the big slides and then sliding down (sitting on a member of staff) with the biggest, brightest smile on his face.

Final thoughts

Carl W. Buehner once observed, 'They may forget what you said – but they will never forget how you made them feel.'

Be aware of that true sixth sense. Note how a child navigates space, performs gross and fine motor tasks and how they speak. Seek the advice of an occupational therapist or speech therapist if you have concerns. Have sensory integration equipment available and consider creating a 'sensory diet' (if needed) to support individual needs.

CHAPTER 20

The Child who Chews

Strategies for the Child who Chews Toys or Clothes

I do not ask the wounded person how he feels, I myself become the wounded person.

Walt Whitman, *Song of Myself*

Chewing can be distressing and frustrating for *us* to observe so imagine how parents must feel.

Imagine if your child continually came home from school with soaked, chewed up, raggy sleeves. How would you feel?

- *Frustrated:* School sweaters are not cheap.

- *Worried:* Is your child anxious, afraid or bored?

- *Suspicious:* Is your child being supervised?

- *Isolated:* Why is your child the only one who does this?

Communicate openly. Let parents know that you recognise the issue and reassure them. You are going to need to work together to resolve it.

We know that chewing can be a sign of Sensory Processing Disorder, autism or anxiety. Refer the child to an occupational therapist for specialist advice.

Why is the child chewing?

Exploring

Mouthing toys is a natural developmental stage. We provide babies with toys specifically designed for this. Often the first thing a baby will do is try to put something in their mouth. A child who is chewing may be exploring in the most basic way.

Sensory

Chewing and biting provide a child with lots of tactile proprioceptive input. They may have a sensory need to chew. Provide something they can chew to fulfil this need. Create a 'sensory diet' for the child. Provide a small trampoline, a large ball to bounce on, access to deep pressure through massage or weighted blankets, swings and so on.

Anxious or frustrated

Observe when the child chews. Do they do it when the class gets noisy? Do they chew during transition times or when they are frustrated by not getting their own way? If the chewing is 'reactive' then we must think 'restorative' or 'redirective'. Set up a 'best day' scenario and see if reducing demands helps reduce chewing.

Bored

Your educational setting may seem far too exciting and stimulating for this to be the case, but observe the child. Try 'Intensive Interaction' to discover *their* interests. Follow their lead. Try an 'Attention Autism' session. Get a whole lot of wonderful, exciting things and see if you can grasp their attention. If chewing is due to boredom then tune in to what interests the individual child.

Habit

Whatever the initial trigger once a child is chewing regularly it can become a routine or habit. We cannot stop the chewing immediately, but can break the habit in stages.

Offer alternatives

There are now products that are specifically designed for children who chew. We tend to use chewy tubes with our class, but there are also chewy necklaces, chewable toy straps, chew bangles and chew gadgets. Take due care and read the safety advice for each individual product. Always supervise and replace if damaged. Wash them regularly.

Snacks such as breadsticks and carrot sticks can offer the same sensory feedback.

Ten tips to tackle chewing

1. Note when chewing occurs. Find the root and respond.

2. Provide sensory equipment for a 'sensory diet'.

3. Create a retreat if chewing is linked to noise or anxiety.

4. Provide access to headphones, fidget toys and deep pressure.

5. Provide something the child can chew when they need to.

6. Ensure the child can communicate: 'I want to chew'.

7. Redirect, suggesting, 'Chew hammer', rather than 'Don't chew'.

8. Try not to make the chewing too much of an issue.

9. Reduce the ease of access, for example roll up the child's sleeves.

10. Communicate and reassure parents. Work together.

Case study: Anto's need to know
Observation
Anto liked to know exactly what was on our schedule. He was a clever little boy and would try to negotiate by removing and replacing symbols on our visual schedules.

Anto did not just want to know what was happening next, but liked to know our plans for his day, the plans for after school, the week ahead and weekend.

When Anto did not like the information given he would try to negotiate by changing symbols around and when this did not work he would head bang and chew at his jumper and sleeves. It was painful to observe. He was so distressed...

Solution
I realised that part of the build up was the trying to change things around and that discussion only increased his frustration and anxiety. I placed a chart up high on the wall. It showed daily activities and also what Anto would do after school each day. Was he staying with his dad, his mum or going to respite? Staff agreed to point up to the chart and read 'Monday, Anto goes to respite'. Once it had been read we would simply point.

Outcome
The chart worked well. Not being able to manipulate the visual removed the need to keep trying to negotiate what we could not change. Anto knew the answer would remain consistent and the obsession with discussing it was reduced. As Anto's anxiety was reduced so were the meltdowns and associated chewing.

Case study: Shimmy's sensory diet
Observation
Shimmy liked to climb, to bounce, to run and was forever on the move. He would also mouthe and chew anything and everything – buggy handles, plastic toys or bottles. He had

an incredibly strong bite. The usual teething toys would not last more than a few minutes; tops of water bottles would be destroyed in seconds. At mealtimes Shimmy loved to eat and was quick to grab food from other children's plates.

Solution

We immediately gave Shimmy access to a chewy tube so that he had something safe to chew. We noticed that he loved to sit in our class buggies and enjoyed the sensory feedback of deep pressure. We introduced a one-to-one individual timetable for Shimmy all based around his sensory needs. He would have short motivating activities followed by physical activity such as bouncing, exploring our woodland area or swimming. At mealtimes we discovered that Shimmy coped best when sitting in our class swing. He seemed to feel more secure and started to use a fork to feed himself, which required more time and focus.

Outcome

Shimmy still needs to chew a lot, but by giving him things he can chew and creating an individual programme based around his sensory needs we are seeing him access learning opportunities and develop positive relationships.

The extract that follows was written by Lorraine Scott Young. Her daughter Jamie is diagnosed with autism. Trying to find an alternative to chewed uniforms led her on an interesting journey:

Jamie has always chewed, it was like she never stopped teething. She was a clothes chewer. She would ruin her t-shirts, bite buttons and zips off things and then when she started at school her polo shirt collars and school jumper cuffs were full of holes where she chewed them. She would also have a constant wet patch on her jumper where she mouthed it at school. I honestly didn't think anything of it until the path started taking us down the route of an autism diagnosis and we had to see a speech and language specialist. She suggested that we try 'Chewelery' as it wasn't good the amount of saliva Jamie was losing and this could make her dehydrated. Not to mention the mess she was always in being wet and uncomfortable. So I searched and searched online but couldn't find anything that would be acceptable to her peers (this was a huge thing for me – probably not so much for Jamie). I couldn't find anything in the UK either. This was in a time before you could order anything you wanted from Amazon and it came on next day delivery! So I eventually settled for a necklace and bangle set from the USA, it took 6 weeks to arrive and it looked like coiled telephone wire from when I was a kid. We couldn't choose the colour so when it arrived in yellow (a colour Jamie hates – that was not a good start). She did take it school and I think it helped, but she would flick saliva everywhere with it and it was such an obvious aid that she was singled out and children were starting to ask questions. The school asked me to look for something else as this wasn't working as we had hoped, so I frantically started scouring the internet again and in a last ditch attempt turned to the Netmums website for help, where I found an ad for teething jewellery. Gumigem Teething Jewellery was fashionable silicone jewellery for Mum to wear and baby to teeth but as soon as I saw the lightning bolt I knew that my Harry Potter mad daughter would love it. I ordered and it arrived the next day! This time the saliva stayed where it should, the other kids thought it was really cool; something that I hadn't realised happened…chewing helped her! When she was anxious it would calm her, when she was frustrated she could bite down hard, when she was concentrating it aided her… I was amazed. So I contacted Gumigem Teething Jewellery and told them what amazing products they had for a completely different audience. Gumigem then sent me a selection of products for Jamie to test and see how she got on. Back then she was a really aggressive chewer so the products didn't last long, but that didn't matter to me. The price of a necklace over a school uniform was cheaper and it was safe and discreet. Gumigem decided that with my help we would market the range at a completely different audience and Chewigem evolved from there. Over the years our products have evolved as we've come to know the chewing market in great detail. We have a huge selection in the hope that we can cater for all chewing needs. Jamie is nearly 12 and at mainstream secondary school now and she still chews. She has now learned to control her chewing so she knows which type of chew she needs depending on her mood. So when she is really frustrated and angry she will chew on a Button as that's the strongest most robust product but when she is chilling out on You Tube or doing some homework she'll opt for something like a twister which is soft and flexible. (Scott Young 2015, personal correspondence)

Final thoughts

Chewing can be distressing and frustrating to see and we must react in a loving, respectful way. Build the child's feelings of trust and security and provide alternatives. Observe, adapt, reduce demands, add visuals and the means for communication. Trust your teacher instinct and do not fear trying out that new idea.

As Lord Byron once observed, 'There is no instinct like that of the heart'.

CHAPTER 21

When Clothes Hurt

Helping Children with Sensitivity to Clothes and Shoes

Those who know, do. Those that understand, teach.

Aristotle

Sensory issues surrounding hats, coats, shirts and shoes must be handled with care.

Clothes sensitivities are real and can cause overwhelming distress, which is heightened when you add in the unfamiliar or unexpected.

Most of us have got that outfit hanging in the wardrobe that we will *never* wear. Maybe it's too tight or feels too hot. Maybe it's too formal, too casual or associated with a bad memory? Keep it in mind.

Now imagine that you're full of cold, hot, tired and generally want to hide under a duvet. You've struggled through work and hadn't planned on going anywhere. Suddenly a colleague is at the door, telling you about a karaoke night you didn't know was planned. They're expecting you to go and sing on stage. Next they produce *that* outfit and say that you must wear it. The whole thing will be broadcast live on television too – no pressure. How would you feel?

When a child resists changing into boots or a coat to go outside in the rain, it could be due to sensitivity or anxiety. Clothes sensitivities are real and can cause overwhelming distress, which is heightened when you add in the unfamiliar or unexpected.

The last thing you should ever do is force a child into something that alarms them. Even if you cannot see or feel or understand what is causing the issue, do believe that there *is* an issue. That label might feel like a razor blade scratching their neck, the idea of wearing a different colour T-shirt might seem to them how you would feel wearing a skimpy black dress to school.

So, look for ways to reduce the sensitivity by adapting the clothes. Reduce your expectations and choose your battles. Listen to the child, speak with their parents, their past teacher or childminder. When we try to overcome issues with clothes that 'hurt' we must do so in the most sensitive and respectful way.

Case study: Ned's new shoes

Sensory issues

Ned had huge sensory issues about clothes and shoes. He would wear the same style of T-shirt and trousers to school every day. Over the summer Ned's feet had grown and his Crocs (the only shoes he would wear) were too tight. Ned's mum had sent in an identical pair hoping that we would be able to get Ned wearing the new ones.

After a lot of convincing and a Social Story™ about growing feet, Ned agreed to try them. He put one foot in, but instantly pulled it out as if it burnt him. He could not keep wearing the old Crocs. They were too tight. What were we going to do?

Communication

I spoke to Ned's teacher from the previous year looking for ideas, and came upon a solution. She said that she had eventually used sandpaper to make the soles of Ned's Crocs smooth. Lots of sanding followed.

When Ned tried his new Crocs again he walked about in them. They were much better and clearly not causing him pain, but then he went back to his old reliable Crocs and would not let them go. The new Crocs felt okay, but Ned was still resisting change.

Outcomes and solutions

The next step needed to be final. We spoke with Ned's mum, who agreed to accidentally break the old Crocs so that they had to be thrown away. Now Ned had no choice but to accept the new ones!

Sometimes cutting, stitching and even sanding(!), as in this case, are necessary, but other strategies can work too. Consider using Social Stories™ to prepare children for new clothes, as well as schedules to give warning of any impending activities that require a change. Make use of children's interests – such as a favourite character, or even a colour – and model the desired behaviour. Finally, don't be afraid to compromise to make progress; take your time and build trust.

Case study: Setting Sam up to succeed
Potential problems

When Sam started nursery it was clear he had some sensory issues. He would become really upset by other children's noise and would cover his ears to keep out the sound. Sometimes noises even made him cry. He liked to take his shoes off when inside. I noticed, too, that over the first few weeks that Sam attended nursery he was wearing the same Disney T-shirt, tracksuit bottoms and shoes to school every day.

Investigating further

I wanted to find out whether Sam was also sensitive about his clothes, so when speaking to his mum on the phone I took the opportunity to ask about why Sam always came into nursery in the same outfit. Were the T-shirt and tracksuit trousers the only clothes he would wear? Sam's mum said that, actually, he was fine with clothes and didn't have an issue.

Taking action

Armed with this knowledge I asked Sam's mum if she wouldn't mind varying what Sam wore to school each day. I've seen too many children get 'stuck' with clothing over the years, and I wanted to avoid this becoming a problem for Sam.

Sam's mum understood, and from then on she varied the clothes he wore. Sam came to school in different shirts, trousers and shoes without a problem. It may never have become an issue, but I was glad we had acted (just in case).

School uniform

For the child with severe sensitivity to touch introducing school uniform can seem to be an impossible task. Suddenly that child who will only wear that one type of trousers, T-shirt and shoes is going to be expected to wear a stiff shirt, trousers, sensible shoes and maybe even a tie. Where do you start?

First and foremost, if there might be an issue do not wait until the first day of term to find out. Try the uniform on long before (if you can get that far).

Michelle is an occupational therapist (OT), who started a fantastically useful website.[1] She suggests an OT referral, but has these useful tips for those still waiting:

> **First**, use TONS of fabric softener!! Wash and rewash and rewash as many times as you can with a lot of liquid fabric softener… soak them for days or multiple times if need be. This is a 'magic pill' for many.
>
> **Second**, buy clothes (even school uniforms) at a consignment shop or used clothing store; where they may have been worn and washed many times, naturally making them softer.
>
> **Third**, have [the child] do firm rub downs during and after their shower/bath. Start with lotion, move to baby washcloths, then rougher washcloths and towels, to scrubbies and loofahs as [they] increase [their]

---

1   *www.sensory-processing-disorder.com*

tolerance and decrease [their] touch sensitivity/defensiveness. But, make sure it is done consistently and as often as possible – working up to several times a day, if possible.

Fourth, give [the child] some deep pressure lotion massages to her arms, legs, hands, neck, back, and feet (avoid the stomach). Use firm, even pressure.

Fifth, sew some very soft material (same color) of the inside of the shirt on the collar and seams of the shirt. Have [the child] feel different materials at the store and decide which one feels best. (We did this for the waistband of a pair of jeans for my daughter... she chose a silky material, and it worked!!)

The **last thing** you can try is a tight fitting lycra/ spandex undershirt or a 'compression shirt' underneath [the child's] shirt to give her some calming deep pressure input and keep the 'itchy' shirt off [their] skin directly.

Although accommodations are a good idea and usually necessary, they are a temporary fix. Therefore, I do encourage OT treatment to address and change the underlying touch sensitivity (tactile defensiveness).[2]

The ouch factor!

Ten reasons children may respond negatively to clothes:

1. *Labels* – this can be resolved easily by cutting labels out.

2. *Textures* – the material might feel horrible to the child.

3. *Temperature* – experiencing extreme reactions; being hyper- or under-sensitive.

4. *Reasoning* – for example, 'Why must I wear a coat and gloves in winter?'

5. *Anxiety* – if you can change their clothes, what else might you change?

6. *Newness* – children may be unwilling to try anything new for fear it might hurt.

7. *Colour* – some children will only wear one or two colours.

---

2   *www.sensory-processing-disorder.com/touch-sensitivity.html*

8. *Sound* – does the fabric of the offending item of clothing make a sound when it rubs together?

9. *Routine* – children may be used to always wearing set clothes in certain situations.

10. *Control* – children may not want to be *told* what to wear.

Final thoughts

If clothes sensitivities are not tackled thoughtfully they can become a huge issue. Be on the look out for the child who has all their labels cut out or wears the same thing every day (whatever the weather). Introduce games that involve dressing up, putting on hats, wigs and sunglasses, and if you spot a potential issue communicate with the child's parents. There is a window of opportunity when children are little. We can significantly reduce the chances of them becoming 'stuck' wearing only one colour, one outfit or one pair of shoes.

CHAPTER 22

Personal Care Scares

Supporting the Child with Anxieties about Hair Washing, Hair Cuts and Brushing Teeth

The only thing we have to fear is fear itself.

Franklin D. Roosevelt

Parents of all young children can find hair care a battle. It's wrapped up in a bundle of fears of what is new, what is not understood. But add in anxieties linked with sensory issues, heightened sensitivity and communication difficulties, add autism into the equation and the word 'battle' has new meaning.

A child is coming to school with long, matted, smelly hair. There is clearly an issue. So how can we support parents with this?

Communication

Speak to the parents, if the issue has not already been discussed. A direct question works best. 'Does Billy have any sensory issues about his hair care?' Offer your support.

Observe or request details

Try to learn more about what's causing the issue. Is it sensory? If so is it relating to the sound, the sensation, the smells or all of these? Is it fear of the look of the scissors, of water being too hot or too cold, of water or hair getting in the eyes? Is the fear associated with a bad memory?

Form an action plan

Meet with parents and discuss a plan to tackle this. This will be tailored to the child and everyone must be aware that there is no quick fix. These things take time.

Hair washing

Case study: Lenny – overcoming anxiety and washing hair scares

Lenny was extremely anxious about hair washing. His parents were open about how difficult this was and I said we would make it a priority. Lenny was absolutely refusing to wash his hair at home. Lenny was a sensory child, but I had learnt that he was able to conquer anxieties if they were tackled in a playful way. The way with Lenny was to make the fear conquering and desensitising into a game. Rather than ask Lenny and tell him it was going to be okay we needed to actually show him it was okay through incorporating it into play.

Tackling the issue

We had two hydrotherapy swim sessions built into the timetable. We would start the session with developing swimming skills and then end with either a play session or a sensory session with music and colourful lights. I decided to extend playtime with lots of play involving getting each other's hair wet. We made it a game. He loved pouring the water on my head and as it was a game he got used to his hair getting wet too. We did this each week and he loved it. After swimming I would get some comments on my red-eyed, drowned rat appearance, but I was absolutely thrilled at the progress we were making. Lenny's tolerance grew and grew. As his hair was already wet he started to be okay with showering and pretty soon we added in the shampoo.

Overcoming anxieties

I spoke to Lenny's mum about his progress and suggested building the water play into home bath time. I explained how he was at school. I reassured them that he really wasn't frightened any more, but needed to generalise this to home, where being anxious was a learnt routine. They just needed to be confident and make it fun. Lenny's parents tried this at bath time and were really happy to see that he had overcome the anxiety. Hair washing had become one more issue Lenny had managed to overcome.

Splash anxiety

Every case is different. My instinct with Lenny was to turn things around through play, but that could be completely wrong for another child. There is no one solution.

The author Donna Williams explains:

If a person with 'autism' has anxiety about being splashed by others then this may become part of the hair-washing anxiety too, so if you are washing someone's hair when such a person is experiencing high anxiety (due to lack of control) the person may feel his/her head is sensitive. One way to tackle this anxiety may be to give control back and reduce stress. Guiding the person's hands through actions of the hair washing may help some people feel in control and an active part of what is going on. This may also help them map out the actions physically, establish a routine and eventually maybe even choose to take over (if you progressively 'fade out' your part in these actions so that the other person ends up pre-empting the actions and guiding your involvement rather than you guiding theirs). (Williams 1996, p.292)

Time for a hair cut

I'm lucky enough to job share our Early Years class with a dear friend. Clare Walker is a teacher who is as enthused as I am about every aspect of teaching children with SEN and will always go that extra mile to support a parent in need. I was chatting to her about this chapter and she told me of a little boy she'd taught and how they used a gradual approach to desensitise him to whatever fear he had of the hairdresser. I asked her if she could spare the time to write it down so that I could share it in this book:

Case study: Alex, a 'hairy' tale

Alex came in one day with very short hair, I commented to his mum about what a smart boy he looked. Her face drained of colour as she retold the harrowing story of their ordeal at the hairdressers. It became clear that Alex's fear of having his hair cut manifested itself in hysteria, screaming and wriggling and kicking to do anything he could to get away from the man with the clippers. Apart from the obvious distress to Alex and his distraught mother, the hairdresser was understandably terrified of going near him with anything sharp and the other waiting children fled from the barbers in tears with unsympathetic comments from the parents.

This was an unsustainable situation. At four years old, Alex had been barred from many a barber and his mum was too embarrassed to revisit the same one more than once. It was agreed that neither his mum or Alex should ever have to experience that trauma again – we had until the next haircut in six weeks to make a difference.

Identifying the issue

- We identified that Alex was fine having his head touched and different pressures applied.
- We identified Alex was terrified of the noise of the clippers.
- We identified that Alex's biggest motivator was the iPad.

Working towards a solution

We allocated a key member of staff (Jo) and Alex was always given her photo when working with her. Every day, Alex and Jo would have time together. Initially Jo exposed Alex to the sound of hairdryers and clippers in a safe environment. There was no pressure on Alex except to be in the large room. Alex would be allowed to play on the iPad during the sessions.

Alex did lots of work with mirror play getting used to seeing himself in the mirror, wearing an apron and having Jo comb his hair, so he could see her behind him. Jo would use gentle vibrating toys against his head – always demonstrating on herself or another adult such as Alex's mum first.

Gradually Alex could cope with the sounds of the clippers and hairdryers in a much more confined space and coped with seeing Jo hold them in the room in the mirror near his head.

Alex was allowed to turn on and off the hairdryer and clippers and be in control. He ran them over a balloon. He watched a doll have her hair cut.

Alex was always shown the symbols and a schedule of what was happening and a finish symbol at the end.

Alex's mum came into most of the sessions. This was important to empower her.

I phoned a few barbers and found one who was willing to support us. Alex visited with Jo and Mum, initially just going in and leaving soon after. The next visit involved going in and sitting in the chair with his iPad – Jo massaged his head, then the barber. Things were done at Alex's pace and in fact he moved faster than we anticipated. As tempting as it was to speed up the process, we stuck with the schedule and never changed it on the day. This was important to give Alex control and show that we would not move the expectations.

The result

Six weeks later Alex went to the hairdressers with his mum and Jo and came back to school a happy little boy sporting a new hair cut. Alex's mum came in beaming and extremely proud (not to mention relieved!) Since then Alex's mum has been able to take Alex to the hairdresser and it is now part of regular family life.

Hair-dressing anxiety triggers

Anxiety triggers include:

- sounds, such as clippers, hair dryers, lights, chat and so on
- the idea that it will hurt or a memory of being hurt
- fearing hair or water in the eyes
- the itchy feeling of chopped hair
- discomfort and having to stay in one place; waiting
- not knowing how long it will take or what will happen next
- sensory issues surrounding touch; having a sensitive scalp and skin
- smells such as shampoo, hairspray or perfume
- an unfamiliar place, people and routine
- attachment to their current image; resisting change.

Point to consider

Adults with autism have given personal accounts of face blindness (prosopagnosia) in many books and blogs. The hair style or hair colour can be a big tool for recognising other people. Hair style helps the child know who they are.

Ten tips to help with hair cuts

1. Use head massage to desensitise.

2. Invest in quiet clippers.

3. Create a routine and be regular.

4. Have a visual schedule to show 'when'.

5. Have a schedule breaking down what will happen.

6. Be as quick and as quiet as possible.

7. Use distractions – television, iPad and so on.

8. Let the child see others having happy hair cuts.

9. Use tokens, timers and rewards.

10. Remain calm, consistent, patient, but persistent.

Brushing teeth

Our little class each have their own toothbrush and every day after lunchtime toileting we support them one-to-one to brush their teeth. We show the child a symbol first and allow them time to process. We show them a visual schedule so that they can understand our expectations at each stage. They can also see how many more steps there will be until we say 'Finished'.

We know that establishing tooth brushing can be tricky with any child, but when a child has sensory issues or heightened anxiety this can be taken to a whole new level. If we can establish good routines when they are in Early Years or Primary and if we can focus on giving support in this important area, we could establish enough tooth brushing and aural care to save them agonies and torment when they get their big teeth. The baby teeth allow us time to right things and make such a difference to their experience when the tooth fairy days are in the past.

Case study: Joshua and teeth brushing

Michelle (a mum, who wanted some help) contacted me. She has three sons on the spectrum. Her seven-year-old, Joshua, had issues with brushing his teeth. Michelle was keen to use Social Stories™, but wasn't sure where to start. She thought that if I helped her write one then she would have a model to follow.

Her request made me think of that old proverb, 'if you give a man a fish he is hungry again in an hour; if you teach him to catch a fish you do him a good turn'.

Investigation

First I asked a series of questions. How old is Joshua? Does he read/ or enjoy words or is less language better? What is the exact issue with teeth brushing? Is it the getting him to do it at all, the length of time? Has he now got quite a few 'grown up teeth'? Is the issue new or has it gone on forever? Would Michelle be willing to buy him a new toothbrush to go with the story? All this information will help make a story. You must investigate first to write a good story. A new toothbrush could help him see a new start or a case to keep his toothbrush in. I also suggested mild toothpaste and a mild mouthwash.

Michelle informed me: 'He's a typical boy; into Minecraft and dinosaurs.' She was happy to buy a new toothbrush and sent me a link to the dinosaur one she had chosen. She said, 'He has always had issues and it's very much sensory based. I buy him a very mild toothpaste, put on the tiniest dot then flatten it. He's very particular with textures and doesn't like strong flavours either. I'll look for a mild mouthwash.'

Action

Michelle ordered a special dinosaur toothbrush and I got to work on a Social Story™. I also created a daily sticker chart and sent them both to see if they were suitable. I advised Michelle that she could have a reward for so many stickers, but not to make it dependent on them all being in a row as there may be a 'wobble' day. Michelle was really happy with them and had not heard of 'Symwriter' (the writing with symbols program I had used). I sent her a link to investigate this further. It's great to use symbols with stories for children who do not yet read as they gain attention, add interest and can even promote reading.

Outcomes

The following week I had a message from Michelle, 'I just wanted to let you know what a great toothbrushing week Joshua had! He earned a little treat today as he's been so good. Night time brushing is still an issue but he came up with his own solution today; he now has the LEGO® ninjago theme tune playing while he brushes. Thanks so much for all your help!'

A year later Michelle reports: 'On the whole he will brush now as part of his morning routine but on occasions, usually school holidays and when we're away, the Social Story™ will be used again. He now has a Social Story™ for homework and I'm trying to do one for tidy bedrooms. The personalisation of the stories is key for Joshua to relate to them.'

Ten tips for brushing teeth

1. Let the child choose their toothbrush. Link motivators.

2. Choose a really mild toothpaste and change if it's 'yuck'.

3. Introduce a timer once brushing is established.

4. Let them see other children and adults model brushing teeth.

5. Have a big set of teeth and toothbrushes for play brushing.

6. Introduce a song for each time they brush.

7. Establish a daily routine, doing it at regular times of the day.

8. Show a brush teeth symbol before brushing and allow time to process.

9. Have a schedule of the steps to break down information.

10. Praise and reward the child as they make progress.

Final thoughts

When a child resists hair cuts, teeth brushing or any other personal care we cannot know just how anxious or sensitive they are. We must never judge the parents of these children. They need our understanding and support because they will most likely be worn down and frustrated by this ongoing battle. Talk to the parents, listen to them, observe the child and use your instinct. And when the child does make small steps ensure they get the praise and rewards they deserve. James Joyce commented on how many of the most inspirational battles are ones that we do not see (the battles that happen inside the head). When a child succeeds in overcoming their fears be incredibly proud of them. We can only guess just how great the mental battle they have won is.

CHAPTER 23

Food Phobia!

Children Who Refuse to Eat or Have Extremely Limited Diets

Nothing in life is to be feared, it is only to be understood. Now is the time to understand more, so that we may fear less.

Marie Curie

What do you do when that special child refuses to eat in your setting? We cannot base what other children will do on our personal experience; we need to take each case individually. Try to see mealtimes through the child's eyes and help them past any barriers.

Mealtimes can be a terrifying ordeal for little ones, and particularly those with SEN. The idea of eating 'yuck' foods in a foreign environment may cause them extreme anxiety. At home, set routines will have built up without parents really being aware. The supports a child expects are already in place. Maybe they will not eat at all if they've had a snack; maybe they will not eat without the TV on, or food must be in a Thomas bowl, with a specific set of ingredients, blended to an exact consistency and heated for exactly one minute in the home microwave... Oh, and did I mention that they will *only* eat for Mum? Needless to say, if a child refuses to eat at school or nursery, knowledge of home routines can be invaluable.

It's important never to judge children who struggle at mealtimes. Maybe you had children who sat beautifully at the table and ate every meal. Maybe you could go anywhere and know your child would eat up, and they knew that if they were remotely fussy there was no leeway. But maybe you were lucky.

No matter how much we want a child to eat, no matter what pressure we are under, retaining a child's trust is paramount. Be firm, but never force a child to eat.

Case study: Home visit for Henry
Refusal to eat at school

Henry came into school with food he would eat at home, but absolutely refused the same food at school. He would avoid the spoon with great skill, moving his head and squirming under the table. Lunchtimes were an ordeal and the refusal to eat was a real concern for everyone.

Mum told us that Henry was very fussy at home, but he would eat. She was worried too. Henry was doing whole days at school. It was too long for him to go without eating and we did not want not eating at school to become routine.

The home visit

We went to see Henry having lunch at home. We noticed that his mum used a very firm voice with him: 'Henry eating'. We also noted language she used for his foods. For instance, she would call his yoghurt 'yog yog'. Henry ate his food in a little seat in the lounge with Baby TV playing on the big screen to distract and motivate him.

Mum let us step in and feed him at home. This allowed us to meet him halfway. We were so happy when Henry ate for each of us.

Progress

The next time Henry had lunch at school we were armed with all his mum's home strategies. We also knew that getting him to eat was achievable. Over the next term Henry made great progress and eating at school became less of an issue. He even sat beautifully at the table for our whole school Christmas dinner. Henry now eats some of our school dinners pureed. He will feed himself yoghurt using the spoon. Watching him do this makes me so proud. We would never have anticipated this progress. What a difference a home visit and good home/ school communication can make.

Case study: Pudding first for Eddie

Mealtime meltdowns

Eddie was not impressed with lunchtime in the school hall. He wanted to eat the biscuit and did not seem to get that the savoury should come first. He ended up having a meltdown about it and needing to leave the lunch hall.

A new approach

We had a team meeting and talked about what to do. We decided to move our lunchtime to the Early Years classroom while our class developed food tolerance and sitting skills. The eating was more important than sitting in the school hall. I suggested we try to let Eddie have both the lunch and pudding on the table at the same time, to see if he would eat lunch after pudding.

Progress

Eddie ate up his biscuit and then tried the baked potato. He would not eat from a fork, but lifted the potato with his hands. He would only eat the potato, but we continued to have other foods on the plate.

In time Eddie started to try other things on his plate. First these were hidden under the potato, but as time went on he was lifting bits of ham and putting them in his mouth. He was also sitting at the table during lunch with very little support. We started to not have the pudding in sight and he ate up the lunch first without any issue. He would go into the lunch hall and request 'pudding' by handing over a PECS® symbol.

The next step was to introduce eating off a fork, which again he mastered. We started to support Eddie with feeding himself off the fork by loading it with food and gently directing his arm to lift it. Eddie amazed us all when he started to lift these mouthfuls up on the fork and get them in his mouth. What a difference a compromise can make!

Case study: Carla, who refused food and drink

Starting point

Carla's parents had mentioned eating issues at our initial home visit so we were expecting that we would need to work to support this. As snack time approached Carla became very fretful. She refused to come to the table and did not eat or drink. Lunchtime was much the same. We felt awful phoning home to say that she had not had anything. Her parents were clearly anxious too. As the week went on we noticed that Carla would often fall asleep just before lunch. Was this another way of opting out or was the eating anxiety exhausting her?

Building trust

Carla clearly had huge anxieties over food so we decided to build trust and reduce demands. We wanted her to be happy at school. Instinct told us that this was the best way. So instead of expecting Carla to come to the table at snack or lunchtime one of us would open her lunch box and place a biscuit near her. At lunchtime a member of staff would spread Carla's chocolate spread on Carla's bread and leave it near her. There were no demands. Carla watched out of the corner of her eye, but ate nothing. Days turned into a week. Her parents were concerned, but we were convinced that this was the way.

Progress

The following week Carla nibbled a biscuit and then some toast. She did it when she thought we weren't looking. Her eating got better and better. Still the same sweet diet, but she was eating. We found that Carla would drink if it was a part of play. She drank water from a paint brush. She was getting the water so we went with this. We never said she was drinking or made any issue of it. At parents evening we talked about the eating and drinking. I wondered if Carla was picking up on her parents' anxieties. I said that although Carla did not yet speak she could probably understand everything they said so they must not talk about food or drink issues in front of her. Her dad was taken by surprise. He clearly did not know that his little girl could understand.

Outcomes

Carla will now sit at the table at snack time and lunch. Her diet is still restricted to lunch box contents, but she is starting to explore other foods through sensory play and cooking. She does not get anxious at mealtimes and rarely sleeps in school. She may always be a picky eater, but it is lovely that she knows she can trust us when it comes to food.

Ten tips to address problems at mealtimes

1. Communicate with home as soon as you see an issue.

2. Try to do a home visit to observe how the child eats in their comfort zone.

3. Begin with home foods served in the same pots at the same temperature.

4. Try mealtimes away from noise and too many people.

5. Allow a longer time to reduce pressure.

6. Use distractions such as a big screen (if that has been used at home).

7. Tackle one issue at a time and communicate this to home.

8. Have plates, cups and cutlery that suit the child – for example, the Kura Care Children's Cutlery Set available from NRS Healthcare.[1]

9. Use rewards and praise or tokens (if the child will understand them).

10. Try to let the child make choices. Accept that there are some 'yuck' foods or textures they will *not* eat.

Final thoughts

Eating can be a huge issue. It's not like getting a child to cooperate with doing an inset puzzle or thread a string of beads; if they don't eat they could die! Unfortunately, our adult concerns will feed the child's anxiety. There are children who have taken food refusal to extremes and ended up tube fed. This is rare, but still happens. We cannot relax and think that they will eat if they are hungry enough. But they must not ever sense adult anxiety – we must radiate calmness and control.

If a child does not eat at school, address the issue immediately. Communicate with parents and try to find some middle ground.

---

1   *visit ow.ly/HC4ZK*

CHAPTER 24

Recipes for Success

Cooking with Children with SEN

Tell me and I forget, teach me and I may remember, involve me and I learn.

Chinese proverb

Cooking offers amazing learning opportunities for every child regardless of their learning style.

Cooking is something children of *all* abilities can experience. It is hands on, sensory and can introduce a variety of different foods. We should start teaching our children that *they* can cook creatively as early as possible. We can promote independence by allowing children to do as many of the processes as possible. It's not enough to give them a mixing bowl to pass around or pre-cooked biscuits to decorate. Give each child their own set of utensils and ingredients, and see what they can do. Don't stick to sweet treats, either – cooking can get children experiencing a huge variety of new smells, tastes and textures that they might not ever access at home.

Savoury recipe ideas

First things first – here are two simple savoury recipes to try in your setting.

Sunshine pies

INGREDIENTS

1/4 sheet of puff pastry

tomato purée

1 tbsp of grated mozzarella cheese

1 piece of sun-dried tomato, chopped

2 pitted black olives, sliced

1 cube of feta cheese, crumbled

egg

METHOD

Preheat the oven 180°C (fan) and add one tbsp of flour to a board. Cut out two large circles of puff pastry, then roll them out on the board to make bigger circles. Spread with tomato purée and sprinkle with mozzarella cheese. Now add the chopped tomato and sliced olives. Crumble feta cheese on top, then fold in the edges of the pasty. Brush the edges with egg, then cook in the oven for 10–15 minutes.

Tuna fishcakes

INGREDIENTS

1/2 cup of cooked potatoes, peeled and diced

2 tsp of crème fraîche

1/4 cup of tuna in brine, drained

1 tbsp of tinned sweetcorn, drained

1 tbsp of chopped parsley

2 tbsp of bread crumbs

METHOD

Preheat the oven 200°C (fan). Tip the potatoes into a bowl, and mash them with a fork. Add the crème fraîche, tuna, sweetcorn and parsley to the bowl and mix. Sprinkle the bread crumbs on a plate. Make a ball with the mixture from the bowl, then press it onto the bread crumbs. Turn over to cover both sides. Place the fishcakes on a lined baking tray, then cook for 20–25 minutes.

No-cook sweetie recipes

Here are two recipes for treats which don't need to be cooked.

Nutella truffles

INGREDIENTS

4 tbsp nutella

1 tsp butter

6 chocolate chip biscuits

3 tbsp cornflakes

cocoa powder – for dusting and rolling

TIP

When making these with my class I used half these ingredients for each child and those that resisted eating the mixture ended up with five.

METHOD

Combine the nutella and butter in a bowl.

Crumble in the chocolate chip biscuits (I used Maryland). These are hard and six take a long time to crumble by hand. You could use a grinder or share the work.

Crumble in the cornflakes. Mix together.

Form small balls then roll in cocoa powder. We put ours in sweet cake cases.

Pop in the fridge for two hours (if you can resist). They can also be eaten straight away.

No egg peppermint creams

INGREDIENTS

1 cup icing sugar

4 teaspoons milk

1/2 teaspoon green food colouring (optional)

1/4 teaspoon peppermint essence

extra 1/3 cup icing sugar, for dusting (do not mix it with the rest)

Tips

I would halve these quantities for individual class recipes. I also made up a peppermint and green food colour mixture and they each added half a teaspoon of this to keep it simple.

Method

Mix the icing sugar, milk, food colouring (if using) and essence until they stick together. Add more milk if the mixture is too powdery. Add more sugar if it's too moist.

Dust the kitchen counter and rolling pin with icing sugar.

Form little balls and squash gently with a fork.

Set peppermint creams on wax paper to dry overnight. The following morning, turn them over to dry the underside.

You can then dip half in melted chocolate if you want to make them really special.

Strategies for successful cooking

Colour-coded bowls, utensils, measuring spoons and cups are great for getting a child looking and copying. Children can begin to experience weighing and measuring out ingredients. These can be left in a sand or water tray so that children can explore capacity. Adding coloured rice or pasta will add interest. I use the Primary Science Mix and Measure set from Learning Resources because its spoons are chunky – ideal for little hands – and the cups are shaped to show a whole, half and quarter.[1]

It's easy to create visual recipes with step-by-step instructions. I use SymWriter and add in photos of specific equipment.[2] It helps to break recipes down into chunks so children can create their own creations from scratch. Remember to model each step of the recipe, so that the children can see what they are expected to do.

---

1   www.learningresources.com
2   widgit.com/products/symwriter

Top ten tips for cooking

1. Make sure you have everything ready before you start.

2. Stay cool and calm if they get a bit sensory with the ingredients.

3. Be overly enthusiastic – they will pick up on your mood.

4. Use a visual recipe and show them a picture of what you are going to make.

5. Let them try to do things that are not dangerous independently.

6. Build a bank of recipes that work well – they will enjoy choosing a recipe.

7. Remember they will enjoy watching ingredients pour so do it slowly from above.

8. Create a personal recipe scrapbook with photos of your little chefs.

9. Praise the end results.

10. Be prepared for a bit of mess – clothes and surfaces wash.

Case study: Charlie – a miniature whirlwind

Charlie was a bright, bouncy, full-on four-year-old, who needed to be occupied at all times. If he was busy and being stretched, his behaviour was great; if he was left to his own devices and allowed to become bored, he would look for ways to mix things up – dismantling whatever he could get his hands on, causing damage or general disruption. He was a bit like a miniature whirlwind.

At pre-school this was okay because there were lots of activities to investigate and staff to help him with social clashes. However, it was much harder for his mum to keep things exciting, challenging and engaging at home – especially as Charlie also had a baby brother, who was occupying much of Mum's attention. Charlie loved being in the middle of things and preferred the 'real' to pretend play. Cooking really engaged Charlie at nursery, so we suggested it to his mum.

Charlie and his mum started planning things to cook together. They lived near a local shop, so after they had made their plans, they would take a walk to get the ingredients. Cooking was something positive they could do together and both felt that they were achieving something by doing it. It not only helped Charlie's behaviour, but built a positive relationship between Mum and son, which did wonders for Charlie's self-esteem and his ability to build relationships with his peers.

Case study: Lenny

Lenny had a diagnosis of autism. His limited diet was beginning to cause concern. He would refuse to eat anything other than cornflakes at snack time. Conversely, he was more than happy trying to eat non-food substances such as play dough. In art lessons he would quickly grab the glue, so our reactions had to be fast.

We started our cooking sessions making individual biscuits. Lenny enjoyed the sensory aspect of these sessions and would have a cheeky taste of the mixture afterwards. Next we moved on to cupcakes. Again the mixture was sweet and tempting.

Following this we started making bread rolls. We began with simple white bread rolls, before starting to add ingredients such as cheese, onion and sun-dried tomatoes. The smell of freshly baked bread wafted down the corridor and Lenny began to eat the bread, including the extras. Pizza was next. One of my best teacher moments was seeing Lenny devour a pepperoni pizza!

When we started our 'Under the Sea' topic, I wondered what Lenny would make of our salmon fishcakes. I was delighted to see him try the smoked salmon and then enjoy eating his fishcake. Through cooking he was soon eating spinach, sweetcorn, nutmeg, potato, egg, smoked salmon and even prawns. All of these healthy foods that previously he would not have touched were suddenly okay.

This was not limited to school either. At weekends, Lenny cooked with his family. He was gaining lots of practical skills while also eating a growing variety of foods, leading him to have a healthier, balanced diet and, hopefully, subsequently improving his health as an adult. (This case study was originally published in *Colour Coding for Learners with Autism* by Adele Devine (2014a).)

Learning opportunities

With cooking, children can practise:

- following a visual recipe
- visiting a shop to get ingredients
- using the internet to find a recipe
- writing a list of ingredients
- waiting during preparation and cooking
- cooperating and following instructions
- listening and taking directions
- taking turns and working as a team
- measuring using cups and spoons
- sharing creations with others.

Final thoughts

Children love to role play 'grown-up' activities. They may not be getting 'involved' at home, so it is essential that they get ample practical opportunities to 'learn' at your setting.

CHAPTER 25

Eating Out

Taking Children with SEN to Restaurants

Nothing ever becomes real 'til it is experienced.

John Keats

Teaching 'restaurant skills' can afford more social freedom to both children and parents.

We must step out of our comfort zone and allow children with SEN to experience the reality of real restaurants.

You are in a top restaurant. Glasses sparkle and the tablecloths are pristine. Fellow diners are dressed to impress and know exactly which fork to use first. There is a high-society buzz about the place and you examine the menu with anticipation.

Unfortunately, there's one slight snag. Sitting opposite you is the wriggliest, squiggliest boy you have ever taught. You can see that tell-tale glint in his eye, and worry what he might do. Suddenly, those five delicious courses seem less appetising. The dreaded behaviour begins and disapproving glances from other diners cause you to break out in a hot sweat. You don't sense sympathy, just hard, cold judgement. Oh, and did I mention that leaving early is not an option?

Eating out with any child can be a challenge, but factor in a hidden disability such as autism and it can feel far harder. To the casual onlooker, a child with such a condition seems old enough to know better. Parents feel as if they are under the spotlight and may simply opt out of eating out. But there will come an occasion when they want to take their child out to eat – perhaps to a family wedding or on a birthday. Teaching 'restaurant skills' can afford more social freedom to both children and parents.

Case study: Kam, the number thief

The waiter left our plate of chips on the table. My class were mostly pre-verbal and the idea was that they would use their PECS® to ask for individual chips. As the waiter walked away, Kam let out an ear-piercing scream and sobbed uncontrollably. Kam's anxiety escalated to the point where we had to take him out of the restaurant. I stood outside counting down from 100 to calm him.

The next day I sat by Kam and started to instigate a Carol Gray-inspired comic strip conversation. I drew a simple stick figure sitting at a table to represent Kam. Kam was familiar with using Comic Strip Conversations™ to help discuss social situations and explain his thoughts. Kam grabbed the pencil and drew what I recognised as a wooden spoon in the middle of the table. He then gave me the pencil and told me to draw '7' on the spoon. I had forgotten that when we ordered chips the waiter had left a wooden spoon in a pot on our table with a number 7 on it. This was so that they could quickly see which table had placed the order. I drew the waiter and the chips. Kam took the pencil and started scribbling over the waiter, then the table number. That's when I understood. When the waiter left our chips, he had taken our number spoon away. Kam loved numbers! Understanding the issue meant I could prepare Kam for our next outing.

After a week of role play, we returned. Kam now had a Social Story™ that explained how number spoons matched customers to orders. We read the Social Story™ and watched a workman wait. There was a number spoon on his table. Eventually the waiter brought his food. Holding our breath, we watched him put down the plate and take away the spoon. I felt Kam's relief and later when the waiter took *our* number spoon he was okay because he understood.

What if we had decided to not take Kam to the café again, or this number issue never revealed itself until he was a teenager? An anxious teen can do a lot more damage than a five-year-old...

Case study: Survival pack Billy

Billy was a loveable rogue who could quickly go from adorable to totally disruptive. The trigger was usually not enough attention or feeling bored. The idea of him sitting in a restaurant seemed unlikely, as he could not sit still *anywhere* for any length of time...

Billy's mum and dad had been invited to a family wedding and they wanted to be able to take Billy to the service *and* the meal. We needed to find a way to get him to stay the course, without disrupting. After an initial group 'Eek!' we set about creating a bag of motivators containing all sorts of things that Billy liked. He was into dinosaurs, so we linked a lot of things to this theme. We filled the bag with toys: Duplo dinosaurs, mini dinosaurs, play dough and a box of raisins packaged as dinosaur food. Anything we could think of that would buy quiet time went into the bag.

Some people might see a bag full of rewards as spoiling the child, but the need for motivators usually fades as the child's self-control improves.

We took Billy out to a restaurant for a practice run and it went well. His mum, however, was still unsure... She thought that Billy was only being good because he was with us. I encouraged Billy's mum to have a practice run herself (armed with a bag of motivators). It did not go as well as I'd hoped. Billy's mother said she had handed Billy the bag and the novelty had worn off before the end of the meal. I suggested that she use the mystery of the bag and produce things from it as rewards for 'good sitting', 'good waiting', and so on. I gave her a set of visuals including a visual 'volume control'.

The wedding day arrived and we waited with bated breath on the Monday morning to hear how Billy had behaved. Mum arrived at school with a beaming smile. Success! Billy had not managed the whole church service and Dad had taken him out halfway, but with the help of the visuals and rewards, he had behaved during the meal *and* speeches.

Restaurant rituals

The idea of hosting a birthday party can be daunting to the parent of a child with SEN or autism and to help with this our special needs school will often offer to host the party or run the outing. A visit to a favourite fast food restaurant is a popular choice. But be warned – children seem to get set routines and expectations about familiar eating places very fast. I recall one time thinking that I would be able to get my children who used PECS® to request 'chips' using their visuals. They were outraged because they were in the routine of getting a full portion instantly. We did not stay in the restaurant too long. The class consisted of students with complex autism aged 9–11 and they were causing quite a storm. I had one who was 'stuck' watching the screens at the counter, one who wanted to slam the door shut each time someone came through it and so on...

We were getting a few stares from people wanting to enjoy their food without the floor show. Part of my aim for the outing was to get my class to transition a little further in public. I knew that a specific fast food restaurant would be a motivator.

As the children all got onto the minibus a lady came up to me. 'I was in the restaurant just now...' she said. I was about to offer a quick explanation for the behaviours she'd seen and offer her one of our school explanation cards with the school contact details for further explanations, but she continued and what she said surprised me. 'I wanted to come and tell you what a wonderful job you are all doing. I was watching the way you all were and I was so impressed.' I thanked her and got on the bus. When you are out in a restaurant you probably will get looks and judgements, but they are not all negative. A lot of the onlookers will be silently admiring you, getting what you are doing and silently willing the children to conquer their anxieties and succeed.

I recall a teacher returning from taking her reception class on an outing and saying how one of the children had had a massive meltdown because he had expected a Happy Meal. He had probably never been to the restaurant and not got a Happy Meal.

I've heard Roz Blackburn speak on several occasions. She is an adult with autism who gives the most insightful, entertaining talks about her life with autism. She explained how she was almost unable to do one talk because there was not a McDonald's nearby.

If you are planning on taking children with SEN to your local fast food place it's well worth asking parents if there are any specific routines their children are used to.

Judy Endow is an author, artist and consultant. In a blog post titled, 'Autism and Eating Out,' she shares some useful strategies:

> When the atmosphere isn't so perfect, I ask for a booth if the place has booths. A booth ensures that nobody will walk behind me and surprise me. A tall-backed booth greatly cuts down the noise. If a booth is not available, I ask to be seated along the perimeter of the dining room.
>
> If there are any sort of blinking lights, TVs or lots of movement, I know I will get dizzy. Chairs with arms are great to help me stay anchored. Even if I don't get dizzy, I often have trouble feeling where my body is located in crowded noisy places. If I don't have a chair with arms, I will find something to lean at least one side of me against – wedge in with the table or, if in a booth, lean against a willing friend.
>
> There usually isn't much a person can modify about lights in a restaurant, but I try to avoid down lights if at all possible. Sitting on the perimeter of the dining room helps reduce the noise input. There is not the surround sound with a wall behind you! (Endow 2016)

Ten tips for eating out survival

How to make your restaurant visit a success:

1. Go with someone supportive, who understands the child.

2. Sit near the edge of the restaurant or in a booth.

3. Take a visual schedule and a visual volume control.

4. Take a timer and reward chart (if used).

5. Try to relax a bit about what others think.

6. Prepare a card to hand staff or diners, explaining the child's diagnosis.

7. Take food to suit the child if the menu won't.

8. Limit initial waiting by ordering ahead – small steps.

9. Forewarn the waiter for an empathic response.

10. Take motivators and also have an 'emergency only' *big* motivator.

Final thoughts

Think about the children in your setting. Is there one you would *never* want to take out to a restaurant? Now think of that child's carer and imagine them being forced to avoid all social gatherings. It is up to us to set children up to succeed beyond the school gates. Go on, be brave!

CHAPTER 26

Retail Therapy

Taking Children with
SEN to Real Shops

Children are living beings - more living than grown-up people who have built shells of habit around themselves. Therefore it is absolutely necessary for their mental health and development that they should not have mere schools for their lessons, but a world whose guiding spirit is personal love.

Rabindranath Tagore

Shopping with children with SEN can be a challenge for even the most patient of parents, but with practitioners' support it can be made far easier.

Parents of children with SEN may need practical help – they might not have the strength, support network or training to address shopping issues alone.

Situation: Your tearful toddler is clutching some sweets. They missed their nap and it's been a long day. The queue is massive and the shop is busy. Do you...

a) stand your ground and risk a full blown public battle

b) cave in, buy the sweets and make a quick exit, or

c) not go there! Shop online during the tricky toddler stage?

Remove your 'childcare' hat for a moment and be honest – which option sounds most appealing? Online shopping has offered a lifeline to some parents – many simply don't 'do' shopping with little people. They avoid the battles. It's not worth the stress! Instead of riding *through* the storm they wait until their child is past the tantrum phase.

Of course, most children will naturally grow out of the unreasonable stage. In time they learn that they can't have everything they want. But there are some children who will never learn without real life experience.

Shopping with special children can be challenging. They might decide to rearrange displays, spend hours 'stuck' watching the escalators, or absolutely refuse to give up a wanted item. They may have an enormous tantrum or drop to the ground in a busy doorway. They could even trash a shop or attack a passer by. To support parents we must step out of our comfort zone, away from the pretend play area, and see how our children with SEN cope with real-life shopping.

Case study: Sam's toy strop

I had given the five minute warning, four minutes, three, two, one. 'Toy shop is finished,' I said. Sam had *really* enjoyed playing at the Thomas trains table. My support staff gathered up the other children, but I could see Sam trying to glue his feet to the ground. 'Sam,' I said calmly, but definitely, 'toy shop is finished. Café is next. Five, four, three, two, one…' I showed him the visual schedule and held out my hand.

Our usually happy, cheeky chappy totally flipped – he had the most almighty temper tantrum. He lay on his tummy kicking his legs up and down and crying. He wasn't hurting himself, so I stood a short distance away and waited. What a drama! He was squeezing out the tears and making loud crying noises. Occasionally he would pause for a second and check my reaction. There was none. The other staff and children had moved on to the café (next on our visual schedule).

Eventually the tantrum started to lose steam. It wasn't working. A space of calm contemplation followed... Then, 'Train?'

Sam was negotiating. (Buy me this train, then, and I'll leave quietly). I pretended not to understand: 'Yes, train,' I agreed taking the train from his hand and speaking to it. 'Train – Thomas?' I asked.

'No! Percy!' exclaimed Sam. My daftness had amused him and that cheeky twinkle was returning. Redirecting him with train names was working.

'Percy. We are going to the café to meet the rest of Blue class. I hope they haven't eaten all the chips. Bye Bye, Percy. We will see you next week.'

Sam was engaged with my chat with the train and he'd heard the bit about the chips. 'Bye Bye, trains. Chips.' he said. We left the shop, waving goodbye to the trains.

Case study: A DVD a day for Alec

Alec's mum confided to me that every time they went to the shops he would drag her to the DVD shop and want the same DVD. He had a huge collection of this one DVD at home. He always unwrapped the outer packaging so his mum couldn't return them. Imagine the frustration! 'No' resulted in such dangerous head banging on the floor that his mum gave in.

We didn't go straight to the problem shop. We started by going to buy a DVD in a DIY shop. I knew his favourite DVD wasn't there. This outing went smoothly...

Next we visited the 'problem' shop to buy a DVD to link with our topic. I had prepped Alec with a Social Story™. No issue! I was pleased, but perplexed. I even walked past his 'favourite' DVD. He clocked it, but moved on.

Back at school I drew a Carol Gray-style comic strip picture. It showed Alec by the DVDs. I added a lady to the picture and wrote 'Mum' below so he would know it wasn't me. Alec grabbed the pencil and drew the DVD in his hand and a smile on his face. I asked what happened next. Alec drew a big 'M' shape, a circle and two smiley stick people. 'McDonald's?' I asked. His huge smile was answer enough...

A chat with Alec's mum revealed they 'would usually – well, OK, *always* go to McDonald's after shopping.' Was there a connection?

The following week we scheduled the DVD shop followed by McDonald's. This time Alec did go and get the DVD. He brought it to me as if I would buy it. I showed Alec a picture of the DVD we were looking for. He took the schedule and pointed to McDonald's. 'Alec, we do not need that DVD.' He did not seem convinced, but put the DVD back.

As we approached the doors I could feel Alec's reluctance, but he did not make a fuss. Next outing, Alec's mum joined us. She couldn't believe it. From then on his mum used a visual schedule and their shopping trips were easier. The unwanted DVDs stopped piling up.

We still don't know if the DVD collecting was caused by obsession, need for routine or association (trying to re-enact a happy day), but by addressing the issue we resolved it.

Olga Bogdashina is internationally renowned for her research, books and talks on autism and sensory perception. In an article published in Aukids Magazine, titled 'Aisle be back', she shares the strategies she used to help her autistic son Alyosha cope with the supermarket. She's kindly allowed me to share some of it here:

> I knew my son could not tolerate fluorescent lights, babies crying (the high pitch of the babies screaming was drilling through his ears), and people moving in different directions. What was I to do...go in beforehand demanding all the lights were switched off, while escorting all mothers with young children out and ordering the rest to move one by one in a straight line, keeping their voices down. That wasn't exactly an option.
>
> Operation Supermarket was likely to be long-term and needed a lot of planning and organisation. We decided that every Sunday morning we'd go shopping in a big supermarket (the same supermarket at the first stage of the adventure, equipped with tinted glasses and ear defenders against visual and auditory 'offences'.

Starting with small doses of the shopping experience, we hoped to desensitise my boy's ability to tolerate the stimuli other people were comfortable with.

The first time was the most successful. However it was too early to celebrate. Yes, Alyosha did cope with his first visit of the supermarket, but his stay there lasted all of 30 seconds. We went in with a trolley (and determination) yet had to leave pretty soon afterwards. Still it was a start!

Next week we managed to reach the first aisle and spent nearly two minutes inside. The following weeks our shopping experience lasted longer and longer and longer and I realised he was finally beginning to get accustomed to the foreign nature of the place and the stimuli.

Fast forward a year: our shopping trips were no problem (not only in this supermarket but at any other shop). Aloysha happily pushed the trolley, zig-zagging along the aisles correcting 'wrongs' on his way (picking up misplaced things and putting them where they should be, straightening the rows of tins and cans etc.). (Bogdashina 2016, p.7)

Ten tips for shopping with 'special' children

1. Be prepared to wait out the tantrum. Stay calm and controlled.
2. Have a routine end reward, like a visit to a cafe.
3. Talk through a visual schedule of shops. Stick to the plan.
4. Use shopping lists and involve the child.
5. Know where the toilets are (plan ahead).
6. Take a bag of 'just in case' motivators, symbols and Social Stories™.
7. Ask parents to tell you about shopping issues. Choose your battles.
8. Wear ID and have a ready made explanation card.
9. Avoid busy times when there will be crowds and queues.
10. Carry mobile phones with each other's phone numbers.

Educating the public

Parents may have had to deal with some very unsympathetic, unkind responses when they are out with their children. Being the teacher of the child who has chosen to drop to the ground or have a huge meltdown in the door way feels so very different to being the parent. We can field ignorant comments with little cards explaining that we are from a special needs school and that they can contact school for further information.

The more we take our children with SEN out the more we are able to educate the public and ensure they are supportive.

Jane McCready's ten-year-old son Johnny has autism and learning disabilities. She took to the website Mumsnet for support after finding the attitudes of the public so difficult when out shopping.

She explained:

> He looks like any other child, but he behaves oddly – for example, he might sit there banging two toys together – and he sometimes makes strange noises. Especially when he was younger, he might have a massive meltdown – at the supermarket checkout, for instance. I'd feel 300 pairs of eyes on us – all watching us, all judging us for being disruptive and difficult.

In this same article Jane states, 'I have friends with special needs kids who don't even take them out any more' (Moorhead 2013).

Supporting parents

We must support these parents to go out with their children. Ask them about the issues they face. Many parents will not tell you until you ask, but you can uncover all sorts of things, which if addressed early will not bubble into huge issues later on. Children with SEN must not be kept away from shops because they cannot cope. The sooner they start to overcome fears the less set they will become. We must reassure parents that they are not at fault and no one has the right to judge. Arm them with quick, polite come backs and also little explanation cards to hand over because (no matter what the provocation) a confrontation may be the worst thing for an anxious child to see. The child must always come first.

Final thoughts

It's important to remember that parents of children with SEN may need practical help – they might not have the strength, support network or training to address shopping issues alone.

CHAPTER 27

Pet Therapy

How Animals Can Encourage Interaction, Communication and Calm

Animals are such agreeable friends — they ask no questions;
they pass no criticisms.

George Eliot

Imagine that you are sitting in a waiting room. The room has a few other people, but you have a dreadful cold and are not really in the mood for social interaction. You are feeling a bit anxious and uncomfortable. There's not much to do so you find something else to focus on. Maybe your phone?

A lady walks in. You glance up and see she has an adorable puppy with her. He is sniffing your boots. You love dogs. You smile. You instinctively reach down and pat him. Suddenly you can't help but interact.

Animals have this effect on people. They encourage communication and social interactions.

Pets' therapeutic qualities

There are a number of emotional and physical therapeutic benefits children can gain from access to pets as therapy:

- *Touch* – We know that the sense of touch can provide cosy warmth and comfort. Stroking a pet can lower blood pressure, release endorphins (oxytocin), relax us and alleviate our anxieties.

- *Needs* – Meeting pets' needs can raise a child's self-esteem. Being needed helps the child feel important. They feel less dependent and more able, which can promote a 'can do' attitude in other areas. Pets need to be cared for. They also need exercise and this may encourage the child into exercising.

- *Listening* – Pets listen. A child does not need to speak. They pet will understand and pick up on their feelings. They may even learn to alert the child to their own feelings.

- *Communication* – Pets understand verbal and pre-verbal communication. They do not use confusing language. They can also provide something to talk about. A child can learn social dialogues associated with the pet.

- *Trust* – The pet will never judge. There is no anxiety linked to social blunders or mistakes. Pets demands are linked to their needs, making them reasonable, predictable and easier to understand. The trust between child and pet can bridge trust with other people.

- *Humour* – Pets can be funny. Their antics can make us laugh. Laughter is so important for mental health and happiness.

- *Distraction* – Pets can distract from the child, alleviating pressure associated with feelings of being in the spotlight and having to act a certain way to fit in.

- *Time* – Pets seem to have unlimited time. Providing that their basic needs are met they will give and accept affection for extended periods.

- *Unconditional love* – This is the most important thing a pet can provide, the most vital thing to the child's well being.

Pat dogs at playtime

I love to see the way some of our students interact with therapy dogs at playtime. They walk around with the dogs, pat them, groom them and enjoy them. When they are with the dogs they smile more, talk more and seem so much calmer. There are children who find times with little structure really difficult. They don't yet have the social play skills to join in with role play games. They don't know what to do. But when a pat dog appears it can be exactly the type of companionship they need.

As they engage with the pat dogs they are developing so many skills, which will help them develop interaction, communication, cooperation and care. As these skills develop they move closer to being able to interact with others and develop their play skills.

Bing with Bunny, his autism service dog

Case study: Bing and Bunny, the autism service dog

Bing is a 14-year-old boy with autism, who has a very special autism service dog. She's a Boston terrier and he's named her

'Bunny'. Bunny came to live with Bing when she was four months old and was in training for the next 14 months to become an autism service dog. I wanted to learn a bit more about how having a trained service dog could be helpful. Bing explained this brilliantly and also offered some really useful advice, which he has kindly agreed for me to share.

Adele: How does Bunny help you?

Bing: For one, she alerts me when I'm doing some weird ticks or when I get stressed out. She's a very comforting dog.

Adele: How does she alert you?

Bing: She taps my side. She also comforts me while I'm out and makes it easier to socialise and communicate with others. Plus, she gives me something to talk about. So there's that.

Adele: She sounds amazing.

Bing: She is. She's a sweetie. When I get super stressed, she has an instinct to run up to me and try and comfort me, like a 'Oh no, what's wrong Bing?' Dogs are very good listeners, as they have a stronger sense of hearing.

Adele: That is so lovely. She just knows.

Bing: She also helps me get more exercise, as I enjoy taking her on walks through my neighbourhood. And she's very silly.

Adele: Is she?

Bing: Yes. All the time.

Adele: What a great companion. We all need a bit of silly.

Bing: Indeed we all do.

Adele: Do people stop and talk to her?

Bing: We have people ask before they can pet her though. She has stop signs on her vest, which say 'Please don't pet, I'm working!' so that nobody can just come up and begin to pet her out of the blue.

Adele: What a great idea. So you don't have to explain.

Bing: Speaking of explanation, I usually have small cards that tell about her and explain what she is doing with me, with me to hand out to people so I don't have to verbally explain what she does with me. Sometimes I don't really like to explain things on the fly, especially if it's something that others may perceive as 'Something you aren't supposed to do.'

Adele: That's a great idea.

Bing: It very much is.

Adele: I know you homeschool now, but did you ever go to school?

Bing: Yes. My elementary years. And pre-school. Never forget about pre-school.

Adele: How did you find it?

Bing: I was on good terms with learning and teachers. The children were sometimes a different story for me though. But I do believe that if I had Bunny with me, she would help me very much.

Adele: Ahh – how would she have helped?

Bing: She would have made me a bit more comfortable being out.

Adele: At playtime? Or just out of the house?

Bing: Pretty much both. She goes with me to activities and In-seat classes I take.

Adele: Do you think she helps with learning?

Bing: Sometimes I hold her in my lap while I'm learning, and she's pretty much a teddybear.

Adele: That would be comforting. Did you ever have dogs in your schools?

Bing: No. I did not have dogs in school while I was in state school.

Adele: What would you say to someone thinking about getting a dog like Bunny?

Bing: You will want to not only figure out what kind of dog is right for training, but what is right for you. Because in all honesty, I'm more of a smaller dog person, so I prefer dogs like Boston terriers. If I were to get a bigger dog, I don't really think I would have bonded to it as much as

I did Bunny. And that's not to mention, nothing can replace the sweet little dog's personality.

Adele: It sounds like you found the perfect match though. I'm really happy about that. You are very lucky.

Bing: But another thing to remember, it's a lot of hard work. It may seem like that your dog's training is going nowhere, but the longer it takes, the sweeter the inevitable success.

Adele: It's a bit like the children I teach. With enough time and patience they can achieve so much.

Bing: Indeed. I appreciate your care for service dogs.

Adele: I care very much. Maybe you doing this will help some other child gain access to a dog. That would be a great thing. Thank you Bing.

Case study: Sol's guinea pigs

The storm

Sol seemed to like creating a bit of chaos. I observed him bouncing around the classroom, climbing on the tables and throwing things up in the air. He seemed to have learnt all the things that triggered other children and would use this knowledge to create yet more chaos. We could not go on like this...

The right pet

I called Sol's home to get some more information about his motivators. Was there anything that we could use as a motivator? Were there any times when he was calm and settled? His mum said that the one thing that settled Sol at home was sitting with his guinea pig. He absolutely loved it.

The calm

I spoke to Sol about his guinea pigs. He really enjoyed this topic and I was able to create more motivating work using a guinea pig theme, but what I really wanted was for Sol to be able to access a guinea pig at school.

It took some time and a lot of persuasion, but eventually we got two guinea pigs for school. Sol loved to help with them, but most of all he loved to sit with them on his lap. He would be quiet, content and calm as he stoked the guinea pigs and spoke to them. It was wonderful to watch. Having access to the guinea pigs made such a difference to Sol's school days.

Research

Marguerite O'Haire, a PhD candidate at The University of Queensland, Australia, led a study on the comparative interaction of children with autism when given toys and guinea pigs. O'Haire observed that, 'Children with autism engaged in 55% more social behaviours when they were with animals compared to toys.' She also said the amount they smiled doubled and concluded that, 'Including an animal in children's playtime or home activities may be an effective way to encourage socialization with other children as well as adults' (Pearson 2013).

Cat therapy

J. Manerling has written a touching article about how he took his son, who has autism to an animal shelter. After looking at dogs and getting no reaction they stopped in the cat area. 'Suddenly my four-year-old non-verbal son pointed to the cage and said, "Cat!" That was it. That day we took the cat home' (Manerling 2016).

Imagine having a four-year-old who didn't speak and suddenly hearing him correctly label an animal. Manerling explains that he had not even considered looking at cats. He's always had dogs as a child and his mother was not a fan of cats at all. Manerling also explains how the cat seemed to encourage his son to speak:

> From day one, we heard Richard having conversations with Clover when no one was looking. He had language. He needed someone with the patience to listen and who did not ask him to repeat himself or explain what he meant. Clover had all those qualities. (Manerling 2016)

Final thoughts

Alfred A. Montapert once observed, 'Animals are reliable, many full of love, true in their affections, predictable in their actions, grateful and loyal. Difficult standards for people to live up to.' The more you think about it the more it makes sense. School can be a terrifying social minefield, full of demands, unpredictable noise, boisterous children and no time to process. An animal can shift this focus, places no demands and offers affection. It is no wonder that so many of the children at our special school smile when they see a pat dog companion arrive at playtime.

CHAPTER 28

Dealing with Different Days

Strategies and Supports for Halloween, Dress-Up days, Sports Days, Fireworks Night and Other Events

Man is not worried by real problems so much as by his imagined anxieties about real problems

Epictetus

Dress-up days, sports days, Halloween and other changes can cause anxiety. This chapter offers strategies and supports to help children with autism, sensory issues or anxiety cope with the changes.

Schools seem to be having more and more 'different' days where children are expected to dress up for the day. This may be role play linked to the topic. As a busy parent you see the note in the book or read the newsletter with some dread. Is it 'Victorian Day', 'Pirate Day', 'Roman Day', 'World Book Day' or a charity day such a 'Comic Relief' or 'Children in Need'? These days are scattered throughout the year and sometimes they seem to come up all of a sudden.

Some children cope very well with this, but there are children who will find these different days a trial. Maybe they have sensory issues and cannot cope with the scratchy costumes, maybe it's the volume or the change in structure (or removal of structure).

It's not only the children who suffer these days. Parents of the child with sensory issues or anxieties will read the newsletter and loathe it when these days arise. They know that their child is being a little hero getting through school on the usual days. Why throw this into the mix? Seeing all the children going into school on World Book Day inspired me to write something directed to one of those parents whose children find dress-up days difficult:

TO THE MUM OF THE CHILD WITH AUTISM, WHO DID NOT DRESS UP FOR BOOK DAY

This morning I saw a few Harry Potters, a Red Riding Hood, a bear, a tiger and a teacher and headteacher dressed up as 'Where's Wally'. It's Book Day and EVERYONE is getting in the spirit.

I also saw a few children who were not dressed up. There was the Granny saying loudly, 'Oh Mummy must have forgotten'. There are a few guilty parents who have a zillion other things to think of, who will rush home, turn the house upside down and return, red faced with a costume.

Other parents may judge the non dressed up. Did they forget? Do they not care? Or maybe they are just thinking (like me), 'Thank goodness I remembered.'

But then there is the mum walking into school holding hands with her child, who NEVER does dress-up days. The child who hates these different days... The child who struggles with a 'normal' school day and today fills him with anxiety and dread.

This mum has tried EVERYTHING! This mum is actually really pleased her son will wear the uniform and she really hates these days too. This mum knows how her son is feeling. She feels it with him. This mum and this son are actually being incredibly brave.

They say 'Never judge a book by the cover'.

Maybe the child who did not dress up is an original, a non conformer.

Maybe the child who did not dress up is the one with the potential to make our world better.

To that mum of that child who did not dress up for book day, I'd like to say…

I think YOU are doing the most amazing job and in the scheme of things dressing up and silly judgements don't matter.

Be proud of yourself.

Be proud of your child.

Walk tall.

You may not have taken Harry Potter to school this morning, but you may just have dropped off the bravest and most magical child in the whole school. (adapted from Devine 2015a)

Sports day

The following information also appears in my *SEN Assist* blog.

To support the child with autism on sports day try stepping into *their* shoes.

Imagine that you are a non swimmer, but five days a week you MUST go on a sail boat. You have been doing this for some time.

- It is less terrifying than it was at the start because there are certain things you now know about the journey.

- You have learnt the familiar landmarks to look out for.

- You have learnt how long the journey will last.

- You are secure in the knowledge that at the end of the day you will be back home and safe. These 'knowns' make you feel braver and safer.

Today is different though…

Today you have been asked to wear different clothes and shoes.

You are nervous and reluctant, but you get on the 'boat'.

The journey starts off the same, but them the boat takes a different direction.

The weather is changing.

You can feel a storm is starting.

You look around for the life saving rings usually hanging along the side (just in case), but they are gone.

You have not experienced this before.

What if you sink?

What if you are knocked over board and no one sees?

Suddenly you realise that you are not safe.

You look around for some reassurance, but things get worse and worse. You begin to panic, but no one sees it.

You feel you have three options:

1. Fight.

2. Flight.

3. Retreat.

It is too late for fight now. You are already on the boat.

Flight is impossible for a non swimmer in the middle of the sea.

You choose 'retreat' and hide in a little nook.

You put your head down, cover your ears and close your eyes hoping that you will survive the storm.

Or maybe you do nothing different, but you do still FEEL the fear and discomfort.

The best way to help a child with autism deal with a 'different day' is to understand, prepare, inform, reassure and compromise.

A teacher might think that on sports day there is less need to put up their visual schedule. They replace the whole timetable with a 'sports day' symbol. Worse still they leave the previous day's schedule up, which will completely confuse the child.

The child with autism arrives at school. Change is in the air and they look to the timetable for reassurance.

Knowing what is 'next' is part of what makes them feel safe and able to get through the school day.

On 'different days' the child with autism needs visual supports and information more than ever.

Ten tips for sports day success

1. Visual schedules are more important than ever on 'different days'.

2. Show on a calendar that the change is only for one day.

3. Prepare to compromise on different clothes.

4. Prepare for disappointments with Social Stories™.

5. Have a sticker, medal or reward ready for every child who takes part.

6. Try to build in some 'normal' routines the child can cling to.

7. Praise the children who do not win for excellent sportsmanship.

8. Reduce expectations to suit. Do they need to sit through every race?

9. Build in some fun activities such as throwing water sponges at teachers.

10. Speak up and be proud of what the child *is* achieving by taking part.

(adapted from Devine 2015b)

Halloween

Walking around the shops in October it is impossible to escape the ghoulish Halloween theme. The supermarkets are full of masks, deathly hands and creepy cobwebs. A child may shrug this off as you walk them quickly past displays that are a little too creepy for comfort. But let's think about the child with autism. These children often have a different way of processing, heightened or jumbled perception and sensory issues. How might they perceive those costumes, decorations and unexplained changes?

The best way to understand is to try walking in their shoes...

Shops

You are now a child with autism entering a supermarket.

The volume has been put up and every individual noise is becoming unbearably loud. The sound of a trolley is like thunder clashing, those sliding doors are nails down a chalk board screeching as they open and close, open and close. Colour is gone and the lighting creates a nightmare strobe effect coupled with a continuous, loud hum, which feels like bees moving about and buzzing inside your ears. Your senses are all muddled. Revolting shop smells of food and body odours do not stop at your nose, but become sickening tastes. Your mouth is dry. The floor seems to wobble and your clothes begin to grate and chaff and burn into your skin. You anticipate these feelings, but at least you know this shop. You know the routine. You've been here before and survived…

But wait!

Suddenly there is an aisle of terror where the toys usually are. That piano with the coloured buttons, which is the *only* reason you've ever endured this shop has been replaced by a cauldron full of skeletons and black spiders. That LEGO® set you've been told to 'wait for until your birthday' is *gone* too! You zoom in and take in every detail – image after image like the 'click, click, click' of a camera. It's fascinating, but also terrifying. You'll think about it later. It is all too different and uncomfortable right now. Images will be stored for when are home and feel safe – maybe bedtime?

Dressing up

Maybe you hate dressing up or seeing other people dressed up. Maybe you recognise people by what they wear and the sameness of style makes you feel more secure. Maybe dressing up makes you feel you must become that character. If you are dressed as a tiger, then you feel like a tiger. Grown ups don't seem to get this and keep telling you off as you leap about roaring and scratching.

Face paints

Maybe you find face paints frightening – the sad clown with a painted smile. Is it happy or sad? Good or bad? Facial expressions are already confusing, without throwing face paints into the mix. Maybe someone wants *you* to wear face paints, but you have a sensory fear or do not realise that those paints are only temporary. Maybe the face paints are okay, but you have a deep, scratchy memory of the face washing after.

Trick or treat?

Now there are knocks on the door after dark and you see your mum or dad giving away *your* sweets to other children. When will it end? Maybe Mum and Dad turn the lights out and neighbours know not to knock on your door. But then there are the neighbours, who still welcome trick or treating. They make this clear with decorations – a friendly pumpkin or a full on fright house...

What can we do to help?

Whether you choose to get involved with Halloween or not it is important to prepare a child with autism for the run up to 31 October. Here are my top ten tricks:

Ten tips for Halloween

1. Highlight Halloween on a visual calendar.

2. Use photos and talk through seasonal changes.

3. Take care! Internet searches are unpredictable.

4. Encourage communication – prepare PECS®.

5. Choose your battles. It's meant to be fun.

6. Model using face paints and taking them off.

7. Do not model fear. The child will copy.

8. Dispel fear of the dark through fun torch hunts.

9. Explain through Social StoriesTM and role play.

10. Pave an empathic'trick or treat' route.

(adapted from Devine 2014d)

Fireworks!

Night time is consistent – until one night when *everything* changes.

The sky is full of big banging explosions and crowds of people gather to look at the sky.

Fireworks – we love them or hate them. People with SEN or autism may love fireworks for the colour, the sensory experience and the excitement. However there are those who hate the noise and the change in routine. They cannot see where they are coming from. Like so many things, fireworks do not make sense.

We cannot control natural light. When it is late at night it gets dark. Day and night happen. The world gets darker and quieter at night.

We bath, we go to bed. The curtains close and people sleep. This has to be accepted (it happens).

Ten tips for surviving the fireworks

1. Provide a visual schedule so the child can prepare for what will happen and know your expectations.

2. Let them watch fireworks on TV or from inside.

3. Prepare them by showing them as fireworks appear on sale in shops.

4. Agree with them that they are sometimes too loud or screechy.

5. Use count downs for the noise (hold up ten fingers) so they have a visual to focus on.

6. *If you brave the display:* try to go to a more visual 'choreographed light show' than a loud one.

7. Aim to go to the same one again the following year so they can build tolerance.

8. Arrive early to avoid queues and find a good spot with quick access to an exit.

9. Take your own snacks and treats to avoid queues.

10. Take an MP3 player and ear defenders (just in case). These can be used together.

Daytime fireworks

I spent three years teaching at an autism specific school. Every year the school would put on a daytime fireworks display. There are some children who are very frightened by the idea and the noise of fireworks. They find the whole thing alarming and difficult.

During the daytime fireworks display we could encourage, cajole and praise. Seeing daytime fireworks may remove some of the difficult factors about annual fireworks displays. We remove the dark and we remove night time. We let them see fireworks in a safe, familiar environment where they are used to facing challenges and overcoming hurdles.

We have all the strategies they are used to and the support of staff they trust.

Final thoughts

Nelson Mandela wrote: 'I learned that courage was not the absence of fear, but the triumph over it. The brave man is not he who does not feel afraid, but he who conquers that fear' (Mandela 1995). Dress-up days and changes are a part of life and here to stay. Over time the anxious child can even really enjoy these days.

Mary McLaughlin, author of the blog *Mom-Not Otherwise Specified* reflects on how her son ended up loving one of the school dress-up days:

> A couple of years ago, Wacky Hair Day was scary for Bud. Nobody looked the way they were supposed to look and he didn't know what to expect. But, over time, he started to get used to the idea, and now he loves Wacky Hair Day. This morning when I dropped him off, he told me he was going to laugh all day.' (McLaughlin 2010b)

Teachers must understand that these days can be a real trial, think carefully when planning them, be aware of the children who find them difficult and communicate with and support parents. A little empathy can go a long way.

CHAPTER 29

Planning for Christmas

Why Christmas Causes Anxieties and Ways to Help

Nothing is so painful to the human mind as a great and sudden change.

Mary Shelley, *Frankenstein*

We teachers get together and plan a whole lot of Christmas activities. There will be tree decorating, classes covered in tinsel, structured lessons changed to play rehearsals, decoration making or baking. There are so many ideas out there and we all love making Christmas extra special. But there are some children who will find all these changes alarming, discomforting and distressing. They will find the waiting impossible and every activity can become a reminder of that waiting, making school intolerable. Even if they hold it together throughout the school day they might go home and have a meltdown.

When planning all the Christmas 'fun' it is vital that we think of every child. A little thought, a little respite time from all things Christmas, a little more sticking to structure can make such a huge difference to a child.

A fictional case study: Christmas through the eyes of a child with autism

Decorations

School decorations trigger memories and make my heart beat faster. My mouth is dry and my palms are suddenly sweaty. I *love* Christmas. I *love* our home decorations, but I don't like waiting. I cope with school by knowing a lot of the routines. I mentally prepare and plan my day, but now none of my strategies or safety supports are going to work. When the school hall changes I know that we are at the start of that unpredictable run up to Christmas. Other children's faces light up with joy, but I feel alone and anxious.

Good morning

There won't be time today. We are decorating our class tree. We are supposed to be happy. It's going to be fun. The teacher doesn't talk through our schedule because 'we don't need to'. We are in mad Christmas mode.

Numeracy

This is still up on our schedule but it is suddenly 'play rehearsal' instead. We stand about and listen to teachers talking and then moving us about. There is the awful singing and kids 'playing' random instruments. Why?

Staff absences

Our teaching assistant is off sick with flu and has not been replaced so I have to wade through this minefield without my all smiling, all knowing guide...

My eyes hurt, my head aches, but I'm not ill enough to stay at home – 'attendance records', the 'importance of routine' and all that...

Science

We are adding glitter to snowflakes. I usually like science. Mrs White has been replaced by Mrs '?', who seems to find fun in getting glitter everywhere... The mix it up kids take advantage and could do *anything*, any minute... She starts to shout. Shouting is my worst thing. Why is she punishing me? Injustice and pain!

Literacy

We are making Christmas lists, but the things I *so* want are *not* in their catalogues. I need to go on the computer to make my list, but get an instant 'No'. I try to get to the computer anyway because my list needs to be right. Now the teacher is really cross and gives me a sad face to hold. I feel really, really sad and do nothing while the other children make their lists. 'You won't get presents if you don't make a list' – that throwaway comment from the parent helper feels like a knife stabbing my heart.

Santa watching

'Santa is watching' they say and I know I'm not managing Santa's 'good', but I'm trying so hard with all the noise, the change, the anxiety and the sensory overload.

Then there is that final straw – the Christmas fayre (in front of everyone)

Time to see Santa. I wait and I manage the noise, the smells and those flickering lights... I take the gift. I say 'thank you' as rehearsed. I endure the flash of the camera, shading my eyes with my flat present. And that's when I realise – Santa has given me a picture book! After all that!

I feel so mad. All those strategies they've taught me about counting, deep breaths and asking for time out don't help me. My foot flies up out of nowhere and before I know what is happening I've kicked him. I've kicked him right in the knee and he's hurt. I can't look at him. I want to sink into the ground and disappear. I've kicked Santa! I feel bad – totally and utterly bad all through. And suddenly I'm hitting out at everyone because I'm angry with myself and I want them to disappear too.

Home

I know that my parents are 'disappointed', but they say nothing. They let me be – not because they are soft or think kicking Santa is okay, but because they know me.

They know I need some time to process, to think, to work the whole thing out and I already feel really, really sorry…

It wasn't even Santa that made me mad, it was the muddle, the confusion, the list and all that talk.

Still on the good list

I might not manage 'good', see things or react as you expect me to, but I do try harder than anyone can know.

Christmas changes are hard to handle.

Listen to me, watch me and try to understand.

Give me time, give me unconditional love, get to know me as an individual and set me up to succeed because with your support I *can*!

This case study is based on the experiences of the many children with autism I have taught. It will not be the experience of *all* children with autism, but is written to highlight some issues which can cause anxiety and trigger challenges.

My ten tips for Christmas

1. Have a Social Story™ explaining that it will all go back to normal after the holiday.

2. Have a visual calendar counting down the days to the end of term and showing changes to the usual schedule.

3. Have an area that remains normal so a child can escape Christmas. Show them. Say you go there when Christmas gets too much.

4. Keep as much routine in place as possible. Let them know they can tell a teacher if they feel worried or overloaded.

5. Avoid leaving tempting treats on display and mystery gifts wrapped up until the end of term. Waiting is hard.

6. Unfamiliar noises, textures, smells, taste, touch and lighting may be disturbing. The usual things can become upsetting too.

7. If they don't want to see Santa let them opt out – it's meant to be fun. Make some allowances, reduce some demands. Choose your battles.

8. Be aware of sensory issues when dishing out parts that need costumes. Dressing in different clothes can cause real discomfort and anxiety.

9. Communicate with home and be aware of triggers. Let parents know they can email you if something is causing anxiety.

10. Show you understand that it is hard – give praise, stickers or additional reward time. Be proud of them.

Julie Pates explains how Christmas changes affect her daughter:

My little girl said to me that the problem with Christmas is everything changes. Teachers are rushing so little tasks get overlooked or given to someone else because it is easier than waiting for a slower child to complete it. Teachers shout more and don't want you to tell them problems because they don't have the time to sort them out. The decorations are distracting and make her anxious because she knows she can't concentrate (she says it's like they are shouting out to her to look at them and when she does it makes her brain hurt). Lessons are disrupted and no longer make sense because she is so anxious about the changes that she can no longer focus on what is happening. The worse thing is the school performance. She knows everyone's part and gets frustrated that the other children cannot remember their lines. She wants to do more but is only allowed a small part. She wants to sing the part that her character is supposed to sing but instead everyone sings it. She becomes negative to everything that is happening but in school you would never know. Add this to the usual daily anxieties of dealing with friendships, feeling isolated from social groups and the stressors of everyday school life. She struggles through the day holding herself together but once she's home the frustration and anxiety overwhelm her and she lies in her room and screams and bangs her head until she is exhausted. As parents we have to be there to pick up the pieces. We try to makes things right, or at least better but in our hearts we know that there is little that we can achieve (and believe me we have tried). We are the boat's anchor in a very stormy sea. We don't ask for everything to change to facilitate our child, just that they remember that she is there. (Pates 2014)

Final thoughts

As Julie Pates explains we may not see the impact that all our Christmas chaos has, but parents will. Communication can make such a difference and allow parents to set their children up for a much less anxious time. Phone parents, email them, let them know you are there to listen and that your care extends beyond their expectations. Support and strengthen parents because this time of year can be a real trial. Just knowing that there is someone to listen, someone to ask can make a huge difference.

CHAPTER 30

The Christmas Play

Helping that Special Child Shine

Those who trust us educate us.

George Eliot, *Daniel Deronda*

Christmas can be a trial for children with SEN. As the rest of the school gets into the spirit they may be overwhelmed by sensory challenges and anxieties.

The Christmas play may seem like the time to showcase those children who cooperate, speak beautifully, sing, smile brightly and love getting dressed up. Their parents may have high expectations and you strive to create the perfect performance they anticipate. You want parents to congratulate themselves for finding such a wonderful place to nurture their wonderful child.

But what about the parent of that child who does not yet speak, the child who hates any noise, the child who needs routine, the child who will point blank refuse to wear a costume, the reluctant performer who will resist stepping foot on stage? What if the Christmas play fills one of your parents with dread? They imagine that they will be watching through their fingers, feeling their child's anxiety, anticipating what might go wrong. They'll feel the glares from other 'perfect' parents, who they believe are questioning why 'that *one* child has to be there, messing everything up'.

Ten tips for an inclusive play

1. Think about what the child can do. Jiggle the script. Consider a recording if the pressure will be too much.

2. Pre record a pre-verbal child's line on a Big Mack switch.

3. Teach all the children Makaton™ signs to go with songs.

4. Use symbols for 'Good sitting', 'Good standing', etc.

5. Don't over rehearse if there is lots of sitting around waiting.

6. Use microphones to help little voices get heard.

7. Don't pass on adult anxieties to children. Have fun!

8. Don't get too hung up on perfection. Take risks.

9. Let every child show what they *can* do.

10. Ask the audience to wave hands quietly in the air instead of clapping.

Play pressures

Children with SEN may be pressured by the following aspects of the Christmas show:

- anxiety
- noises
- decorations
- lights
- change
- costumes
- face paints

- audience

- boredom

- exhaustion.

Case study: Zane, a special narrator

Stage fright

Christmas changes made Zane anxious. As we planned our Christmas play we wondered how we could set him up to succeed. The previous year the play had caused him such anxiety. Despite making it to some rehearsals when it came to the day he refused to leave class. His mum did understand when Zane did not appear, but we wanted her to enjoy the play with other parents and see what her little man could do.

Finding the right part

Zane had excellent speaking skills and liked technology. I wondered if we would be able to record him being 'Narrator'. We knew it would take time so we recorded his narration bit by bit. Sometimes Zane refused, sometimes he was not in the right mood, but over time and with a lot of editing we got a lot of the narration recorded.

Another thing that had made Zane anxious the previous year was that during the play his mum was in the school hall and he could not be with her. To counteract this, we arranged for him to watch the play with his mum. He had recorded his part already. Zane had a Social Story™ and a schedule so he knew exactly what to expect. I didn't bring Zane in until we were ready to start so we would avoid too much waiting.

Play day

Zane came into the hall and sat next to his mum. I stood near by ready to support (if needed). He watched the whole play cuddling into his very proud mum. His Narrator part was played on a big screen at the front of the school hall. Zane stole the show without ever stepping on stage.

At the end of the play Zane went back to class leaving his mum to chat to other parents, who were genuinely impressed with his narration.

I contacted Zane's mother for consent to include this case study and her words below explain what this meant to her:

>...he was really part of that play and the first time I sat comfortably and enjoyed just being a parent watching their child in a school play like everyone else There are so many times as a parent you just want to feel like a 'normal parent 'and doing what everyone is doing and feel so proud. I'm so proud my 'Zane' was included in the play is this amazing way. It was the first time I'd ever sat and enjoyed watching my son in a school play without getting upset that he was having a meltdown in his class or the corridor with anxiety. He was truly amazing. Thank you Adele it really takes special teachers to think outside the box and allow our beautiful children to show their abilities without causing them distress and allowing parents to enjoy the moment. (Dyer 2015, personal correspondence)

Case study: Luke – Teddy Bear, Teddy Bear turn around...

Emerging speech

We had been using PECS® with Luke for a year and his speech was starting to develop. Words came out as a series of sounds, but those who knew him could find the meaning. He was ever so quiet...

Finding the right part

When it came to organising the Christmas play I really wanted to find a way for Luke to show his developing speaking skills.

We chose to do 'The Three Bears' and my plan was to somehow get Luke saying a line. In truth it was going to be quite an achievement to get our wriggly, squiggly, anxious Luke to stay on stage.

One day we were using the 'Teddy Bear, Teddy Bear rhyme' in class and the children acted it out. Luke really enjoyed this and it got me thinking...

Play day

We practised and practised and on the day of the play Luke (who was playing baby bear) took the microphone in his hand and went centre stage. He looked so cute in his little bear suit. We could hear the 'Ahh's' from the parents...

Everyone watched, wondering what he was going to do. Luke lifted the microphone, 'Te y Beh, Te y Beh, Tur Arow...' I held my breath as Luke acted out the whole poem and spoke the words into the microphone.

The audience of teary eyed parents all knew what a massive leap Luke had made. Luke's grandmother was in the audience clapping and crying. Afterward a still teary Gran came and told me that this was the first time she had ever dared to hope that Luke would learn to speak. Ten years have passed and thinking of that moment still brings tears to my eyes.

Little stars celebration

Every year our Early Years class have taken part in the primary play, but with our numbers growing and quite a few children we knew would be extremely anxious, we decided try something completely different. We wanted the parents to come into school and we wanted them to see what little stars their children are, but in a way that would not cause anxiety.

With our star theme in mind we created lots of starry crafts and art work. We then set out tables with activities – there was card making, green sensory rice where the children could decorate little Christmas trees, icing star biscuits and play dough Christmas trees to decorate. Dress code was 'optional'. All we asked of the parents was to share with us a song or piece of music that their child would like.

The atmosphere was relaxed. Some children were a little thrown by parents being in class, but that was nothing to how they would have felt being in front of an audience. Children and parents were free to choose what to do. Some chose to be outside balancing and bouncing. That was fine. This wasn't about showing off. It was about celebrating our wonderful class for who they are.

Towards the end of the morning we gathered in a group and played the music the parents and children had chosen. Each child hung a little star (with their picture) on our Christmas tree while we shared their individual triumphs.

This was a lovely morning. There was no stress, no pressure and yet we managed to create some really special Christmas memories.

If you think that your class won't cope with a traditional play then think of what they will cope with. Get creative. Think of a way to share their gifts and celebrate their individual 'can dos' with their families.

Video

We have touched on this already in the case study about Zane's part as narrator. It may be that you have a number of children in your class or school who will not cope with the play. Another way I've found is to video them doing something in class. Maybe they could all make puppets and do a puppet show or create decorations then hang them on the school tree. These videos work really well with a little music and (if you are feeling very techie) adding some well chosen words to annotate. I've seen parents watch these videos and be moved to tears because instead of watching their anxious child being made to stay on stage they can actually see the child in their element. Anxiety is catching. There is nothing worse than seeing our children set up to fail and not being able to do anything about it. We must assess our children and set our expectations with empathy for both parent and child.

Final thoughts

Salvador Dalí once suggested that we should not fear 'perfection' because we will never reach it. When arranging Christmas plays it's natural to want everything to be right. You may be inclined to choose the reliable Mary who will rock the baby Jesus rather than swing him by the leg. But stop and think about what makes these plays magic. Think about how *all* those parents and grandparents in the audience will feel. Imagine how you would feel if you had the child who was least likely to sit, to sing or even make it on the stage. This time when the play comes around, shift your focus. Rather than thinking 'perfection' focus on creating those 'can do' moments. The play may not go as smoothly as usual, but it will leave parents deeply moved. They'll see that your school has somehow got the point of all this crazy chaos. You've thought about each individual child and made sure that every parent gets to experience those reoccurring happy tears. School plays are not about creating 'perfection'. They are about supporting, loving and ensuring every child can shine.

CHAPTER 31

Present Danger!

Teaching Children to Handle Gift-Giving Times

The manner of giving is worth more than the gift.

Pierre Corneille, *Menteur*

Gift giving can be a social minefield for all children, but especially for those with SEN and autism. The first thing we must do to help small children deal with present times is to understand how they feel.

Imagine a gift. It can be anything you like – maybe it is a new phone, a pair of shoes or an outfit by your favourite designer. The only limit, other than your imagination, is that it must fit in a box (big or small). The gift will be beautifully wrapped and left on your table. There will be bows, ribbons, feathers (whatever you can think of). There is one slight snag... You can't open it, and in two weeks' time it will be given to someone else – someone you know, who irritates you. *They* will be getting the present and opening it right in front of you.

Presents can be wonderful. They can cause almighty rushes of joy to both the giver and getter. But they can also spell disaster. Presents can cause tears, frustration, disappointment, embarrassment and even rage. Children may need to learn how to react when they are given 'wrong' gifts. Waiting is difficult, and at certain times of year temptation is everywhere. The first thing we must do to help small children deal with present times is to understand how they feel...

Case study: Ashton and the great unwrapping

It was a couple of weeks before Christmas. Ashton's mum woke and went downstairs to find him in the lounge surrounded by opened presents, ripped wrapping and crumpled cards. He had got up early and opened every present and every card. His mum was distraught. It wasn't just what he had done that upset her, but that she had been so angry and almost lost control too. It frightened her. She said she was 'just so mad'. Everything she had done to keep on top of Christmas... All that work undone in an instant. Ashton was already in class, behaving as though nothing had happened. It was school time now and he had moved on.

I suggested his mum went into town to buy some new cards, then visited a coffee shop to write them. She deserved a treat and some 'me time'. She was a calm, loving parent, but everyone has a final straw moment!

And Ashton? After his mum left we sat together and I drew him a Carol Gray-style comic strip picture of a peg person, a tree and some presents. I found out he wasn't being malicious, but that he just couldn't cope with the mystery. He *had* to know what was inside the wrapping paper. Then he had got into a sensory unwrapping frenzy and the cards just followed. He was sorry, but I was pretty convinced he could do the same thing all over again.

I spoke to a much calmer mum later in the day. She had gone to the coffee shop, written and posted the cards. She sounded refreshed, even happy.

I suggested that she wrap the presents, but this time with Ashton, so there would be no mystery. She would get him to select paper for different people and add photo labels to aid his memory. There were no Ashton presents under the tree to start with.

After the weekend we decided to test him further. Ashton's mum wrapped an Ashton present and left it under the tree. She made sure it was a squishy, not-too-exciting present. She told him it was clothes. The wrapping stayed on. His mum praised Ashton every day and he glowed with pride because not unwrapping that present did take some self-control. On Christmas Day, Ashton enjoyed handing out the presents, using his photo labels and telling everyone exactly what was *not* in their present.

Case study: Wilf, who waited and waited and waited

Wilf was *so* excited about opening those presents under the tree. He waited and waited using his advent calendar to count down the days. His mum had already explained that he was not going to open every present as soon as he got up on Christmas Day. The family were spending Christmas with Wilf's grandparents, and Mum wanted him to open some presents with them.

Wilf's mum had a sister who lived on the other side of the world, and when they were apart for Christmas they would speak on Skype, so they could see each other opening presents. Wilf loved LEGO® and there was one gift with that tell-tale plastic rattle waiting under the tree. This was the one he kept asking and asking to open, and it was from his aunty in Australia. During the call, Wilf was allowed to go and get his LEGO® present and unwrap it. He gave a great reaction and ran off delighted, leaving his mum to chat to her sister in peace. All was good.

But when Wilf's mum went back to the lounge after the call, she discovered why Wilf had been so quiet. He had been unwrapping every single one of his other presents. Paper and labels were everywhere and his mum had no idea what present was from who (and neither did Wilf, of course).

Wilf's mum managed to resist getting cross because Wilf had thought the Skype call signalled the end of the big Christmas wait. She tried to match paper and labels to presents for 'thank you' notes and filed the experience – another lesson. Next year she would explain more clearly to her very excited and oh-so-literal son...

Ten tips for being prepared

There are ten simple steps we can take to help children cope with gift giving:

1. Do not leave gifts out on display too long, or at all if a child won't cope.

2. Colour code wrapping, so a child knows what's for whom.

3. Wrap presents in front of the child to remove the mystery.

4. Use photos on labels so pre-readers can help hand out presents.

5. Relax when a child tells a person what's inside their present.

6. Role play waiting and good reactions to bad gifts (make it fun).

7. Ask other adults and children to model good reactions and praise them.

8. Don't be afraid to suggest 'good' gifts to people who ask.

9. Show you understand their feelings. Praise and reward them.

10. Have one last present hidden, ready for when the unwrapping is all over.

Gift tags

Gift tags can be an opportunity for that final reminder. Make up a little visual reminder and stick it to each tag. Have three stages and add pictures above the words:

1. Open gift.

2. Look.

3. Say thank you.

If a child uses PECS® you could prepare a 'Thank you' symbol so they can remove it from the book and hand it over. If they use Makaton™ signs you could use a pictorial representation of the sign or a photo of them doing the 'thank you' sign on gifts.

This may all take a little time and preparation, but it will be structuring the child to learn to say 'thank you'. The effort will be appreciated by gift givers, but it will also be teaching them how the child communicates.

These tags can even be kept and used the following year or for a birthday. They will not be in use forever. Over time the visual and routine will become a part of gift giving.

An extra helpful teaching assistant might even be willing to make a set to send home to get parents started. It means such a lot to parents when they know that our care for the child and for them as a family extends beyond their school day. Children are always learning and we are always supporting.

Children need to learn our social rules. Children with SEN and autism will need extra support to do so.

Santa fears

So parents have taught their child about 'stranger danger'. They may have given additional focus to this if a child has SEN or autism. Then suddenly the child is told that Santa will come to their house, enter through the chimney or by 'magic' and leave gifts. Surely alarm bells should ring. A 'stranger' is going to leave gifts in their house, while they are asleep. And people think this is a good thing? Really?

To counteract Santa fears we must suit what we do to the individual child. If they cannot cope with the idea, we must accommodate them. There is simply no point in having a child living in fear of Christmas Eve.

Social Stories™, Comic Strip Conversations™ and visual schedules can all help. Some children simply need to know and that is okay.

As teachers we can guide and support families, but we must also be extremely sensitive. There may be siblings or cousins involved so do take care. Some lessons are for parents to time and to teach. Teachers can be there as a support, but not as the initial instigator.

Case study: Remy's reactions

Avoiding disappointment

Remy would get extremely anxious about gift giving. He was a very articulate little boy so his reactions could present as rude. At home he would always know what was in a gift before he opened it. That was how he would enjoy the experience and not get the extreme disappointment or the anxiety related to the fear of extreme disappointment. That was how a huge meltdown (on what should be a happy occasion) was avoided.

Preparing for disappointment

In life we will not always know what a gift will be. In life he would one day be presented with a gift; he would not know the contents and he may be disappointed. We had to ensure that he had experienced this and learnt to modify his reactions.

So when it came to school gifts we prepared him with a Social Story™, explaining good reactions and explaining that he would not know. The story explained that his teachers would try to get a gift he liked, but it might not be exactly what he would choose. If he did not want the gift that was okay, but if he was disappointed it might help to go outside and take some time out. He was unimpressed, but gave the resolved sigh I'd come to know as acceptance of a Social Story™.

Dealing with disappointment

The time came for Remy to open his gift. School budgets do not stretch to huge presents, but we try our best to get something that will make the children happy. Remy ripped off the wrapping and I could see that he was already anticipating 'extreme disappointment'. He opened the gift, flung it on the table, growled and went outside. After about five minutes he returned and started to open the box to explore the contents. I was so happy with Remy. The disappointment could have resulted in flying furniture, but he had remembered the story and taken himself off to calm. We would still need to work on the perfect reaction, but what a result. What a brilliant little man!

Being fair

Children are constantly measuring how fair things are. If you have had siblings or are raising siblings you will know this. We dish out bowls of ice cream. Scoops must be equal size with equal amounts of sauce. It is important to keep in mind just how important all this is to children. They might not vocalise it, but they will know. So when it comes to gift giving we must try to set them up to succeed by making things fair. We might know that one gift is more expensive, but in a smaller box, but a child may have no understanding of this. When giving Christmas gifts see them through the child's eyes before they have ripped off the wrapping. Think about how the child will feel. Think about that special child, but also think of their siblings. Believing that things are fair can make such a huge difference to a child.

Final thoughts

Children grow up too fast. Those quirky, dreadful things they do and say today will, one day, be the memories we cherish. Present times can be tricky. Try to understand a child's triggers and set each child up to succeed. Oh, and if they do get it completely wrong, learn a lesson and see the funny side. 'Everyday is a gift. That's why we call it the present' (Anon).

CHAPTER 32

A Change of Setting

Transition Tips for Your Special Children,
Inspired by the Experiences of a Rescue Cat...

*Belief in oneself is one of the most important bricks in building
any successful venture.*

Lydia M. Child

Our cat, Albie, was three when he joined our family. His previous owner gave us his usual bowl, his blanket and his carry cage, so that he would have objects around him that he was familiar with. We asked about his routines, his likes and dislikes, and stocked up on his favourite food.

Albie was naturally fearful when he arrived in our home. His first act was to retreat behind the nearest curtain, and he stayed there until late in the evening. We let him be, understanding that he needed time to adjust to new surroundings and new people. He was clearly anxious and he needed space – not to be made to sit on a lap, chased around the house or assailed with squeaking toys.

Going through this experience with Albie made me think about all those tough transitions special children make when they are starting at an early years setting, or are moving onto a new class or school. Are such children always afforded the accommodations they need? Are they given the time, the space, the familiar foods and comforts that will help them to adjust to their new environment? Do they have access to a safe retreat to escape the madding crowd when things become too much to cope with? Or are they expected to take such challenges in their stride, regardless of their needs?

Case study: Settling Billy

Home visit

Billy's parents were doing everything they could to help him develop play and communication skills. His mum had been learning Makaton™ and was giving him access to great craft activities and toys. At the home visit we realised that Billy used some unique hand signs that had developed between him and his mum. We tried to learn what they were so that he could use them successfully at school.

The familiar

Billy's mum helped settle Billy into his new class. He had a comfort blanket and his own snacks and drinks. Billy did find it strange at first, and the noise of his classmates made him anxious and tearful. He took an immediate shine to our laptop and DVDs. I gave him a set of laminated pictures to choose a DVD. He chose *Peppa Pig* and we put it on. Sometimes he signed 'Peppa Pig'. He enjoyed being able to communicate.

When the educational psychologist observed Billy using the pictures, she said that in his previous setting all the DVDs had been kept on a high shelf. They did not have pictures but written labels. Billy recognised the labels and would reach up towards the one he wanted, but would be told, 'Now is not the right time'.

The present

Billy showed great potential and his ability to communicate by asking for the DVD, and we honoured his requests. If *Peppa*

Pig helped him feel safe, secure, communicate and settle, we could live with it.

After a while Billy stopped asking for the DVDs. He would use a symbol to ask to go outside or for help opening the door to the toy room. We got some *Peppa Pig* books from the library and Billy would enjoy looking through those too.

Billy now has a PECS® book full of symbols that help him communicate. As he gains confidence, we're starting to hear more speech too. Access to symbols, comforts and the means to communicate allowed Billy to show us all how brilliant he *could* be.

Case study: Winnie the whirlwind
First impressions

During our home visit, we barely saw Winnie as she zoomed across the room, narrowly avoiding some shelves. She was fast, but seemed to be aware of the danger. Her mum told us that Winnie had bumped her head before, ending up in A&E. She had learnt that the shelves could hurt. Winnie's mum also said that Winnie had lasted only an hour in her mainstream nursery before they had phoned to say they could not meet her needs!

Taking action

Winnie was very active and into everything. She liked to eat, bounce, climb, chew and run. We realised quickly that Winnie needed an individual programme with a one-to-one assigned to keep her as busy as possible. Activities were short and matched to her attention span. She had lots of physical activities built in to create a sensory diet and Intensive Interaction to develop communication skills. We adapted to her needs and kept on adapting.

Progress report

Winnie is an affectionate child who likes lots of cuddles. She seems a lot happier and is settled in school. She continues to be very active, is starting to use PECS to ask for what she wants and will now sit with the group during 'Good Morning', 'Story Time' and, particularly, our daily 'Attention Autism' sessions.

Access to an active programme designed to meet her needs has allowed Winnie to make great progress.

Ten tips on new arrivals

Here are ten ways you can ease transitions:

1. Get to know the child through a home visit.

2. Take photos of the new place and create a transition book.

3. Use visual schedules and have symbols or photos available.

4. Have the child arrive after the mad rush and stagger settling in.

5. Request that the child brings a comfort blanket or toy, familiar cup and snack.

6. Allow the child plenty of time. There is no need to rush!

7. Have a retreat ready and show the child where it is.

8. Select activities that will spark a child's interest. Bubbles often win!

9. Ask a parent or past teacher to stay around while the child settles.

10. Keep parents posted, because their anxiety is catching.

Colour coding their way

Developing a colour coding system can make for a more comfortable learning environment, especially for learners with autism.

Through the classroom door

Transitioning into class can be a big hurdle for a child with autism. They have no idea what will happen beyond that door and the 'unknown' triggers alarm bells. We must also factor in some of the sensory issues, which often partner autism.

Turn up the volume of everything so that it is way above 'uncomfortable'. Unfamiliar voices echo and what is that tidal wave sound? Is there a toilet flushing? The lighting seems drastically different – flickering as it does in horror scenes, building a frightening atmosphere. Clothing that felt fine before has become itchy, sticky and hot. The child may not be able communicate or make sense of these nightmare feelings. They realise there is no going back, but moving forwards suddenly seems overwhelming.

Show them the way

Preparing visuals to explain our expectations can help make everyday transitions seem more achievable. We must try to avoid the child reaching that overwhelmed state by paving each step with a visual support. Matching photos and symbols can give the child a task to focus on. The visual clarifies our expectations and reduces the need for complex language.

Visuals help the child feel safer and more in control.

A child uses an individual schedule

Provide individual schedules

The child enters the classroom with a clear idea of what they should do first. They match their photo to the one at the top of their personal schedule.

We must make sure schedules are placed somewhere prominent within the child's reach.

Next the child removes the first symbol from their schedule.

We teach the child to do this by gently guiding them and providing hand over hand support.

For example, they might first remove the blue table symbol and if so they will transition to the blue table from the top of their schedule.

Using transition boards

On the blue table there is a transition board with other 'blue table' symbols. The child places their symbol on the board.

There is a photo on the back of the chair indicating where the child could sit. They may not choose to sit. That is okay. They can learn to sit later. Right now we want them to feel safe, in control and that they are on the right track.

A child places a symbol from their schedule on a transition board

At the blue table you can set up an activity for the child to do, this should have a clear structure so the child knows the expectation. They should be given hand over hand help with learning a new task so that it does not frustrate or overwhelm them. Showing the child will be more helpful than a verbal explanation. Do not do the task for the child over and over; instead reduce your support each time and allow them to build their independence.

When the blue table activity is 'finished' the child is given their photo. They return to the schedule to match it and check what is next.

Using symbols, schedules and transition boards reduces the need for too many verbal instructions, helps the child transition and promotes independence.

Schedules

A visual link can be created through colour. The individual schedule is purple, the symbols and the transition board are outlined in purple. The class timetable is also backed in purple. The hope is that the child may start to make a connection between their individual schedule and the class timetable.

A class timetable

A child may use a 'Now and Next' or 'First and Then' schedule to break down the expectations. These schedules are also backed in purple.

A Now and Next board

Using a colour code for schedules, timetables, Now and Next boards and transition boards helps create a category. Children with autism are often very good at sorting by category, tuning into colours, shapes and patterns, but they can have difficulty generalising.

The colour purple creates a category for schedules. When the child wants to know 'what we are going to do next' they look for purple. We use the child's strengths for categorising to create a stepping stone towards generalising.

Visual structure can bring order to chaos and help set the child with autism up to succeed (Devine 2014c).

Starting at a mainstream primary school without a diagnosis

When Kenneth Hall started primary school he had not yet been diagnosed with Asperger's Syndrome. He explains:

> The start of my primary school was very traumatic for me, because it was so new. I hated nearly everything about it. Having to sit still. The other children. The handwriting. The work. It was very easy and very boring. I hated the noise of school but I am not sure exactly what part of it I hated. Playing was boring. In the playground I always tried to find a quiet corner. In the classroom I mostly tried to find a quiet corner and

do nothing at all. I can't say anything at all about what my behaviour was like because I can't remember.

There were a lot of problems and I had difficulty trying to cope. I thought I would get used to it but I didn't. I never quite adjusted to it and I was even sent to the headmaster. This got me very annoyed because I was definitely blamed wrongly. (Hall 2001, p.20)

Kenneth was diagnosed when he was nine years old then home schooled. He passed his maths G.C.S.E. six years ahead of time.

Final thoughts

Sir Isaac Newton once observed, 'Men build too many walls and not enough bridges'. How true that is. The child who clings or cries or climbs is not trying to be awkward. The child who doesn't join in at 'circle time' may simply need more time, space, consistency or compromise. The key is to be patient and subtle, but to keep sparking such children's interest so that, when they are ready, they cannot resist coming to take a closer look.

CHAPTER 33

Reasons to be Hopeful

Changing Our Attitudes and Language
Can Change Outcomes

Hope is the thing with feathers
That perches in the soul
And sings the tune without the words
And never stops at all.

Emily Dickinson

The consequences of positivity and a willingness to respond to the needs of our special children can last a lifetime.

Compelled by curiosity Pandora *had* to open that jar and 'out flew all the evils in the world, but one thing remained – a tiny white flicker called hope'.

A child with SEN may not start pre-school with a label stating that they require extra help, but they can really change how things run. Perhaps they upset the other children by knocking down brick towers or struggle with following routines. Maybe you think the working day would be a lot easier if that child were placed somewhere more suited to their needs. But wait! Maybe your setting is *exactly* what that child needs and by seeing all their 'can do' possibilities you could change their future. Maybe you have the potential to be that tricky child's 'flicker of hope'.

Case study: Archie and his special cushion

Archie was easy to spot. He was 'the boy with the cushion'. After seeing him squiggling about, sliding and fiddling with the tassels on the cushion I asked why he had it. I was told that the autism advisory lady had said that children with autism would often sit better on a cushion and so Archie's mum had provided one. Archie had the cushion at all times. Whenever the children sat, he sat on his cushion, and he had been taught to carry it when transitioning. The cushion concerned me. I knew the thinking behind it, but I could also see Archie was being singled out and wondered if, in the future, he would become dependent on it. I suggested we see how he was without the cushion. Archie was not bothered at all. He sat on the floor and did not seem any more or less fiddly or squiggly than before, but he did look more like one of the group.

I created some visuals for 'good sitting', 'good looking' and 'good listening', making sure that we had different sitting visuals for the floor and on a chair, as children with autism can be very literal; they will look and copy the visual exactly. I laminated the visuals, punched holes in them and put them on key rings so they could be available at all times. I also printed them out so they were in view next to the teacher at circle time and at eye level in the front of the assembly hall.

The visuals reminded Archie how to sit in a more effective and subtle way than the 'special cushion'. Think carefully about the individual child before you introduce any new strategy; discuss it with your team and keep reviewing its effectiveness over time.

Case study: Eli's answer

Eli was causing quite a storm in his little village nursery. The staff had never had a child like him. He seemed to enjoy creating chaos. His antics included throwing sand in other children's faces at the sand tray, knocking over brick towers, riding the tricycle directly into other children, tripping up, winding up, and making unnecessary noises during story time. The list of negatives went on and on...

His use of language was advanced. He was not afraid to ask questions loudly and his knowledge (especially of dinosaurs) was amazing. He was really bright.

Was Eli ever quiet? I asked. The teacher said he would sometimes spend long stints alone in the book corner. He loved looking through each book, taking in every detail. He had a particular fascination with one book. I flicked through the book – *Don't Be a Bully, Billy: A Cautionary Tale* by Phil Roxbee Cox (2008) – and saw what could be a problem. The story went through all the times when the central character, Billy, bullied other children and ended with him going off with the aliens in a space ship. This story could be confusing. Eli was either getting ideas or trying to use it as a 'Social Story'™. The pictures only showed unfavourable behaviours and it was not going to help Eli get it right.

I suggested that the teacher remove this book as it was not helping and replace it with Social Stories™, which clearly illustrated behaviours people want to see at school. They could also use visuals to show Eli how to behave at the sandpit, on bikes and teach him how to build bricks and turn take with another child. They should praise other children getting it right in an obvious way so that Eli could learn the expectations.

A month later I met with the teacher to see if things had improved. The teacher said that Eli was still looking at *that* book and still disrupting. She had not implemented any of the suggestions I'd made. It was as though she'd never heard them. I asked why and she explained that they could not do things differently for *one* child.

Sadly, sometimes you realise that the best thing to do is move the child to a place that has more understanding of children with SEN and a willingness to meet their needs. Happily we found this setting for Eli and he has been supported brilliantly ever since.

TIP: Try this book – *How to Be a Friend: A Guide to Making Friends and Keeping Them* (Brown and Brown 2001).

Hopeful comments

Slightly altering our wording to be more positive can create 'hope' where there would otherwise be despair:

Ten tips on changing negatives to positives

1. Change 'violent' to 'challenging'.

2. Change 'disobedient' to 'anxious'.

3. Change 'impossible to teach' to 'individual learning style'.

4. Change 'disruptive' to 'developing play skills'.

5. Change 'rude' to 'assertive'.

6. Change 'controlling' to 'little leader'.

7. Change 'lazy' to 'laid back'.

8. Change 'slow' to 'gaining ground'.

9. Change 'loner' to 'enjoys their own company'.

10. Change 'non-verbal' to 'pre-verbal'.

Imagine how you would feel as a parent hearing the descriptions on the left of a list, compared to those on the right.

Lauren Warner, in an article on her blog *Sipping Lemonade* entitled 'What I didn't Know about Down Syndrome', explains how she feels parenting her daughter with Down syndrome:

> I know that the sun rises in the east and sets in the west and that Kate will giggle when I tickle that one spot on the side of her tummy. I know that she will fuss a dramatic cry if one of her siblings gets put in time out, simply because her nature is one of peace-maker. I know that if a door is open, she will shut it. If a drawer is open, she will unload it. If a heart is open, she will fill it with a great sense of love.
>
> I have seen with my own eyes the way she melts the faces of grumpy old men into tender smiles. I have seen the way that by simply being herself, she brings out an authenticity in others. I suppose we all have the qualities to affect the world this way if we could so easily be ourselves. (Warner 2015)

Author and speaker Sharon King has three children. Rosie and Lenny are on the autism spectrum and Daisy has a rare condition called Kabuki.

She explains:

> I've never pitied my children. I've made mistakes over the years, but this is one thing I instinctively got right from the word go. I feel they are perfect just as they are, and the only change necessary is in the attitude of people around them. Whatever we choose to bathe in attention will grow, so why would I ever pay attention to what I am told my children lack? I have always focused on their strengths and I know that my parenting style has helped them in many ways.
>
> When Rosie was a little girl I told her that Asperger's was her superpower. She believed it and I did too. (King 2016, p.14)

King saw that she would need to find a different route for her other two children, who she describes as 'non-verbal':

> Daisy and Lenny spoke a language of facial expressions, gesture, behaviour and body language – they *were* communicating with me! And it wasn't a language that I would have to laboriously learn, it is an innate language that we all use, I only had to re-attune to its nuances.

Furthermore I learnt that one of the reasons that words came into being was to disguise our true feelings. Words were duplicitous and unreliable. The deeper language that my children used could only ever be frank and open. I fell even more deeply in love with them.' (King 2016, p.15)

Little by little

Daniel Tammet, who was diagnosed with autism as a child and achieved fame due to his remarkable brain, reflects on how his parents supported him in the early years in his memoire *Born on a Blue Day:*

In spite of all my many problems, all the tears and tantrums and other difficulties, they loved me unconditionally and devoted themselves to helping me – little by little, day by day. They are my heroes.' (Tammet 2007, p.35)

Final thoughts

As a child I was always drawn to the non-conformist, 'naughty' children. I once overheard a teacher complaining about my friends to an elderly nun who supervised our school mealtimes. The response I overheard has stayed with me for life. Sister Hawkins told that teacher very firmly: 'There is no such thing as a bad child.' The teacher, who had expected agreement or sympathy, was silenced. I skipped off with a smile on my face and a desire to prove that wise old lady, who believed in *every* child, right.

Your words will create ripples, so choose them with care. Ensure your feelings and your comments are hopeful and positive, so that children remember you as that special someone who believed in them and loved them without condition. Be the person who that special child hopes to prove right.

CHAPTER 34

Extending Learning

Extra Information on Attention Autism,
Intensive Interaction, Makaton™, Social
Stories™, PECS® and TEACCH

Throughout this book I have touched upon some of the training and strategies which make a huge difference when teaching children with SEN or Autism. Training in each of these can take several weeks and the information on each could fill a book or several books (as some do). My aim is to take a brief look at each strategy and highlight some practical examples, tips, ideas and starting points then point you in the right direction where you will learn so much more.

Attention Autism

Attention Autism was developed by renowned autism expert and specialist speech therapist Gina Davies. I have never known a course to get teachers more enthused and excited.

Benefits of the Attention Autism approach

Attention Autism sessions are a fantastic, motivating way to gain a child's attention, inspire them to want to join the group, develop attention, listening, communicating, cooperating, turn taking, waiting, independence, thinking skills, awareness of self and others and raise self-esteem. The list goes on…

The clear visual structures, exciting objects and the visually appealing 'show' that form a part of the session appeal to children with a visual learning style. The sessions do not appear to be 'work'. Gina Davies suggests that 'we could think about the autism learning strengths rather than the things that are going wrong. These children are fantastically visual and this gives us a way forward and they have the most amazing memories…' (Davies 2014).

Anxiety reducing structures are also in place – there is the visual schedule, repetition, praise of good behaviour, activities which are modelled and opportunities to show what the child can do.

Attention Autism allows teachers to get the children working on all the skills they most need. It's amazing to see how the children progress.

These sessions are also great for developing work with support staff. They see how much of a difference their enthusiasm, modelling, support and selective use of language can make to the children's learning. Team morale is so important and these sessions have an energising effect on all involved.

Like many of the strategies developed for children with autism Attention Autism is effective with most children with learning difficulties. I implore all teachers to investigate this further. Be inspired by some of the online videos of Gina Davies and attend a course if you can.

Steph Reed is a passionate teacher who shares her good practice through her *ASD Teacher* blog. She has written a great blog post about Attention Autism, which includes a YouTube video of Stage 1:

> After I completed the Attention Autism training last year, adopting the approach in my class has made a HUGE impact on the children's attention and interaction levels, the staff teams skills in working as a group, and most importantly, it has been a whole lot of fun for everyone!
>
> Attention Autism is a highly motivating and creative approach to building attention and early communication skills and I highly

recommend any parent, carer, family member or anyone working with children with autism, to learn more about Attention Autism.[1]

Attention Autism has four stages to build and sustain attention. These stages build up over time as ability to sustain attention improves.

Getting started

Provide a visual schedule similar to the one shown in Figure 14.1. This can be drawn on a whiteboard or on a large piece of paper stuck to a cupboard. It doesn't matter as long as the children can all see it and keep the pen to hand so that you can cross out the stages as they 'finish'. You will draw the schedule in front of the children at the start of each session.

Prepare a sign for the door explaining that a session is in process. This should avoid unnecessary interruptions. These sessions are carefully structured to build attention, which justifies the sign completely.

Stage 1: Focusing attention

Have a bucket or box of toys and activities suited to what motivates the group. It must have a lid to keep contents hidden away. I've listed some examples of things that can be in the bucket below, but it is how the leader shows their own engagement, excitement and wonder at the things they take out of the bucket and the excitement modelled by other staff that really gets the child's attention.

Begin by drawing the visual schedule with stages and a simple picture. Keep speech clear and simple.

'BUCKET' OR 'BOX'

I use the song that Gina Davies uses in her training:

I've got something in my bucket, in my bucket, in my bucket.

I've got something in my bucket.

I wonder what it is.

---

1   See http://asdteacher.com/attention-autism-stage-1-attention-bucket

You can use your hands to pat the bucket in rhythm to the song to build excitement and anticipation. You can also incorporate Makaton™ signs to gain attention and aid understanding.

Have everything ready and close to hand before you start. The children will soon learn to anticipate the session. Even if there is a reluctant sitter they will come over for a look once they see everyone else engaged. They will want a better view. Ensure that the non sitting child has a slightly obstructed view.

If a child tries to grab something from the bucket put it back in. The toys in the bucket are controlled by the person who has the Bucket. Do not let the children have free reign to play with bucket toys as they will lose their magic.

Examples of 'bucket toys'

- wind up toys

- singing/ dancing toys

- light up toys

- vibrating toys

- party poppers

- balloons

- projector torches

- spinning tops

- pop up toys

- sound repetition toys.

When this stage is 'finished' show this by crossing 'box' off on the visual schedule.[2]

---

2   A video example of stage 1 can be found here: http://asdteacher.com/attention-autism-stage-1-attention-bucket

Stage 2: Sustaining attention

This is the part where you must get creative. Have everything you will need for the activity in a box or bag so that each new thing you pull out is a surprise. Preparation is everything and the bigger and bolder your ideas the better. Gina Davies explains: 'What I try to do is look at my activities first and ask, is my activity absolutely irresistible?' (Davies 2011).

The more visual, the more unusual, the more appealing you can make this, the better.

EXAMPLES OF ACTIVITIES TO 'SUSTAIN ATTENTION'

- *Sensory play dough:* Sensory play dough doesn't have to turn out perfect! Pour oil and water from above, sieve the flour from above. This will make a mess, but children love to see their naughty teacher make a mess. It's not what they expect. Add colour. Add smells. Add glitter. Just make it all completely, wonderfully, visually fascinating.

- *Spider's web:* Pour PVA glue onto a large piece of black paper to form a spider's web then sprinkle on silver glitter. This is so simple, but so effective.

- *Flower pots:* This is a favourite with shaving foam erupting through the holes in flower pots. I saw this one modelled by Gina Davies in a YouTube video.[3]

- *Paint races:* Take a large roll of display backing paper and stick it up as high as you can reach. Angle it if possible and then take different coloured paints and squirt them at the top. See which colour races the fastest. Add glitter for additional mess, mischief and sparkle.

- *Volcanoes:* Create an eruption using a bottle of lemonade and mints such as Polos or Mentos. (Look up what happens online before trying this with a class.)

---

3   See 'Gina Davies at The Walnuts Milton Keynes', *www.youtube.com/watch?v=J8h12X4sPTY*

- *Large scale junk modelling:* Use cardboard to build a bridge, a house, a cow, a Christmas tree… The only limit is your imagination.

Have a few activities that take less setting up because in reality sometimes we lose the time allocated for getting things done and we don't want the children to miss out on the session. Marble runs, bubbles, Elefun or a favoured sensory story can all be good standby activities.

Stage 3: Shifting attention

At this stage you introduce an interactive turn-taking game. Keep it simple to start. We might start turn taking with something familiar like wearing a hat and looking in the mirror. This stage can be a great way to introduce or reinforce waiting, turn taking and learning not always to be first or even (as time goes on) children can learn to cope with not always getting a turn.

IDEAS FOR 'GAMES'

- *Wearing a hat* (vary hats to match the time of year): You may want to include a song such as 'Who is going to wear the hat, wear the hat, wear the hat, wear the hat. Who is going to wear the hat? Who oh who will it be?'

- *Being rolled in a blanket:* 'Roll you up, roll you up like a sausage roll… Then we roll you back again like a sausage roll.'

- *Rockets:* The child stands on a stool and you count down to 'Blast off!'

- *Ten green bottles:* knocking bottles off a wall.

- *'It's raining, it's pouring':* umbrella and water spray.

- *Party poppers:* '1,2,3 pop'.

- *Rocket launch* (well worth buying): Again count down and stamp to blast off.

- *Letting cars go down a big ramp.*

- *Posting a letter in a box* ('Pop it in the post' game is great for this).

- *Hanging baubles* on a Christmas tree.

- *Blowing out a candle.*

Stage 4: Focusing, sustaining and shifting attention including a transition to independent working

It may take some time to build to this stage as it requires children to watch an activity or task and then independently copy what they have seen. It may mean splitting a group so that those ready can learn this. Tasks must be made up ready in advance. I tend to use those zippy bags we get in school. Each child will have their own kit. You will also have a kit so that you can model the activity to the group and one or two for support staff to use so that children can look at what they are doing with their kits and copy rather than depending on a physical or verbal prompt.

Tasks must be suited to the ability of the group. I use a lot of simple play dough tasks with our current class. The more complex the task, the less likely all children will be able to follow the instructions. We want them to succeed.

TASK KIT

I keep a kit of items we use for tasks and reuse them often (this saves a lot of time). Contents include Zippy bags, coloured pipe cleaners, play dough, glitter, scissors, glue sticks, googly eyes, coloured card, coloured pens and pencils, dry pasta, twigs, paper plates and cotton wool.

IDEAS FOR TASKS

- *Play dough*: spiders, snowmen, aliens, funny faces, animals, cupcakes and so on. Make use of the googly eyes and pipe cleaners. Animal ears can be precut from card.

- *Card making* (keep it simple): Valentine's, Father's or Mother's Day, Christmas, St Patrick's and so on. You can provide things already cut out so that the children simply stick them.

- *Craft*: puppet making, decoration making, additions for displays for example.

These sessions do take a bit of time to set up, but once you see the way the children progress you will agree that it is time well spent. It's well worth looking up some YouTube videos of Gina Davies or even better attending her training. The Attention Autism approach is expertly geared to set every child up to succeed. Children must be free to explore ideas, question, invent, experiment and create, while teachers build their self-esteem and sense of wonder.

Intensive Interaction

Intensive Interaction is all about natural, instinctive human communication.

Think of how a parent interacts with their newborn baby. Before there is any understanding of language the parent communicates with their child by making a connection through mirroring facial expressions and movement. The baby gurgles, the parent gurgles back, they copy and they smile back at one another. The parent responds to the baby's needs naturally and instinctively. This early communication forms the basis for Intensive Interaction. This technique works with all ages and stages. We will use it with our children in Early Years, through to Post 16. The technique is also being used with elderly people and has been notably effective with patients suffering with dementia.

Case study: My earliest experience with Intensive Interaction

Many years ago when I was 15 our school was asked for volunteers to go on a holiday for children with SEN. They wanted some students to go along as carers and companions. When I was on this holiday I met a young man, who I will call Eli. He was about 14 and had no speech. He could be very loud, he liked to run off (sometimes after stripping) and when sitting he would rock backwards and forwards. Over the five day holiday I became more and more connected with this boy. We would sit together rocking back and forth on chairs together, smiling and laughing. There was never any language, but our communication and connection intensified over the week to the point where when I said something simple to him he would follow my instruction, showing that he understood. What I did not know at this time was that I was instinctively using what I would later learn was Intensive Interaction.

Since that meeting with Eli I have continued to use Intensive Interaction with the children I have taught and find it the most amazing, freeing approach. I love it when I am showing parents around our school and we see staff having these wonderful natural, non-timetabled times with our children. Rather than leading students along the corridor the staff may be mirroring how they are walking or singing along to their tune.

We are lucky to have a teacher at our school who is so enthused about Intensive Interaction that she runs an Intensive Interaction club, where we can sign up our students and staff to develop communication. At the very start we will make a video baseline showing interaction and then make later videos to show progress. These can be a wonderful way to show parents how Intensive Interaction can develop communication and interaction, which will encourage it to be used at home.

Intensive Interaction is never the same twice so there is no set of fast rules to follow. Sometimes it will involve sitting quietly, waiting, but it may also involve those simple games we play with babies such as using a scarf to play 'boo', copying sounds, songs like 'Row, row the boat', tickles, rocking or rough and tumble.

There is no set place or time for Intensive Interaction. We grab the opportunity when it arises. We may be helping with dressing, we may be in the swimming pool or we may be transitioning between rooms. The length of a session will always be led by the student. They will get to a point when they decide that they have had enough and may disengage or walk off. When they do this we may wait a minute and see if they return. Usually they will not. The session is finished. It's all about communication on their terms. This is what I love – that it is so student led. We are giving them the controls – not trying to change them, but going with them at their pace and showing them that we love who they are.

There is more information on the Intensive Interaction website (see the 'Useful Websites' section at the back of the book) and there are many books and there are courses. If you can access any of these it will be very worthwhile, but until then keep those newborn interactions in mind. It is a technique we all can draw on because it's based on our natural instinct.

Makaton™

Makaton is 'a language program using signs and symbols to help people to communicate. It is designed to support spoken language and the signs and symbols are used with speech, in spoken word order'.[4] Using Makaton signs along with simple language can draw a child eye, help sustain interest and provide a visual clue to decode language.

Baby signing

Many parents are now using Makaton with babies developing speech. Before my own children were able to sound out words they could understand and sign 'please', 'more', 'finished' and 'milk'. I recall a relative voicing concerns when I was communicating using Makaton with our first child that the use of signs could reduce his need to speak. But Makaton is always used along with speech; every time we sign we say the word. The language is constantly modelled in such a clear and consistent way. The child can listen and process again and again, linking the action with the word and as speech develops the need to sign is reduced.

---

4   *www.makaton.org/aboutMakaton*

Makaton™ in our school

Portesbery School was probably one of the first to start using Makaton as it was closest special school to the original headquarters of The Makaton Charity. It is lovely to go to the website and see students and staff from our school.

As you arrive at our school you will see a screen with our staff demonstrating different Makaton signs along with the symbols. This display instantly shows visitors that Makaton is one of the strategies they will see our students use to communicate. We display commonly used signs suited to areas in order to encourage staff and students to gain confidence in using Makaton. In the art room you will see a display showing signs for colour, shape and size, scissors, paper and glue. In the office you will see signs for 'hello', 'goodbye', 'telephone' and 'help'. Displaying these signs encourages their constant, consistent use.

Music and song can be a great way to develop use of Makaton over time. Our speech therapy team developed a Makaton choir. There are examples online of Makaton being used with music for example YouTube videos of 'Signing Hands'.

Something Special

Something Special is an award-winning children's television series developed by the BBC. The main character 'Mr Tumble' (played by Justin Fletcher) uses Makaton signs and symbols. The programmes are often linked to learning topics and are a fantastic way to extend vocabulary and develop understanding of language. It is wonderful to see how *Something Special* has gained popularity with all children so that when they see a child using their hands to communicate they understand what they are doing and will try to find the meaning. The programme also features children with SEN, which can promote discussion about differences and help develop understanding, acceptance and support for these children.

I have found *Something Special* magazine to be a brilliant resource and will often use the contents for our displays. The magazine features pages with multiple photographs of Justin Fletcher showing how to make Makaton™ signs. These can be great to display in a classroom to encourage staff to use them with children.

Makaton in mainstream

It is great to know that more and more nurseries and primary schools are starting to use Makaton because they see how it can promote understanding and help with language development. The signs are not only helpful to children with speech and language difficulties, but can help illustrate meaning for learners whose first language is not the same as that spoken at school. When a parent of a child with SEN sees that a mainstream setting is using strategies such as Makaton with all children it helps them feel that their child is in a supportive, inclusive setting.

Ten tips for encouraging Makaton signing in school

1. Print out the Makaton signs and include them on displays so that staff and children can learn signs linked to stories.

2. Display Makaton signs for likely language in specific areas – for example the school office. Display signs for 'register', 'good morning', 'good afternoon', 'hello', 'copy', 'pen', 'envelope', 'post a letter', 'phone' and so on.

3. Include books containing Makaton signs in the book corner.

4. Open school Makaton training courses up to parents and carers.

5. Teach some basic signs to staff at places children regularly visit – shops, sports centres and so on.

6. Look at episodes of *Something Special*. (There's probably even one that links with your topic.)

7. Find songs by 'Singing Hands' on YouTube.

8. Include Makaton™ signs when reading stories and signing songs.

9. Incorporate Makaton signing into assemblies and school plays.

10. Speak to the Makaton charity if you need advice for good practice or are stuck interpreting a particular sign. (Devine 2016, p.192)

Social Stories™ and Comic Strip Conversations™

While teaching at an autism specific school in Surrey, UK, I was lucky to attend quite a few training days with Carol Gray herself. If you get the chance to do this it is so worthwhile, but she has also set up a website with information and examples of Social Stories™ and written several books on the subject.

Social Stories™

Social Stories™ were created by Carol Gray in 1991 to help teach social skills to people on the autism spectrum. They are short descriptions of a particular situation, event or activity, which include specific information about what to expect in that situation and why.[5]

Social Stories™ can be incredibly powerful because they explain situations in a simple, consistent way and are individual to the child. They take account of the child's interest and understanding. Before writing a Social Story™ we must investigate in order to get it right.

For children who do not yet read using a symbols programme such as Symwriter can allow them to follow the story as there will be images above the words. These can include photos of the child and people or places involved. This takes a little time, but will add to

---

5   www.autism.org.uk/socialstories

the effect. I tend to keep social stories in a file for a child so that staff can pull them out. It can also be a good idea to laminate the Social Story™ if it is preparing the child for something they might not like, for example: 'Sometimes swimming is cancelled when it was on the schedule' or 'Why Jimmy cannot open his Christmas presents until Christmas'.

Comic Strip Conversations™

Comic Strip Conversations™, also created by Carol Gray, are simple visual representations of the different levels of communication in a conversation. For example, they could show:

- the things that are actually said in a conversation
- how people might be feeling
- what people's intentions might be.[6]

Comic Strip Conversations™ can be an amazing starting point to prompt discussion with a child who is either too anxious or does not have the communication skills to explain their thoughts or actions.

To create a comic strip conversation you need just paper, coloured pen or pencils and patience. Draw a simple stick figure to represent the person in the situation. The colours can be used to link speech to feelings.

Child: 'Billy pushed me.'

Teacher: 'How do you think Billy was feeling?'

Child: 'Angry.'

Teacher: 'What did Billy say?'

Child: 'You broke my tower.'

Teacher: (Drawing a tumbled tower and doing a speech bubble above the stick figure.) 'How did he sound?'

Child: 'He sounded angry.'

---

6   Cited from *www.autism.org.uk/socialstories*

Teacher: (Going to select a coloured pencil.) 'What colour shall we use for angry?'

Child: 'His words were angry red.'

As the conversation progresses the teacher is able to unpick the situation so that the child sees why knocking over the tower leads to an angry Billy.

This can be a really powerful way to teach the child the correct response as next time the situation arises they see the images, remember the conversation and change their actions. I've used these again and again and seen them work again and again.

PECS®

Andrew S. Bondy and Lori Frost developed PECS in 1985:

> PECS® begins by teaching an individual to give a picture of a desired item to a 'communicative partner' who immediately honors the exchange as a request. The system goes on to teach discrimination of pictures and how to put them together in sentences. In the more advanced phases, individuals are taught to answer questions and to comment.[7]

I have seen so many, many children learn to communicate effectively through PECS. When a child makes progress it is the most exhilarating feeling. I would compare the feeling to that which sky divers must get each time they take that first leap out of a plane. This never changes, never dulls. It is one of the amazing buzzes of special needs teaching.

If you are a parent or teacher working with a child with significant communication difficulties and can possibly get to a Level 1 two day basic PECS training course it will be worthwhile and empowering. This chapter offers a glimpse into ways I have used my PECS training to improve communication. The case studies and classroom practices I give in this chapter are examples of how PECS can be put to use in school, but they are no substitute for proper training. PECS courses are currently run by certified Pyramid Education Consultants. The

---

7   www.pecs-unitedkingdom.com/pecs.php

PECS® website is the best place to find more information about PECS courses and resources.[8]

Creating a PECS may sound like a lot of work to set up, but it is well worth the effort. If you are starting out with PECS try to ensure that pictures are available to the child in all settings – school, home, respite and Gran and Grandpa's house. This will make so much difference to the child's progress. Once they are using pictures to communicate the child should have access to these resources wherever they are. Be consistent and grab each opportunity because the more practice a child has the faster they will make progress (Devine 2016 pp.163–164).

TEACCH

In 1966 division TEACCH was set up at the University of North Carolina as a research project focused on children with autism and their families. I can only touch the surface of this approach in this chapter. There is no end to what you can learn through TEACCH training so if you can possibly get on a course I would highly recommend it. I am lucky enough to have been on a five day practical training course twice (once as a trainee and the next time as a trainee trainer). The course demonstrates practical ways that we can use visual structures and use individual motivators to help people with autism learn.

Let's take a 'typical' classroom environment. It's one of those times between activities. There is excited noise and lots of unstructured movement. Amidst all of the buzz there is one child, who is not coping. They may not show this, but these times can cause extreme anxiety to children with autism. They may reveal this anxiety through challenging behaviour, through withdrawal or through trying to physically leave. What the TEACCH training does is helps teachers to see this classroom through the person with autism's eyes and then show ways to improve things. TEACCH is not a one size fits all approach. It is all about helping the individual, knowing their personal anxieties and using their personal motivators to create 'can dos' and possibilities.

---

8   *www.pecs.com*

Putting practical strategies and supports in place

In 2005 I returned from maternity leave to job share with another teacher. After the TEACCH course we were able to reassess our classroom set-up. We designated clear areas for 'independent work', 'work with the teacher, 'leisure' and 'snack'. We gave each child an individual visual schedule with their photograph at the top. We taught the children to match their photos to their schedules and then take a laminated symbol and match it to the area shown. At first our class staff were resistant to the changes. It was a lot of work and meant a lot of change. We were trialling new things, but having done the training we were convinced it would work.

We decided to start by bringing the TEACCH structures into our numeracy lessons. We would start the lesson all together and then send the children to check their schedules. The children soon learnt to do this and seemed to enjoy the new structure. The fact that everyone knew what they were doing next stopped the noise and the movement that would usually happen during transitions, which in turn reduced the anxiety of our learners with autism.

At first the play area was distracting the children who were working so we brought in a huge screen to section off this area of the classroom. We also added two workstation screens around the desks to reduce distraction for the children doing independent work.

Within a few weeks, seeing the difference all the structures made to the children was enough to convince our support staff. Our next step was to add these structures to our literacy lessons.

The principles of structured TEACCHing are as follows:[9]

- understanding the culture of autism

- developing an individualized person- and family-centered plan for each client or student, rather than using a standard curriculum

- structuring the physical environment

---

9   *As outlined by TEACCH at http://teacch.co./about-us/what-is-teacch*

- using visual supports to make the sequence of daily activities predictable and understandable

- using visual supports to make individual tasks understandable.

TEACCH in the Early Years

The Early Years classroom is the perfect place to introduce all these structures as we want to create an excellent first impression. Children like visual structures, they like to know the expectations and what is happening next. Early Years classes are set up so that children can learn through play, but for some children this is more of an intimidating social minefield of 'What am I supposed to do?' than an opportunity for freedom to play.

For these children having a visual schedule with symbols or photographs – a 'Now and Next', a clear structure of what they are supposed to be doing and how long they will need to attend to it, when they can eat, when they can rest, when they can go home – can make such a difference. The more personal this is to the child the better. If you know that Johnny loves trains then have the trains out when he arrives, have his photo and trains on his schedule, a train by his peg. The more set up and ready you are to cater for the individual child the better first impression they will have.

We all like it when people notice what we love and are thoughtful enough to remember. Children are no different. So while thinking visual structure also keep thinking about individual motivators.

In our setting we have our workstation tasks set up in a little room alongside the classroom. They are matched to the child's interests. The other day I was working with a child in the room teaching him some new tasks. Another student was outside desperate to get in and do her Disney Princess themed tasks. This is how TEACCH tasks should be – *so* motivating that they make a child excited about doing them. This takes a little time to achieve, but it is so rewarding to see a child, who might otherwise opt out, leap up when you suggest they do some 'independent work'.

Final thoughts

I have only been able to touch the surface of some of the brilliant courses I've attended during my time in special education and there is so much more to learn. There is a list of useful websites at the end of this book. There are also so many wonderful books, blogs and training videos available to explore online.

If you are based near a special needs school I would suggest that you contact them and ask if you can visit and see some of these strategies in use in the classroom. Special needs teachers are usually very open to sharing strategies with teachers from other settings. We want to see mainstream classes being more inclusive. We want to see more children succeeding in mainstream school. We know that with the right supports and structures so many more can.

CHAPTER 35

Happily Ever After

Life itself is the most wonderful fairy tale.

Hans Christian Andersen

There's that famed fairy tale ending, '...and they all lived happily ever after'. The Prince and Princess marry or the chief protagonist returns with the treasure. The main characters get their 'happy ending' and we do not need to know any more, but I've always wondered.

'Happily ever after' may be the end of many fairy tales we know, but it is not the end of the story. Have you ever wondered what happens after Snow White and her handsome prince ride off on that horse? What sort of life do they have? Do they find that the castle roof is rotting and they don't have the money to repair it? Do they want to have children? Do they struggle to conceive a child or have a child with severe disabilities? Does 'happily ever after' (with no trials and no hiccups) exist for anyone? Our children so often arrive after the 'happily ever after' part of our story. Our children, no matter what abilities or quirky unexpected ways, are *our* happily ever after. The lucky parents are those who realise this while they still have their 'happy' at home.

I recall a grandmother speaking about her grandson, who had learning difficulties. She was asked what her favourite memory was of him as a child. With twinkling eyes she replied, 'He would throw his dinner plate'. She was asked to expand on this, to explain why. The reason – she looked back on the times he did this and it made her chuckle. He didn't want the dinner so he just threw it. The reaction was so extreme. This communication, which must have been frustrating at the time, was now a treasured memory because it was completely unique to her relationship with her grandson. It was a part of something they shared together and could now reflect upon and find amusing.

I once taught a little boy with autism who had a real sensory fixation with my hair. He would come up behind me and have a lovely time messing it all up. I'm not precious about my hair. I didn't mind it being messed. The boy was pre-verbal and we noticed that he had different things he would do with different staff. With some he sought tickle play, some rough and tumble, some a repetitive PECS® request. When I spoke to his gran at sports day she said that the hair thing was something special he had with someone else – his mum. I was touched beyond words at his ability to communicate such a huge compliment. Pre-verbal children find ways to communicate when they have no words.

Stories are a powerful teaching tool. Our best loved fairy tales give messages about seeing the goodness, focusing on positives and so often demonstrate that the least likely character can beat the odds.

The Animal School fable

George H. Reavis wrote *The Animal School* to highlight how it is important to allow children to develop what they 'can do', supporting individuals to hone their talents:

> The Duck is good at swimming – better in fact than his instructor – and he made passing grades in flying, but he was practically hopeless in running. Because he was low in this subject, he was made to stay after school and drop his swimming school in order to practice running. He kept this up until he was only average in swimming, but average was passing, so nobody worried about that except the duck. (Reavis 1940/1999)

Hans Christian Andersen

Hans Christian Andersen shows us again and again that it is the different, often seemingly imperfect, characters inspiring the stories. By focusing on writing fairy tales Andersen did something amazing. He was able to reach people at the stage when they are most open to learning and still developing their attitudes and who they will be. Beyond that he was communicating with parents, who would be reading the stories aloud, gaining social insights from their bedtime story time. Was Andersen paving the way for other quirky characters who do not fit the usual socially acceptable mould to be recognised for the differences which often make them remarkable? Was he writing his own set of parables to teach future generations to accept and embrace difference?

The Ugly Duckling

One of our best loved fairy tales is 'The Ugly Duckling' by Hans Christian Andersen. The ugly duckling is made to feel he is lesser because he is different to the other ducklings. Sidelined and ridiculed he leaves his family and leads a lonely, isolated existence. It is not until the end of the story that he sees his reflection in the water and finds he has become a beautiful swan. This story gains new meaning when we know that Hans Christian Andersen has been posthumously diagnosed with Asperger's Syndrome and described the story as 'a reflection of my own life' (Bredsdorff 1975). Does this tale highlight how a child might feel who has a learning difference or disability? They know that they are different. 'Andersen understood that children who were rejected by others could live a very lonely life' (Brown 2010, p.50). Children with SEN or autism need to be in the company of people who love them unconditionally and see the 'swan' in them and encourage them to believe in who they are and who they can potentially be. A child should never feel they are less than their peers. Differences must be embraced and understood. Going back to Andersen's own life Brown explains:

> What I find heartening here is that Andersen, like the Ugly Duckling, did realize he was different, but as he portrayed himself in this fairy tale,

his difference made him not only *special*, but *superior* to the others. Being 'other' to Andersen, was equivalent to being unique, rare, or chosen. (Brown 2010, p.51)

We must ensure our unique children know that we see the swan in them from the very start.

The Steadfast Tin Soldier

I love the story of 'The Steadfast Tin Soldier'. When I first met my husband Quentin in America I loved it when he would play the guitar and sing 'The Little Tin Soldier' song by Donovan.

All the tin soldiers were exactly the same, but it's the one with only one leg who is unique and inspires the story:

> Each soldier was the living image of the others, but there was one who was a bit different. He had only one leg, for he was the last to be cast and the tin had run out. Still, there he stood, just as steadfast on his one leg as the others on their two; and he is the tin soldier we are going to hear about. (Andersen 2014)

The Proud Tea Pot

In the slightly less well known story 'The Proud Tea Pot' Andersen tells of a tea pot which is proud of its handle and spout, but knows that those around him focus on his cracked and defective lid. They focus on what's defective, but miss what's brilliant.

Finding treasures

There are moments when parents will pause and suddenly understand all that they have. These moments take us by surprise: moments when we reflect on just how wonderful and how special our children are and how their quirky ways are a part of who they are, a part of what we love.

My sister once asked me why I am always taking pictures of our children when they are up to mischief. I'd never thought of it before, but it made me think about how much I relish the mischievous spark in each of them, their ability not to follow, to think for themselves...

Miriam Gwynne. a mum who is raising twins with SEN, wrote a very open, in the moment, account on her blog, *Faith Mummy*:

My beautiful boy is a treasure. He takes a tin of baked beans to bed to hold at night. He gets such delight watching drops of rain falling down a window. He gets excited about going out in the rain. He can spend hours simply pouring coins from one cup to another one. He is thankful for the food on his plate…so thankful in fact he will even try eating the plate! He can hand me a photo of an ice lolly when he wants one. He thinks nothing of watching TV with a swimming ring around his neck:

He is a real child. Someone's child. My child. He is loved. He is treasured. He is stunning. He is different. But he isn't less. (Gwynne 2013)

Ellen Seidman writes a blog *Love That Max* about her experiences as a mum of three. She's kindly allowed me to share a post she wrote about her son Max, who has cerebral palsy.

I got Max's school pictures the other day. I opened the envelope, then stared and stared at his photo. He looked so grown up, handsome and happy.

Before Max came, I couldn't have dreamed I'd have a boy this cute. That hair!

I couldn't have dreamed I'd have a boy this good-natured and cheerful. That giggle. That laugh. That *smile*.

I couldn't have dreamed I'd have a boy so determined to do his best, no matter what challenges his muscles threw his way.

I couldn't have dreamed how much I'd end up talking about purple, spaghetti, car washes, Lightning McQueen, firefighters, Chicago or any of his other fascinations, because I couldn't have dreamed up this mind of his that works in wonderful and mysterious ways.

I couldn't have dreamed how excited the sound of a new word could make me, or even just the sound of a letter. The other night, Max was talking once again about his upcoming March weekend trip to Chicago with Dave. 'OK! You're going to Chicago!' I said, then I tucked him in and shut the lights. 'OK! OK! OK! OK!' Max kept saying as he lay in bed. I guess he just liked the sound of it. I loved hearing him pronounce the 'k.'

I couldn't have dreamed how proud I'd be of every single big and little-yet-not-little accomplishment: using his pointer finger, eating independently, reading words, doing math, potty training, saying 'please' and 'thank you,' riding a bike, giving hugs, making jokes, sitting through an IEP meeting, climbing stairs, descending stairs, winking. Yes, winking.

I couldn't have dreamed how much I would love him and Sabrina, so much so that my heart literally hurts at times, especially when I watch them sleep.

Max is 12 years old today.

And he is the boy of my dreams. (Seidman 2014)

Lauren Warner recalls giving a talk about Down syndrome to 100 middle and high school children:

…as I began my talk, the first thing I asked all 100 middle and high school kids on the floor in front of me was, 'How many of you know someone with Down syndrome?'

I was comforted when at least 30 hands enthusiastically rose to the sky. Because this knowledge is what will change the world.

These children didn't know that Down syndrome had a capital 'D' and a lowercase 's.' They didn't know about the chromosomal makeup of a person with Down syndrome or any of the other random facts I shared – but they knew so much more than I did when Kate was born.

They knew *people*. They had friends with Down syndrome. They sat by kids with Down syndrome in school and had neighbors with Down syndrome. They loved and babysat and laughed and played with people with Down syndrome. And that was all they needed to know.

They didn't need a pep talk about potential. Or a handout with statistics. They knew that people with Down syndrome are of great value and worth (like all of us) just as I know that one plus two equals three – because it's fact.

Kate's new favorite phrase comes out of her pink little lips as a habit every time I ask her for a kiss:

'I love you,' she says confidently as I respond with a smile, 'I love you, too.'

And as it is for every parent and every child of every ability forever more – those simple words are the most important thing we need to know.' (Warner 2015)

Parents of children with SEN will often look ahead to the future. This is only natural, but we must ensure that they don't get so fixed on what might or might not be that they risk losing the magic of the right now. Their special child is the 'happily ever after…' whatever they achieve. They must rejoice and enjoy the now moments, rather than fixate on the future and we must facilitate this by giving them every day 'wows' to celebrate.

Fairy tale teacher

As soon as a child meets a new adult they will start assessing whether they are going to 'get' them, support them and love them. Children with SEN may sometimes not seem to even notice new people, but they are often hyper empathic. They may not process words quick enough to respond or react in the usual way to other children, but they will have read their new teacher by instinct from the moment they meet.

They need to know that a teacher is open to them, that they are going to love them, respect them, wait for them, smile a lot and enjoy them. After that a teacher will need to gain their attention. They will not do this by being 'the teacher', but by getting excited by things that interest them. Loving what they love. Creating with them, surprising them, inspiring them and enjoying them.

If I could only offer one piece of advice to each new teacher it would be this:

Love *every* child without condition, listen with an open heart, get to know who *they* are, what *they* love, and follow more often than you lead.

> There are two ways of spreading light: to be the candle or the mirror that reflects it.

Edith Wharton, *Age of Innocence*

References

Andersen, H.C. (2014) *Hans Christian Andersen's Complete Fairy Tales* (trans. J. Hersholt). San Diego, CA; Canterbury Classics.

Attwood, T. (2007) *The Complete Guide to Asperger's Syndrome.* London and Philadelphia, PA: Jessica Kingsley Publishers.

Bailey, T. (2015) 'Autism Toilet Training.' *Mother Geek* blog. Available at www.mothergeek.co.uk/blog/6140/autism-toilet-training-, accessed 4 April 2016.

Billings, J. (1871) *Farmer's Allminax for the Year 1871.* Available at https://archive.org/stream/joshbillingsfar02billgoog#page/n11/mode/2up, accessed on 20 June 2016.

Bogdashina, O. (2016) 'Blog 4 Aisle Be Back! Why we never steered clear of the supermarket.' Aukids Magazine, Issue 30.

Bredsdorff, E. (1975) *Hans Christian Andersen: The Story of his Life and Work 1805–75.* London: Phaidon.

Brown, J. (2010) *Writers on the Spectrum: How Autism and Asperger Syndrome have Influenced Literary Writing.* London and Philadelphia, PA: Jessica Kingsley Publishers.

Brown, L. K. and Brown, M. T. (2001) *How to Be a Friend: A Guide to Making Friends and Keeping Them.* London and New York, NY: Little Brown.

Cox, P. R. (2008) *Don't be a Bully, Billy: A Cautionary Tale.* London: Usborne.

Davies, G. (2011) 'Inspiring Attention and Communication'. Available at www.youtube.com/watch?v=nFYnc4xcZ6k, accessed on 20 June 2016.

Devine, A. (2014a) *Colour Coding for Learners with Autism.* London and Philadelphia, PA: Jessica Kingsley Publishers.

Devine, A. (2014b) 'Change Happens: Teaching a Child with Autism to Handle a Whoops.' *JKP blog.* Available at www.jkp.com/jkpblog/2014/08/change-happens-teaching-a-child-with-autism-to-handle-a-whoops, accessed 4 April 2016.

Devine, A. (2014c) 'How Using Colour-Coded Visuals Can Ease Anxiety When a Child with Autism Starts School.' *JKP Blog* available at www.jkp.com/jkpblog/2014/08/how-using-colour-coded-visuals-can-reduce-anxiety-when-a-child-with-autism-starts-school, accessed 19 March 2016.

Devine, A. (2014d) 'Helping a Child with Autism Handle Halloween.' *JKP blog.* Available at www.jkp.com/jkpblog/tag/halloween, accessed 6 April 2016.

Devine, A. (2015a) 'To That Mum of That Child, Who Did Not Dress Up for Book Day.' *Special blog.* Available at http://senassist.com/blog/?p=69#comment-168, accessed April 6 2016.

Devine, A. (2015b) 'Sports Day – Tips to Support the Child with Autism.' *SEN Assist* blog. Available at http://senassist.com/blog/?p=141#sthash.SM0lLgt1.dpuf, accessed 4 April 2016.

Devine, A. (2015c) 'Helping that Special Child who Hits' *SEN Assist: A Special Blog.* Available at http://senassist.com/blog/?p=137#sthash.PZnJ2VSG.05rZLfVh. dpuf, accessed 19 March 2016.

Devine, A. (2015d) 'Dear Secret Teacher: Why parents need you to support them in all areas (even toilet training).' SEN Assist blog post, A Special Blog, available at http://senassist.com/blog/?p=125#sthash.Qx4kr5hu.dpuf, accessed 20 March 2016.

Devine, A. (2015f) 'What If the Child with Autism Could Fast Forward School?' *A Special Blog.* Available at- http://senassist.com/blog/#sthash.IwaxFZJ9.dpuf, accessed 4 April 2016.

Devine, A. (2016) *Literacy for Visual Learners.* London and Philadelphia, PA: Jessica Kingsley Publishers.

Dyer, W. (2008) When you change the way you look at things. Available at www.youtube.com/watch?v=urQPraeeY0w, accessed on 20 June 2016.

Endow, J. (2015) 'Autism and Changing Classroom Strategies.' Available at www.judyendow.com/advocacy/autism-and-changing-classroom-strategies, accessed 4 April 2016.

Endow, J. (2016) 'Autism and Eating Out.' Available at http://ollibean.com/2016/01/09/autism-and-eating-out, accessed 6 April 2016.

Frey, H.P., Molholm, S., Lalor, E.C., Russo, N. and Foxe, J. (2013) 'Atypical cortical representation of peripheral visual space in children with an autism spectrum disorder.' *European Journal of Neuroscience 38*, 1 2125–2138. Available at www.ncbi.nlm.nih.gov/pmc/articles/PMC4587666/, accessed 12 July 2016.

Gwynne, M. (2013) 'Did You Really Have to Say That?' *Faith Mummy* blog. Available at https://faithmummy.wordpress.com/2013/10/28/did-you-really-have-to-say-that/, accessed 9 April 2016.

Gwynne, M. (2014) 'When Reality Hits.' *Faith Mummy* blog. Available at https://faithmummy.wordpress.com/2014/09/, accessed 19 March 2016.

Gwynne, M. (2015a) 'My Best Friends... The Beautiful Flowers.' *Faith Mummy* blog. Available at https://faithmummy.wordpress.com/2015/03/11/my-best-friends-the-beautiful-flowers/, accessed 20 March 2016.

Gwynne, M. (2015b) 'Who Supports the Parents?' Faith Mummy blog. Available at https://faithmummy.wordpress.com/2015/09/02/who-supports-the-parents, accessed 14 July 2016.

Grandin, T. (2002) 'Teaching ASD Children and Adults.' Available at www.autism.com/advocacy_grandin_teaching, accessed 19 March 2016.

Hall, K. (2001) *Asperger Syndrome, the Universe and Everything.* London and Philadelphia, PA: Jessica Kingsley Publishers.

Hanscom, A. (2015) 'Why Children Fidget and What We Can Do About It,' TimberNook Balanced and Barefoot blog. Available at www.balancedandbarefoot.com/blog/why-children-fidget-and-what-we-can-do-about-it, accessed 4 April 2016.

Heffner, G.J. (2016) 'Social Circles – Personal Space and Safety.' *Autism Spectrum Disorders Factsheets*, available at http://autism-help.org/communication-social-circles-autism.htm, accessed 4 April 2016.

Hodgdon, L. (2016) 'Autism Techniques to Teach Students Choice Making.' Available at http://usevisualstrategies.com/autism-teaching-choice-making, accessed 4 April 2016.

Ingraham, P. (2013) 'Proprioception: The True Sixth Sense. The Vital and Strange Sensation of Position, Movement and Effort.' Available at www.painscience.com/articles/sixth-sense.php, accessed 4 April 2016.

Jacks, L.P. (1932) *Education through Recreation*. London: University of London Press.

King, S. (2016) 'Just the Way You Are…' *Aukids Magazine Issue 30*

Lebowitz, M. (2015) Tips for Calming your Child with Autism – Calm Yourself First. Available at http://marcilebowitz.com/tips-for-calming-your-child-calm-yourself-first/#comment-20, accessed 12 July 2016.

McCan, L. (2016) 'The Right Way to use Visual Timetables.' Available at www.reachoutasc.com/blog/the-right-way-to-use-visual-timetables, accessed 19 March 2016.

McLaughlin, M. (2010a) 'Shake Your Sillies Out,' *MOM – Not Otherwise Specified*. Available at http://momnos.blogspot.co.uk/2010/03/shake-your-sillies-out.html, accessed 4 April 2016.

McLaughlin, M. (2010b) 'Friendly Talk,' *MOM – Not Otherwise Specified*. Available at http://momnos.blogspot.co.uk/2010/03/friendly-talk.html, accessed 6 April 2016.

Mandela, N. (1995) *Long Walk to Freedom*. New York: Back Bay Books.

Manerling, J. (2016) 'Cat Therapy for Autistic Children: The True Story of the Miracle a Cat Brought to an Autistic Boy.' Available at http://cats.about.com/od/youandyourcat/a/catsandautism.htm, accessed 12 July 2016.

Meadows, T. (2012) 'Learning to Wait. *I Love ABA* blog post. Available at www.iloveaba.com/2012/05/learning-to-wait.html, accessed 20 March 2016.

Mele, J. (2012) The ABCs of Asperger's Syndrome: An A-Z Guide to Understanding the Symptoms of Asperger's. Available at http://www.parents.com/health/autism/symptoms/understanding-Asperger's-syndrome, accessed 4 April 2016.

Merchey, J. (2004) *Values of the Wise: Aspiring to the Life of Value*. Centreville, VA: Six Star Publishing.

Miller, S. (2013) *Why Use Symbols?* (video file) Available at www.youtube.com/watch?v=mw-7-N0WGEA, accessed 9 April 2016.

Moorhead, J. (2013) 'The biggest problem for parents of a child with special needs? Other people.' The Guardian, August 16th 2013. Available at www.theguardian.com/lifeandstyle/2013/aug/16/children-disabilities-special-needs-mumsnet-campaign, accessed 6 April 2016.

Murrell, D. (2001) *Tobin Learns to Make Friends*. New York: Future Horizons.

Myers, M. (2015) 'Autism and the Delayed Effect.' *A Slice of Autism* blog. Available at http://asliceofautism.blogspot.co.uk/2015/10/autism-and-delayed-effect.html, accessed 7 July 2016.

Myers, M. (2016) www.facebook.com/sliceofautism/photos/a.388704064652254.107 3741829.388129484709712/477043292484997/?type=3&theater, accessed on 20 June 2016.

Pates, J. (2014) *Comment on blog*. Available at http://senassist.com/blog/?p=3, accessed 6 April 2016.

Pearson, C. (2013) 'Animals and Autism: Pets Help with ASD,' *Huffington Post. Available at*www.huffingtonpost.com/2013/02/27/animals-autism-pets-asd_n_2776373.html, accessed 6 April 2016.

Reavis, G.H. (1940/1999) *The Animal School*. Peterborough, NH: Crystal Springs Books.

Reed, S. (2015a) 'Sensory Needs, Autism and our 'Class' Exercise Activity!' *ASD Teacher* blog. Available at http://asdteacher.com/sensory-needs/, accessed 4 April 2016.

Reed, S. (2015b) *Attention Autism Stage 1: Attention Bucket Video* and comments from creator Gina Davies. Available at http://asdteacher.com/attention-autism-stage-1-attention-bucket, accessed 9 April 2016.

Rhodes, G. (2012) 'Autism: How Computers Can Help.' *Guardian*, 26 February, 2012. Available at www.theguardian.com/lifeandstyle/2012/feb/26/computer-geeks-autism, accessed 20 June 2016.

Rosen, M. (1989) *We're Going on a Bear Hunt*. London: Walker Books.

Rowan, K. (2013) *Why Kids with Autism May Avoid Eye Contact*. Available atwww.livescience.com/37167-autism-avoid-eye-contact-brain.html, accessed 9 April 2016.

Rybak, P. (2010) Toilet Training Young children with Autism or ASD, and Other Special Needs: A Suggested Protocol and Practical Strategies for Caregivers and Educators Using Visual Supports and Technology. Socially Speaking™ LLC.

Secret Teacher (2015) 'Secret Teacher: Why do Some Parents Expect Us to Toilet Train Their Children?' *The Guardian* 18 April 2015. Available at www.theguardian.com/teacher-network/2015/apr/18/secret-teacher-parents-toilet-train-children#sthash.Qx4kr5hu.dpuf, accessed 9 April 2016.

Seidman, E. (2014) 'The Boy of My Dreams.' *Love That Max* blog. Available at www.lovethatmax.com/2014/12/the-boy-of-my-dreams.html, accessed 9 April 2016.

Strauss, V. (2014) 'The Right and Surprisingly Wrong Ways to Get Kids to Sit Still in Class,' *Washington Post*. Available at www.washingtonpost.com/news/answer-sheet/wp/2014/10/07/the-right-and-surprisingly-wrong-ways-to-get-kids-to-sit-still-in-class/, accessed 4 April 2016.

Tammet, D. (2007) *Born on a Blue Day: A Memoir of Asperger's and an Extraordinary Mind*. London: Hodder and Stoughton.

Ulmer, C. (2015a) Special Books by Special Kids. Available at www.facebook.com/specialbooksbyspecialkids/?pnref=story, accessed 4 April 2016.

Ulmer, C. (2015b) SBSK Roadtrip – Jack. Available at www.facebook.com/specialbooksbyspecialkids/videos/692270527541597/?fref=nf SBSK Roadtrip-Jack (Autism), accessed 4 April 2016.

Warner, L. (2015) 'What I Didn't Know about Down syndrome.' Sipping Lemonade blog. Available at http://sippinglemonade.com/what-i-didnt-know-about-down-syndrome, accessed 7 July 2016.

Williams, D. (1996) *Autism: An Inside-Out Approach*. London and Philadelphia, PA: Jessica Kingsley Publishers.

Useful Websites

Attention Autism
www.ginadavies.co.uk

2Build a Profile
www.2simple.com

Intensive Interaction
www.intensiveinteraction.co.uk

Makaton™
www.makaton.org

PECS®
www.pecs-unitedkingdom.com

SEN Assist
www.senassist.com

Sensory Stories
www.sensorystories.com

Social Stories™
www.carolgraysocialstories.com/social-stories

Squease
www.squeasewear.com

Tacpac®
www.tacpac.co.uk

Index

'ABC's of Asperger's Syndrome, The' (Mele) 24
accidents in toilet training 92
ADHD 128–9
'Aisle be back' (Bogdashina) 217–18
Andersen, Hans Christian 11, 95, 292, 294–5
Animal School, The (Reavis) 293
anxiety
    Daniel Tammet's experience of 33–4
    and first impressions of school 19–20
    of parents 35–7, 43
    toilet training 86–7
Aristotle 179
ASDteacher.com (Reed) 164
Attention Autism 273–80
attitudes to autism
    case studies 268–70
    experiences of 271–2
    suggestions for 270
Attwood, Tony 159–60
'Autism and Eating Out' (Endow) 212
Autism: An Inside-Out Approach (Williams) 24–5, 50–1

Bailey, Tina 93–4
Barrie, J.M. 139
bean bags 129–30
behaviour
    case studies 96–8, 103–4
    encouraging positive 102–7
    at home and school 31–3
    observation of 98

    responses to 95–6, 98–100
    rewards for 105–7
    suggestions for 106–7
Billings, Josh 65
Blackburn, Roz 212
Bogdashina, Olga 217–18
Bondy, Andrew S. 287
Born on a Blue Day (Tammet) 33–4, 272
Bredsdorff, E. 294
Brown, J. 294–5
Brown, L.K. 270
Brown, M.T. 270
Buehner, Carl W. 171

case studies
    attitudes to autism 268–70
    behaviour 96–8, 103–4
    chewing 175–6
    choices 1117–19
    Christmas 239–41, 246–8
    clothing sensitivity 180–2
    colour-coded symbols 54–5
    cooking 205–7
    coping with change 69–71
    creative response 47–9, 50
    eating 196–9
    eating out 209–11
    first impressions of school 20–2
    gift giving 252–4, 256–7
    hair cuts 188–90
    hair washing 186–7
    hitting 80–1
    Intensive Interaction 281–2
    investigation 47, 48, 49–50

modelling 77–8, 80–1
observation 46–7, 48, 49
parents 27–9
personal space 156, 157
pets 223–7
proprioception 165–8, 169, 170–1
shopping 215–17
sitting still 122–5
sound sensitivity 145–7, 150–1
teeth brushing 192–3
time keeping 132–4
toilet training 88–9
transitions 259–61
visual aids 62–4
waiting skills 113–14
change, coping with
case studies 69–71
change toolkit 74–5
communication with parents 75
preparation for 72–4
visual calendars 68–72
change toolkit 74–5
chewing
case studies 175–6
Lorriane Scott Young on 176–7
reasons for 173–4
suggestions for 174
Child, Lydia M. 258
choices
case studies 117–19
difficulties of 116–17
suggestions for 121
techniques for teaching 119–21
Christmas
case studies 239–41, 246–8
Christmas play 244–50
Julie Pates' experience of 242–3
Santa fears 255–6
suggestions for 241–2, 245, 248–9
Christmas play 244–50
clothing sensitivity
case studies 180–2
reasons for 183–4
and school uniform 182–3
colour-coded symbols 53–60, 261

Colour Coding for Learners with Autism
(Devine) 58, 136
Comic Strip Conversations™
description of 286
in modelling 82
in toilet training 92
communication boards 38–9
communication books 39–40
communication with children
colour-coded symbols 53–60
and iPad usage 140–2
visual aids 61–7
visual calendars 68–72
communication with parents
communication boards 38–9
communication books 39–40
coping with change 75
email lists 41–2
home visits 42
letters home 42
local media 43
online learning journeys 40
telephone contact 42
tick lists 40
video recordings 41
websites 41
computers see information technology
Confucius 15
cooking
case studies 205–7
learning opportunities 207
recipes 202–4
strategies for 204
suggestions for 205
creative responses
case studies 47–9, 50
description of 46
suggestions for 50–1
Curie, Marie 195
cutlery 200

da Vinci, Leonardo 154
Dali, Salvador 250
Davies, Gina 273, 274, 277
delayed gratification 112–14

Devine, Adele
  becomes special needs teacher
      15–16
  on colour-coded symbols 58
  on Halloween 235
  on hitting 83
  on life of Louise 11–14
  on Makaton™ 285
  on PECS® 288
  on time keeping 136, 137
  on toilet training 93
  on visual aids 65
Dickinson, Emily 267
eating
  case studies 196-9
  mealtime problems 195-6
  suggestions for 199-200
eating out
  case studies 209-11
  challenges of 208-9
  restaurant rituals 211-12
  suggestions for 213
Education Health Care Plans (EHCP)
      28
Eliot, George 221, 244
email lists 41–2
Endow, Judy 125, 158–9, 212
Epictetus 229
eye contact 158–9

fairy tales
  The Animal School 293
  Hans Christian Andersen stories
      294–5
  message of 292–3
Faith Mummy (Gwynne) 36–7, 43,
      296
festivities see special days
'finished' symbol 55–6
fireworks 236–7
first impressions of school
  approaching anxious child 19–20
  case studies 20–2
  home visits 19
  importance of 17–18

inclusive settings 23–5
interests of child 22–3
personalising learning environment
      22–3
simple suggestions 18–19
Fletcher, Justin 283, 284
food phobias see eating
Franklin, Benjamin 138
Freud, Sigmund 38
Frost, Lori 287

gift giving
  case studies 252–4, 256–7
  difficulties of 251–2
  and fairness 257
  gift tags 255
  Santa fears 255–6
  suggestions for 254
'good listening' symbol 58
'good looking' symbol 58
'good sitting' symbol 58
'good waiting' symbol 57
Grandin, Temple 89–90, 140, 164
Gray, Carol 156, 157, 285, 286
Gwynne, Miriam 36–7, 43, 98–100,
      296

hair cuts 188–91
hair washing 185–7
Hall, Kenneth 120, 265–6
Halloween 233–5
Hanscom, Angela 128–9
Heffner, Gary J. 156
'help' symbol 55
'Helping that Special Child who Hits'
      (Devine) 83
hitting 80–3
Hodgdon, Linda 119, 120
home visits
  as form of communication 42
  help with first impressions 19
How to Be a Friend: A Guide to Making
      Friends and Keeping Them (Brown
      and Brown) 270

I Love ABA (Meadows) 110–11
impatience flashpoints 111
inclusive settings
  help with first impressions of
    school 23–5
information technology
  control over 140–1
  and iPad usage 140–2
  suggestions for 142–3
Ingraham, Paul 162
Intensive Interaction 280–2
interests of child
  and first impressions of school
    22–3
investigation
  case studies 47, 48, 49–50
  description of 46
iPad usage 140–2

Jacks, L.P. 51
James, Scott 144–5

Keats, John 208
Kierkegaard, Søren 68
King, Sharon 271–2

Lebowitz, Marci 35–6
letters home 42
Literacy for Visual Learners (Devine) 65
local media 43
Love That Max (Seidman) 296–7
Loyne School 169–70

Makaton™
  baby signing 282–3
  help with first impressions 19
  and iPad usage 142
  in mainstream schools 284
  in special schools 283
  suggestions for 284–5
  use in *Something Special* 283–4
Mandela, Nelson 237
Mannerling, J. 227
McCan, Lynne 66–7
McCready, Jane 219

McKinnon, Gary 140
McLaughlin, Mary 126–7, 237
Meadows, Tameika 110–11
Mele, Josephine 24, 59, 72, 115,
    127–8, 149, 159, 164, 165
Merchey, J. 130
Mills, Richard 140
modelling
  case studies 77–8, 80–1
  and coping with change 74
  hitting 80–3
  opportunities for 79–80
  in staff training 80
  suggestions for 79
Mom–Not Otherwise Specified
    (McLaughlin) 126–7, 237
Montapert, Alfred A. 228
Moorhead, J. 219
Mother Geek (Bailey) 93–4
movement breaks 125–8
Murrell, D. 158
'My Best Friends...The Beautiful
    Flowers' (Gwynne) 98–100
Myers, Michelle 75

Newton, Sir Isaac 266
Nietzsche, Friedrich 161

observation
  of behaviour 98
  case studies 46–7, 48, 49
  description of 45–6
O'Haire, Marguerite 227
online learning journeys 40
Osborne, Jackie 169–70

parental fears 30–1, 35–7, 43
parental support
  behavioural at home and school
    31–3
  case studies 27–9
parental support *cont.*
  communication methods 38–44
  finding moments 295–8
  inviting parents into school 34

parental fears 30–1, 35–7, 43
parents' nights out 35
  shopping 219–20
  simple suggestions 29
parents' nights out 35
Pates, Julie 242–3
Pearson, C. 227
PECS® 54, 59
  description of 287–8
  for eating out 211
  and Halloween 235
  and iPad usage 141, 142
peg labels 22, 23
personal space
  case studies 156, 157
  expectations of 154–5
  eye contact 158–9
  problem times for 157–8
  and social interactions 159–60
  and Social Stories™ 156–7
  strategies for teaching 155
personalisation
  and first impressions of school
    22–3
pets
  case studies 223–7
  research on 227
  therapeutic qualities of 222–3
physical activity 128–9
positive behaviour 102–7
proprioception
  case studies 165–8, 169, 170–1
  development of 162–3
  equipment for 163
  importance of 161–2
  occupational therapy activities
    163–4
  Tacpac® 168–70
  weighted and squeezing objects
    164–6

Reach Out ASC (McCan) 66–7
Reavis, George H. 293
recipes 202–4
Reed, Steph 164, 274–5

restaurants see eating out
rewards for positive behaviour 105–7
Rhodes, G. 140
role models see modelling
Roosevelt, Franklin D. 185
Roosevelt, Theodore 84
Ryelands Primary School 170

St. Jerome 17
Santa fears 255–6
school uniform 182–3
Scott Young, Lorraine 176–7
Seidman, Ellen 296–7
SEN Assist blog (Devine) 56, 83, 93,
    231
Sharpe, Janis 140
Shelley, Mary 238
shopping
  case studies 215–17
  difficulties of 214–15
  Olga Bogdashina's experiences of
    217–18
  parental support 219–20
  suggestions for 218
shouting 152
Sipping Lemonade (Warner) 30–1, 271
sitting still
  and bean bags 129–30
  case studies 122–5
  and information processing 125
  movement breaks 125–8
  suggestions for 130
Slice of Autism, A (Myers) 75
smearing 90–1
social interactions
  and personal space 159–60
Social Stories™
  and Christmas 241
  and clothing sensitivity 181
  in coping with change 73, 74
  description of 285–6
  and Halloween 235
  in modelling 82
  and personal space 156–7
  in shopping 216

in toilet training 92
Socially Speaking ™
    in toilet training 85
Socrates 76
Something Special 283–4
sound sensitivity
    case studies 145–7, 150–1
    common sources of 147
    shouting 152
    suggestions for 145, 152–3
    and supply/trainee teachers 150–1
    visual aids for 148–50, 152–3
special days
    Christmas 238–50
    fireworks 236–7
    Halloween 233–5
    sports days 231–3
    stresses of 229–30
sports days 231–3
Squease vests 165–8
staff symbols 59–60
Stone, Elizabeth 44
stranger danger 160
symbols
    colour-coded 53–60, 261

Tacpac® 168–70
Tagore, Rabindranath 214
Tammet, Daniel 33–4, 272
TEAACH 288–90
teeth brushing 191–4
telephone contact 42
Thoreau, Henry David 61
tick lists 40
time keeping
    case studies 132–4
    child's control over 134–5
    difficulties with 131–2
    and technology 137
    timers for 134, 136
    visual aids for 135–7
'Tips for Calming Your Child'
    (Lebowitz) 35–6
Tobin Learns to Make Friends
    (Murrell) 158

toilet training
    accidents 91
    anxieties over 86–7
    case studies 88–9
    at home and school 89–90
    importance of consistency 88
    increasing independence 91–2
    kit for 87
    readiness for 85–6
    smearing 90–1
    suggestions for 87
    teachers role in 92–3
    Tina Bailey's experience of 93–4
    wiping 92
Tolstoy, Leo 102, 108
transitions
    case studies 259–61
    colour-coded symbols 261
    in mainstream schools 265–6
    suggestions for 261
    visual aids for 261–5
Twain, Mark 116, 144

Ulmer, Chris 127

video recordings 41
    of Christmas play 249
visual aids
    case studies 62–4
    consistency of use 66–7
    to improve communication 64–5
    in Scotland 65–6
    and sound sensitivity 148–50,
        152–3
    and time keeping 135–7
    and toilet training 92
    for transitions 261–5
    waiting skills 109–10
visual calendars 68–72, 264–5

waiting skills
   case studies 113–14
   delayed gratification 112–14
   examples of 110–11
   impatience flashpoints 111
   strategies for 114
   teaching activities 109
   visual aids 109–10
Walker, Clare 188
Warner, Lauren 30–1, 271, 297–8
Washington, George 26

Washington Post, The 129
websites
   for communicating with parents 41
weighted blankets 164–5
Wharton, Edith 298
Whitman, Walt 172
'Why Children Fidget' (Hanscom)
   128–9
Williams, Donna 24–5, 50–1, 90,
   187
wiping in toilet training 92